# Consciousness and the Actor

# European University Studies

Europäische Hochschulschriften
Publications Universitaires Européennes

Series XXX

**Theatre, Film and Television**

Reihe XXX   Série XXX
Theater-, Film- und Fernsehwissenschaften
Théâtre, Cinema, Télévision

Vol./Bd. 67

## PETER LANG

Frankfurt am Main · Berlin · Bern · New York · Paris · Wien

Daniel Meyer-Dinkgräfe

# Consciousness and the Actor

## A Reassessment of Western and Indian Approaches to the Actor's Emotional Involvement from the Perspective of Vedic Psychology

PETER LANG

Europäischer Verlag der Wissenschaften

Die Deutsche Bibliothek - CIP-Einheitsaufnahme

Meyer-Dinkgräfe, Daniel:

Consciousness and the actor : a reassessment of Western and Indian approaches to the actor's emotional involvement from the perspective of Vedic psychology / Daniel Meyer-Dinkgräfe. - Frankfurt am Main ; Berlin ; Bern ; New York ; Paris ; Wien : Lang, 1996
    (European university studies : Series 30, Theatre, Film and Television ; Vol. 67)
    Zugl.: London, Univ., Diss., 1994
    ISBN 3-631-30143-X

NE: Europäische Hochschulschriften / 30

ISSN 0721-3662
ISBN 3-631-30143-X
US-ISBN 0-8204-3180-X
© Peter Lang GmbH
Europäischer Verlag der Wissenschaften
Frankfurt am Main 1996
All rights reserved.

Printed in Germany 1 2  4 5 6 7

## Acknowledgements

I would like to thank Mr. Enzo Cozzi for his open-minded, intense and thorough advice throughout the development of this study. I am also grateful to Professor David Bradby (Royal Holloway, University of London) for several opportunities of discussing my thoughts in the Department of Drama and Theatre Studies postgraduate seminar. Finally, I would like to thank the librarians at Royal Holloway, University of London, Senate House, British Library and SOAS for their support.

## Note

When I use the term actor in this study, it should be clear that I am referring to both actresses and actors. When I use the masculin pronouns he, his, or him to replace actor, I am equally referring to both actresses and actors.

# Table of Contents

# INTRODUCTION

## 1. The Actor's Emotional Involvement

Among the issues discussed in theories of the theatre, the extent of the actor's emotional involvement in the emotions of the character he is playing has gained a prominent position, even before Diderot formulated his famous paradox of acting in 1773. The Spanish theorist Alonso Lopez Pinciano (1597-1627) argued that although the actor

> must transform himself into the character he is imitating so that it appears to everyone else as no imitation, (...) it seems more likely that the best actor would concentrate on technique and move to tears without weeping himself.[1]

Jusepe Antonio Gonzalez de Salas, on the other hand, held that the actor "must truly experience the passions of the play as interior feeling rather than guileful appearance"[2]. Pinciano, then, champions technique, Salas emotional involvement. This dichotomy of technique versus emotional involvement is taken up by the subsequent major theorists of the theatre up to Diderot: Luigi Ricoboni (involvement); Antonio Ricoboni (technique); St. Albine (involvement)[3]. Following Diderot's *Paradox of Acting*-- which consists in the claim that the actor should stimulate the spectator's emotions without being emotionally involved himself--the issue of the actor's emotional involvement has gained further momentum with growing interest in psychology in general since the last half of the 19th century. The key figure in this development is Stanislavsky, who in turn directly influenced Meyerhold, Strasberg and Brecht. Other leading 20th century theatre artists and theorists, such as Artaud, Grotowski, Schechner, Barba, and Brook, all relate to Diderot's paradox, but appear to reach beyond the emotions to vaguely defined states like *translumination* (Grotowski).

The artists have made those experiences in rehearsal or while performing. They then attempt to describe such experiences in the context of such knowledge of Western and / or non-Western concepts of psychology, philosophy or theatre aesthetics that is available to them. If the experiences are considered beneficial, desirable or helpful, the artists may also attempt to regain such experiences by using techniques described in sources available to them, or they combine source material to develop their own techniques. Such source material may be of

Western or non-Western origin, e.g. the writings of Freud, or Indian Yoga-techniques.

## 2. Western and Indian Theories

To fully understand and appreciate the individual theories, the specific intellectual-historical contexts in which they have developed must be taken into account. Since the theorists under discussion are from the West, the Western context must have priority in such a discussion. However, Western theorists are more and more influenced by non-Western concepts of philosophy, psychology and theatre practice. The majority of non-Western influence emerged from India. Therefore, the non-Western, Indian context has to be assessed as well. However, the analysis of Indian performance theory will not serve as a mere background to advance the interpretation of Western theories. Indian performance theory, as documented in the *Natyashastra* and various later comments on it, exists in their own right: it provides challenging views on the process of acting which fully deserve a separate assessment.

In the critique of Western experience-based theory, tracing direct Western and non-Western influences on the theatre artists will provide the framework in which to understand their statements on the actor's emotional involvement. While such a procedure helps to understand how the theatre artists themselves accounted for their experiences, the understanding of those experiences and the theories based on them may be further enhanced by discussing how most recent developments, findings, or insights in Western and non-Western psychology, philosophy or (theatre) aesthetics, would explain the experiences described by them. Both Western and non-Western "points of contact" between Western theatre theory and new developments in scholarship will be assessed separately.

Two sets of concepts are essential for the discussion on both levels of direct influence and "points of contact": first, emotions are studied in the discipline of psychology, as part of the human personality, of mind and consciousness. Some of the major concepts developed by contemporary theatre artists, such as Grotowski's *translumination*, suggest a level of consciousness that is beyond intellect or emotions. Any attempt at understanding the theatre artists' and theorists' views on the actor's emotional involvement necessitates an assessment of the significance of consciousness. Second, the importance of non-Western, Indian influences on Western theatre artists and theorists demands a discussion of interculturalism.

## 3. Fundamental Concepts 1: Consciousness

Within current Western psychology, there appears to be no concerted research program on consciousness. Rather, isolated phenomena of conscious experience and behaviour are theorised and researched. There is, to a large extent, agreement among those involved in the study of consciousness--psychologists, philosophers, brain neurophysiologists, and computer scientists--that the "study of consciousness has considerably intensified during the last decade or so"[4]. However, the more is written on the subject, the more varied the approaches become. According to Bisiach, several factors are responsible for the difficulties in the study of consciousness. The approaches have to be interdisciplinary, and the "involved parties differ considerably in background, area of expertise, and personal as well as group bias"[5]. As a result, the same problems are "simultaneously presented as non-existent, or insoluble, or happily solved in a number of contrasting ways"[6].

Problems with research into consciousness begin on a much more basic level, however: the terms "mind" and "consciousness", often used synonymously, lack precise definition. Battista names three distinct ways the term "consciousness" has been used in the West:

First, as a theoretical construct referring to the system by which an individual becomes aware; second, to refer to reflective awareness of being aware; third, as a general term encompassing all forms of awareness.[7]

Battista further distinguishes three kinds of data about consciousness. The first are phenomenological, gained by direct experience, by introspection. The second kind of data mentioned by Battista are psychological, gained through observation. Observation, Battista argues, implies "the use of the investigator's own consciousness to understand the experiences of another individual"[8]. The data gained will yield information "about the condition under which individuals will be in a particular state of consciousness"[9]. Finally, the phenomenon of consciousness can be approached empirically, "through making measurements on the physical variables associated with it"[10].

Explaining the difficulties faced by scientists studying the phenomenon of consciousness, Bisiach claims that there are two distinct aspects of consciousness, one within the range of scientific enquiry, the other one definitely outside of it[11]. Bisiach asserts that the aspect of consciousness that is not open to scientific research is "no less real or natural"[12]. This assertion, however, appears to be ignored, as shown by Tallis' discovery, in reviewing recent writings in philosophy and psychology on the concept of consciousness, that there has been

> a move to explain away or, indeed, to eliminate consciousness (...) either by redescribing it in terms that bring conscious behaviour closer to unconscious mechanism or by dismissing it as a conceptual leftover from a pre-scientific age.[13]

Marcel, however, justifies reference to consciousness in psychology thus:

> It is demanded since consciousness is a central (if not *the* central) aspect of mental life. It is legitimate since there are as reasonable grounds for identifying consciousness as there are for identifying other psychological constructs. It is necessary since it has explanatory value, and since there are grounds for positing that it has causal status.[14]

Consciousness cannot be defined in isolation from the body. Concepts of the mind-body relationship are vital in assessing theories of acting, because the body has increasingly been regarded as the actor's main tool of training and of influencing an audience. Two main concepts of mind-body relationship have been developed over the ages: dualistic theories regard mind and body as fully distinct entities, whereas monism maintains either that matter is a phenomenon of consciousness, or that consciousness is an epiphenomenon of matter (brain physiology)[15]. A close investigation of the theories of acting in the theatre will demonstrate that the theories are dominated by "concrete dualistic interactionism", a model assuming separate entities of mind and body which can mutually influence each other.

The mind's influence over the body appears to be rather difficult to theorise. As a result, theories holding that the body influences the mind have gained a prominent position in acting theory. It will also be shown that if theories based on dualism are used to account for the actor's emotional involvement while acting, or for experiences beyond the intellect or the emotions, or if dualistic theories are used to interpret Indian theatre aesthetics, the results are ultimately unsolved paradoxes. To solve such paradoxes by rendering them unnecessary involves the detailed proposition of a monistic model of consciousness. It will also be relevant to an profound understanding of Indian theatre aesthetics.

## 4. Fundamental Concepts 2: Interculturalism

The obvious exchange of Indian and Western aesthetic ideas of theatre has to be examined in the broader contexts of interculturalism. Fischer-Lichte distinguishes between three categories of intercultural productions. The first category comprises productions in which reference to the foreign (theatre, culture) dominates, which regard the foreign components as ideal or model for their own theatre, placing the foreign next to the existing forms of theatre. In the second category, reference to the production's own theatre, culture, dominates. Foreign elements enlarge the range of possibilities for expression, aiming at further development or relativation of one's own forms of theatre[16]. The aim of the third category is for a universal language of theatre. It is served by the collage-montage technique which Brook applies.

Carlson offers a different differentiation, distinguishing between "seven steps of possible relationships between the culturally familiar and the culturally foreign":

1. The totally familiar tradition of regular performance
2. Foreign elements assimilated into the tradition and absorbed by it. The audience can be interested, entertained, stimulated, but they are not challenged by the foreign material.
3. Entire foreign structures are made familiar instead of isolated elements. The Oriental Macbeth would be an example of this.
4. The foreign or familiar create a new blend, which then is assimilated into the tradition, becoming familiar.
5. The foreign itself becomes assimilated as a whole, becoming familiar. Examples would be Commedia dell'Arte in France or Italian opera in England.

6. Foreign elements remain foreign, used with unfamiliar structures for *Verfremdung*, for shock value, or for exotic quotation. An example would be the oriental dance sequences in the current production of M Butterfly in New York.
7. An entire performance from another culture is imported or recreated, with no attempt to accommodate it with the familiar.[17]

Pavis likens the interactions of cultures to an hourglass:

> In the upper bowl is the foreign culture, the source culture, which is more or less codified and solidified in diverse anthropological, sociocultural or artistic modelizations. In order to reach us, this culture must pass through a narrow neck. If the grains of culture or their conglomerate are sufficiently fine, they will flow through without any trouble, however slowly, into the lower bowl, that of the target culture, from which point we observe this slow flow. The grains will rearrange themselves in a way which appears random, but which is partly regulated by their passage through some dozen filters put in place by the target culture and the observer.[18]

Pavis recognises two risks presented by the model of the hourglass: if it is only a mill, the source culture will be destroyed, and ultimately of no use to the target culture; if it is only a funnel, "it will indiscriminately absorb the initial substance without reshaping it through the series of filters or leaving any trace of the original matter"[19]. Pavis also recognises that flow of communication of all sorts between cultures is (or at least should be) in both directions. In the theatrical context, the hourglass consists of three levels, each with its sub-categories[20]:

**Level (1)**
The source culture before the process of theatrical adaptation begins.
    (a) cultural modelling, sociological, anthropological
        codification etc.,
    (b) artistic modelling.

**Level (2)**
The theatrical production
    (a) perspective of the adapters;
    (b) work of adaptation;
    (c) preparatory word by the actors etc.;
    (d) choice of theatrical form;
    (e) theatrical representation/performance of culture;
    (f) reception-adapters.

**Level (3)**
Reception by the audience and target culture,
    (a) readability;

(b) reception in the target culture
  (i) artistic modelling;
  (ii) sociological and anthropological codification
  (iii) cultural modelling;
(c) given and anticipated consequences.

These categories provide Pavis with a framework for the analysis of intercultural performance.

Interculturalism in the theatre is at times accused of insensitivity to the heritage of the country from which they "borrow" or "steal" their material; key phrases in this context are "cultural appropriation as theft" and "neo-colonialist paternalism"[21]. Similarly, Fischer-Lichte argues that it is impossible to answer the question whether intercultural productions based on montage techniques imply a denial of cultural imperialism or, on the contrary, a renewed version of cultural exploitation[22]. Since this study focuses in particular on the exchange of Western and Indian ideas of theatre aesthetics, Rustom Bharucha's critique of interculturalism from the Indian perspective will be discussed in depth. Bharucha argues that

the interpretation and use of cultures have to be confronted within the particularities of a specific historical condition. It is naive, if not irresponsible, to assume that a meaningful confrontation of any culture can transcend the immediacies of its history.[23]

Fischer-Lichte asks whether intercultural collage techniques of production might have to be discussed not in the context of intercultural theatre, but in the context of postmodernism[24]. Indeed, collage can be understood as fragmentation, one of the characteristics of postmodernism. Moreover, the growing emphasis of the theatre artists on "myth, ritual, and what might be called the spiritual side of human nature--the subconscious, instinctive and irrational"[25], also features among "the leading characteristics of postmodern theatre"[26].

However, the concept of postmodernism is ambiguous in at least four main areas: some critics put the legitimacy of the concept in question, arguing that the are no new phenomena that might justify the introduction of a new term[27]. The next issue is the field of the term's application. According to Welsch, the term originated in the North American literature debate, then spread to architecture and painting, sociology and philosophy, and by now there is hardly an area "not infected by this virus"[28]. As far as the time of origin is concerned, the debate originated in the USA in 1959, referring to phenomena of the 1950s; in 1975, when Europe had caught up with the development, the *New Yorker* wrote that postmodernism was out and there was demand for a post-postmodernism[29]. In the same line of argument, Welsch quotes Umberto Eco's worries that before long even Homer would be considered postmodern[30]. Finally, the contexts of postmodernism are ambiguous: the age of SDI technology versus a green, ecological, alternative movement; a new integration of a fragmented society versus increased intentional fragmentation and pluralisation[31].

Welsch attempts to define a common denominator for different approaches to postmodernism:

> We can talk about postmodernism where a fundamental pluralism of languages, models, and procedures is practised, not just side by side in separate works, but in one and the same work, i.e. interferentially.[32]

Postmodernism is often associated with Derrida's criticism of Western dualism. Indeed, the paradoxes resulting when Western dualism in the mind-body relationship is applied to theories of acting could be discussed in a Derridian discourse. However, this would be more of a philosophical inquiry, which is possible, perhaps even more efficient, without reference to the theatre, as Coward's comparison of Derrida and Indian philosophy shows[33]. The framework for tackling the paradoxes in this study is outlined below.

## 5. A Reassessment from the Perspective of Vedic Science

The study begins with an outline of major theories of the acting, focusing on the actor's emotional involvement in the theories of Diderot, Stanislavsky, Meyerhold, Strasberg, and Brecht, and on states of consciousness beyond the emotions in Artaud, Grotowski, Schechner, Barba and Brook. These outlines will provide, where necessary, the Western historical background to the theories: which Western concepts in philosophy, psychology, physiology or (theatre) aesthetics have directly influenced the theorists? This major chapter is followed by an outline of further developments in Western psychology and physiology which were not available to the theatre theorists discussed before, but which help to understand their theories of acting better. In the next step, non-Western, especially Indian influences on the theatre theorists are discussed, as well as "points of contact" between Western theatre theory and elements of Indian philosophy and theatre aesthetics unavailable to the Western theorists. This section includes a description of Indian theatre aesthetics as provided in the *Natyashastra*, which can claim explanatory power in its own right. Its discussion thus does not serve only as background material to Western theories-

The exploration of Western and Indian theories of the actor's emotional involvement while acting will lead to several insights; more important, however, a number of open questions will also be raised, pertaining to the conceptualisation, definition and functioning of consciousness. As a result, a set of criteria for a model of consciousness will be developed that enables a cogent answer to those open questions. Since those criteria cannot be met satisfactorily by applying models of consciousness provided by Western psychology, and since they originate in the theatre artists' encounter with Indian philosophy and (theatre) aesthetics, they will be discussed in terms of Indian concepts of consciousness.

During the last thirty-three years, Maharishi Mahesh Yogi has subjected the knowledge provided by the classical texts of Vedic literature to a thorough re-assessment, resulting in what he calls Vedic Science. Among its various disciplines, Vedic Psychology will be of particular interest to this study.

Maharishi Mahesh Yogi is a disciple of the late Swami Brahmananda Saraswati (1869-1953), who held the position of Shankaracharya of Jyotir Math for the last 13 years of his life. He was the head of one of four monasteries in India founded by the sage and philosopher Shankara to safeguard the tradition of his Advaita Vedanta philosophy. Brahmananda Saraswati has been called "Vedanta incarnate" by India's first President, Radhakrishnan[34]. As Brahmananda Saraswati's disciple, Maharishi Mahesh Yogi is in the direct line of Shankara's Advaita Vedanta philosophy.

The relationship of Vedic literature (i.e. the primary texts) and Maharishi Mahesh Yogi's interpretation of the Vedic literature as Vedic Science and Vedic Psychology will be clarified, as will parallels with and differences from Western concepts of psychology. The emergence of this knowledge will be critically positioned within a general "turn to the East" observed in recent years[35], and within the related contexts of interculturalism and postmodernism. On that basis, the model of consciousness proposed by Vedic Psychology is introduced, encompassing concepts of a hierarchical structure of the mind and of higher stages of human development.

Western theories of the actor's emotional involvement are then reassessed from the perspective of Vedic Psychology, followed by a reassessment of the traditional interpretation of Indian theatre aesthetics as found in the major Indian treatise of theatre, the *Natyashastra*. The reassessment of Western and Indian theories of the actor's emotional involvement includes a reassessment of the implications of interculturalism and postmodernism for the theatre. The reassessment also leads to an outlook, comprising implications of the results for the understanding of the process/event of theatre, the function of theatre for the individual and society, implications for actor training, directing methods, and the canon of plays, regarding subject-matter and message.

# WESTERN AND INDIAN THEORIES OF THE ACTOR'S EMOTIONAL INVOLVEMENT

## 1. Western Theories in their Historical Contexts

### a. Diderot.

One of the earlier major Western theorists to tackle the question of the actor's emotional involvement in acting is Diderot. Diderot differentiates between two types of actors. The one plays from the heart, from "sensibility", immersing himself, while acting, in the feelings of the character he plays. According to Diderot, this way of acting yields poor results: "their playing is alternately strong and feeble, fury and cold, dull and sublime (...)"[1]. Moreover, the actor loses his self-control and the acting varies from performance to performance because it depends on the actor's daily ups and downs. The actor is unable to pull together his "individual actions into a coherent whole"[2]. Such acting will have much less effect on the spectators than acting based on the actor's self-control.

Rather than playing from the heart, rather than feeling the emotions of the character while acting the part, the actor "must have in himself an unmoved and disinterested onlooker. He must have, consequently, penetration and no sensibility"[3]. Such an actor, Diderot's ideal, is guided by the intellect. He will have a highly developed ability to observe nature, to imitate it, and to accurately repeat a pattern of acting that has developed during the rehearsal period. He is thus able to create a coherent and unified role. He does not feel while acting, but makes his impression on the audience by "rendering so exactly the outward signs of feeling"[4]. Diderot describes the English actor David Garrick as an example for such acting:

> Garrick will put his head between two folding doors, and in the course of five or six seconds his expression will change successively from wild delight to temperate pleasure, from this to tranquility, from tranquility to surprise, from surprise to bland astonishment, from that to sorrow, from sorrow to the air of one overwhelmed, from that to fright, from fright to horror, from horror to despair, and thence he will go up again to the point from which he started. Can the soul have experienced all these feelings and played this kind of scale in concert with his face?[5]

The paradox is that emotions in the spectators are stimulated by an unemotional imitation of emotions by the actor.

Diderot's paradox is rooted in the history of theatre, science, and philosophy of his time. According to Grear, seventeenth century France saw a "revival of interest in *pronunciatio*", the "theory of oratorial delivery"[6]. Diderot's central concern, "the extent to which an actor should identify (...) with the emotions of the character he portrays"[7], is also the major issue discussed in the *pronunciatio* part of classical rhetorics. Grear refers to Cicero and Quintilian: Cicero advised the orator to use the rules of the art to portray those emotions he wanted to create in the spectators[8] . Quintilian also emphasised the rules of the art, but added to the "rationally prepared pathos (...) an element of imaginative identification (...)"[9]. The mechanism was this:

> The same devices of style and delivery worked out by the orator to move his audience would, during the performance itself, work upon the orator himself, enabling him to imagine the scene and further assist his ability to portray passions realistically.[10]

Grear shows that French 17th century theatre theory initially followed Quintilian as just summarised. However, from 1670 onwards, this "formalist" position was challenged, as part of "a larger movement against hypocrisy and insincerity"[11]. The emphasis shifted from rational principles of acting to an emotional approach[12]. It is against the latter that Diderot's *Paradox* argues.

To evaluate the implications of Diderot's theory, its central term, "sensibility", has to be understood within the context of the theories of psychology and physiology that influenced Diderot. Roach takes up this key term, pointing out that in Diderot's time the word "sensibility"

> resonated through complex layers of meaning in science, literature, and moral philosophy, ascending from the most rudimentary responsiveness of nervous fibres to the highest expressions of humane sympathy and imagination.[13]

In his discussion of the physiological background of the *Paradox*, Roach refers to Diderot's own work in the fields of psychology and physiology[14]. Here, Diderot's views on the relationship between mind and body become relevant.

Despite the variety of approaches in philosophy and psychology to the relationship of mind and body, each with its own terminology, some major strands can be isolated at Diderot's time. Mind and body can be regarded as fully distinct entities. This view is termed "dualism". Within this approach, it is possible to distinguish at least two lines of argument. One is usually associated with Descartes (1596-1650). It has been termed "concrete dualistic inter-actionism"[15], and holds that both mind and body can mutually influence each other. The other line of argument, termed "concrete dualistic parallelism"[16] is associated with Leibnitz (1646-1716). It asserts that mind and body unfold in a parallel but causally unrelated manner.

Opposed to dualism and its varieties is monism. Subjective monism "argues that the physical world does not have an existence independent of either an individual or universal consciousness and thus absorbs physical reality into a consciousness-based monism."[17] This variety of monism is also called "mentalism", and is associated with Berkeley (1685-1753)[18]. Later develop-ments in physiology led to objective monism, which argues that consciousness is based on, and an expression of, the neurophysiological activities of the brain. This theory is called the reductionist or mechanistic model.

Diderot is also influenced by the empiricist philosophers Locke and Hume, in putting forward "a theory of mind which based everything on discrete sensations provided by the senses"[19]. In this context, Diderot regards the body as a "virtually soulless machine" which has "biological drives but not will"[20] The functioning of the human machine depends on the control of the mind over the nerves. When the mind is in control of the nerve activities, the machine functions properly. When the nerves dominate, the functioning of the machine is disturbed: "Rationality and self-possession inevitably yield before the inexorable pressure of strong feelings"[21]. The feelings, in turn, have specific corresponding involuntary effects on the physiology. For example, the feeling of fury "inflames the eyes, clenches the fists and the teeth, furrows the brows"[22]. Diderot believed most feelings to be directly related to what he regarded as the physical centre--the diaphragm. Just as the brain "propels the mechanism of thought"[23], the diaphragm propels the mechanism of feeling. Negative emotions lead to a contraction of the diaphragm, positive, such as happiness, to an expansion. As any feeling has an involuntary effect on the body in general, also the specific reaction of the diaphragm is involuntary and cannot be intentionally suppressed[24]. Once the diaphragm starts reacting, i.e. once feelings dominate, the mental faculties such as reason and judgment are rendered ineffective.

In this context, the term "imagination" is to be separated from the term "sensibility" as discussed above. In the rehearsal process, not during the actual performance, imagination has an important function for the actor. In creating the pattern for a role that is to be repeated performance after performance without emotional involvement, the actor draws on two important functions: memory and imagination. "Memory retains the image, imagination revives it, vivifies it, and combines it with other images to form the living mosaic of the inner model"[25]. Roach explains that this theory again is grounded in Diderot's understanding of physiology: if patterns enlivened in the memory of the actor are increased in their intensity by the actor's imagination, the revived sensations "can duplicate actual experiences"[26]. Thus, during the rehearsal period the actor can feel and physically experience the emotions of the character he is playing, observe those, and develop the pattern of the automatised performance on that basis. This process is intellectually controlled and leads to performance equally controlled by the intellect. By contrast, acting from the heart, dominated by emotions, by the diaphragm, is never controlled, because the cause-effect chains of feeling and physiological reaction are involuntary.

Diderot's basic assumption about the relationship of mind and body, their functioning as one entity in the process of combining memory and imagination, leads to an apparent contradiction:

> If the actor's mind and body constitute a single entity, then how can his mind coldly direct his body through sequences of passions without mentally experiencing the same emotions?[27]

According to Roach, Diderot followed the notion common in his time that mind/body can simultaneously be engaged in two separate activities because "its components resemble those of a stringed instrument"[28]. The more the actor's discriminating qualities of the mind are developed, the more will he be able consciously to detach himself from the emotions of the character, the closer will he reach towards Diderot's ideal. Such a level of acting presupposes, according to Diderot, a nature-given talent and a long process of learning and experience[29].

Diderot argued in favour of mind and body as an entity, at least as far as the process of combining memory and imagination is concerned. His view is therefore more closely related to monism than to dualism. However, clearly associating Diderot with either subjective or objective monism is difficult. Although Diderot's understanding of mental processes is closely related to his understanding of physiology, he does not argue for a dominance of the physiology. Rather, intentional control of the interplay between feeling and physiological reaction is possible through the activity of the intellect.

This position is closer to subjective than to objective monism. Intellectual control of the interaction between feeling and physiological reaction could be explained by assuming that more subtle levels of mind are by definition able to control less subtle levels. However, this leaves the question where to locate the heart, unable to exert such control, within the framework of human psychology.

In conclusion, although it may be fascinating to understand Diderot's views in a historical context, the paradox is not solved. A model of the mind or consciousness is needed

- to account for the concept (and experience?) of the disinterested onlooker within the actor;

- to do justice to Diderot's theory of mind-body interrelation in the process of acting;

- to cogently define, describe and locate feeling, intellect, the heart in its psychological significance, imagination, sensibility, on a "map" of mind or consciousness.

## b. Stanislavsky

Stanislavsky's system of actor training and acting has had a major influence in Western theatre history of the late 19. and the 20. centuries. If it is not directly practiced, the differences most frequently represent conscious developments of Stanislavsky's theories (e.g. Strasberg and his "Method"[1]), or outspoken opposition to them (e.g. the early Brecht[2]). On the issue of the actor's emotional involvement while acting, Stanislavsky appears to take the opposite view from Diderot: "an actor is under the obligation to live his part inwardly, and then to give to his experience an external embodiment"[3]. This obligation of the actor is in line with Stanislavsky's view of the fundamental aim of the art of acting, "the creation of this inner life of a human spirit, and its expression in an artistic form"[4]. The inner life has to be created and lived in every performance, not just in rehearsal as Diderot argued. The important force that has to be tapped to allow such an "inspired" acting, is the subconscious. Thus, the more the actor can use his subconscious forces, the more will he be able to "fit his own human qualities to the life of this other person, and pour into it all of his own soul"[5]. Stanislavsky describes the ideal of acting in the following words:

> The very best that can happen is to have the actor completely carried away by the play. Then regardless of his own will he lives the part, not noticing how he feels, not thinking about what he does, and it all moves of its own accord, subconsciously and intuitively.[6]

This ideal appears to imply that the actor has lost self-control, a state that Diderot had warned against[7]. Stanislavsky recognised that the subconscious and whatever[8] arises from that realm, is not only inaccessible to consciousness[8] but also beyond the control of the will. For that reason Stanislavsky sought to develop procedures allowing the actor to use the subconscious forces through conscious techniques.

In preparing for a part, the actor begins by dividing the play into units "which, like signals, mark his channel and keep him [the actor] in the right line"[9]. Understanding the structure of the play constitutes the outward purpose of the division into units. This outward purpose is complemented by an inner purpose which, according to Stanislavsky, is far more important. The inner purpose is the "creative objective" which lies "at the heart of every unit"[10]. Stanislavsky provides a detailed definition of right objectives. To be able to "live his part inwardly"[11], the actor's objectives must be "directed toward the other actors, and not toward the spectators"[12]. The actor's orientation towards fellow-actors results in the actor's concentration on the fictional reality of the play. This fictional world, through the actor's objectives, is to be "real, live, and human, not dead, conventional, or theatrical"[13]. The objectives must be precise, clear-cut, they should attract and move the actor, and they should be personal to the actor, but still analogous to those of the character the actor is portraying[14].

Establishing the units and objectives of play and character allows the actor to arrive at a comprehensive understanding--both intellectual-outward (units) and emotional-inward (objectives)--of the play and the character he has to portray. The emotional, intuitive grasp of the role is not completed, however, with the association of the objectives resulting from the units of the play. Stanislavsky recognised that "direct, powerful and vivid emotions do not (...) last over long periods or even for a single act. They flash out in short episodes, individual moments"[15]. Moreover, Stanislavsky asserts that we cannot control such "spontaneous eruptions of feeling"[16]: "They control us. Therefore we have no choice but to leave it to nature (...) we will only hope that they will work with the part and not at cross purpose to it"[17]. No matter how irresistible and moving a force those direct, powerful and vivid emotions may be, they are not sufficient for the actor's daily task of performance.

Stanislavsky does not argue, then, in favour of a loss of self-control, in favour of leaving it to nature and hoping for the best. He recognises the creative potential of a spontaneous eruption of emotions, but at the same time he realises the dangers inherent in this eruption: dangers arise because the eruption is beyond the actor's control. It is in this context that Stanislavsky explicitly warns the actor: "Never lose yourself on the stage. Always act in your own person, as an artist"[18].

Once the actor has established the emotion-dominated objectives of his part, he can use the technique of emotion memory to gain controlled and repeatable access to his unconscious. Stanislavsky explains that just as your visual memory can reconstruct an inner image of some forgotten thing, place, or person, your emotion-memory can bring back feelings you have already experienced. They may seem to be beyond recall, when suddenly suggestion, a thought, a familiar object will bring them back in full force. Sometimes the emotions are as strong as ever, sometimes weaker, sometimes the same strong feelings will come back but in a somewhat different guise.[19]

Thus, the actor uses his own past emotions as creative material, assisted by "feelings that we have had in sympathising with the emotions of others"[20]. Stanislavsky all along emphasised that the emotions should be spontaneous: "The work of the actor is not to create feelings but only to produce the given circumstances in which true feelings will spontaneously be engendered"[21].

While the emotion memory is a technique, allowing the actor to suffuse his acting with genuine emotions of his own which are analogous to the emotions the character portrayed is supposed to experience, several techniques in turn are used by the actor to stimulate the emotion memory: initially, the actor has to believe in the validity of the objectives for the play and the character. Such belief, a sense of truth, is spontaneously followed by desire, in turn leading to action[22]. The action takes the form of physical motor-adjustments which are in line with the emotions felt. A further technique to stimulate the emotion memory is an awareness of tempo-rhythm, both of movement and regarding speech. Stanislavsky explains that both our actions and our speech

proceed in terms of time. In the process of action we must fill in the passing time with a great variety of movements, alternating with pauses of inactivity, and in the process of speech the passing time is filled with moments of pronunciation of sounds of varying lengths with pauses between them.[23]

Indeed, there is "some kind of tempo-rhythm inherent in every minute of our inward and outward existence"[24].

Each actor will have to find his or her own tempo-rhythm for both movement and speech, in line with the requirements of the part. Tempo-rhythm is closely interrelated with feelings, the "inward existence": as Stanislavsky points out, "every human passion, every state of being, every experience has its tempo-rhythms"[25]. The actor can either intuitively apply the tempo-rhythm appropriate to a character and a situation on the stage. If the actor, however, lacks such intuition, he can work "from the outside in"[26], beating out the rhythm. By intentionally adopting a tempo-rhythm appropriate to specific emotions, those emotions can be triggered, stimulated in the form of emotion memory. Through an awareness of tempo-rhythm the actor can "be put into a state of genuine excitement and get from it an emotional impact"[27].

The emotions certainly have an important function in acting, but they are not isolated. Feeling unites with mind and will to form a "triumvirate" of motive forces[28]. They can be stimulated independently and in their interaction. Again, Stanislavsky argues that the motive forces sometimes function spontaneously, subconsciously. However, if they do not, the actor can turn to any of the three components of the "triumvirate", either mind, or feelings, or will: if he turns to the mind, the mechanism will be as follows:

> The actor takes the thoughts in the lines of his part and arrives at a conception of their meaning. In turn, this conception will lead to an opinion about them, which will correspondingly affect his feeling and will.[29]

Using the interaction between the three inner motive forces is at the basis of Stanislavsky's psycho-technique. It encompasses emotion-memory to stimulate feelings (and, in turn, tempo-rhythm of movement and speech to stimulate emotion memory). The mind is directly affected by thought. However, Stanislavsky argues that "there is no direct stimulus by which you can influence the will"[30]. There appears to be a contradiction in this point: when arguing for *will* as the third inner motive force, Stanislavsky points out that units and objectives are techniques of "arousing inner living desires and aspirations"[31]. Stanislavsky clarifies the point by proposing that will and feeling are inseparable, and some objectives "influence the will more than the feeling and others enhance the emotions at the expense of the desire."[32]

All elements of the psycho-technique assist the actor's energies to converge towards a holistic and organic expression of a character on the stage. Stanislavsky regards the holistic value of acting on two levels: on the level of action, he coined the phrase "through line of action"[33]. On the level of speech, the equivalent to "through line of action" is the called "subtext"[34]. Stanislavsky defines the subtext as a web of innumerable, varied inner patterns inside a play and a part, woven from "magic ifs," given circumstances, all sorts of figments of the imagination, inner movements, objects of attention, smaller and greater truths and a belief in them, adaptations, adjustments and other similar elements.[35]

All the elements that compose the subtext lead to the ultimate super-objective of the play[36], which gives the play and the characters their holistic and organic shape.

The actor approaches a part both intellectually and intuitively, to stir his motive forces--feelings, mind and will--to reach into the unconscious, the subtext of the play in order to develop a grasp of the play and the character to be portrayed that leads to genuinely felt and experienced performances. The technique of emotion memory appears most important because it most efficiently enables the actor to gain access to the subconscious: the subconscious creative objective is the best, because it takes possession of an actor's feelings, and carries him intuitively along to the basic goal of the play"[37], the super-objective. Such unconscious objectives are consciously "engendered by the emotion and will of the actors themselves"[38]. The unconscious is set to work by a conscious stimulus. The unconscious objectives "come into being intuitively"[39]. If the actor left the unconscious objectives to themselves once they have been consciously stimulated, the actor might well lose his self-control. Stanislavsky however points out clearly that once the unconscious objectives have come into being, "they are then weighed and determined consciously"[40].

Diderot saw an actor who fully involves himself in the emotions of the character he has to portray as being in danger of losing his self-control. He therefore advised actors to act without emotional involvement, but by perfection of the art of imitating real-life emotions. Stanislavsky no less realised the same risk of an actor's loss of self-control. On the other hand, Stanislavsky holds that acting in which the emotions are not genuinely felt, but merely mechanical, does not do justice to the demands of the art of acting. He thus provides the actor with techniques intended to stimulate as much unconscious, intuitive, emotional material as possible, while at the same time ensuring that such techniques did not lead to an undesirable state of lost self-control. Stanislavsky quotes the actor Salvini as saying: "An actor lives, weeps and laughs on the stage, and all the while he is watching his own tears and smiles. It is this double function, this balance between life and acting that makes his art"[41]. Stanislavsky's reference to this double function, the witnessing of the process of acting by the actor himself, might resemble Diderot's call for the "unmoved and disinterested onlooker"[42].

Thus, the paradox takes a decisive shift from Diderot to Stanislavsky. Diderot's paradox is the emotional stimulation of the audience through an emotionally uninvolved actor. In the case of Stanislavsky, the paradox exists not in the interaction between actor and spectator, but within the actor, the actor's art of being both deeply emotionally involved--down to the level of the unconscious-- and yet still in conscious control of the acting through this ability to watch.

The discussion of Diderot's theory of acting has revealed the importance the influence of the state of the art in physiology and psychology studies had for the development of the theory. Placing his theory of acting into a wider framework of philosophical arguments about the relationship of mind and body has also proved useful. The same is true for an assessment of Stanislavsky's concepts.

The importance that Stanislavsky placed on the subconscious for inspired acting reflects the increasing interest in the psyche, pioneered by Freud. The foundation of Stanislavsky's system, gaining access to the subconscious through conscious procedures, has led scholars to draw parallels between Stanislavsky and basic principles of Freudian psychoanalysis[43]. Kesting proposes further parallels between Stanislavsky's theory of acting and Freud's seminal discoveries in psychology: one of Freud's techniques of assessment was the *free association procedure*, in which the patients reported on whatever "thoughts and memories occurred to them"[44]. Likewise, Stanislavsky sought to use the emotion memory of the subconscious as a vehicle to free the actor's inspiration[45]. Stanislavsky's concept of "subtext", those elements implied in the play and the part, but not directly expressed, mirror, according to Kesting, Freud's construct of the *Id*, and the super-objective of the play, in turn, resembles Freud's concept of the *Super-Ego*[46]. Such parallelisms are in danger of being mechanical, however: the subtext, though invisible in itself, can be made visible through the actor, whereas by definition the unconscious cannot be made visible. The super-objective is defined as giving the play and the characters their holistic shape, whereas the super-ego is defined as "the individual's internalisation of societal moral values

(...) preventing the individual from expressing primitive urges publicly, and (...) encouraging the individual to set goals that would establish him or her in a career as a productive citizen"[47].

It is perhaps more appropriate to draw parallels, between Stanislavsky's system and Freud's first topography, where he differentiates the unconscious, the preconscious, and the conscious. The area of the mind Stanislavsky wishes to access, which he calls the subconscious, could resemble the preconscious in Freud's first topography of the mind: whereas unconscious contents are in principle not accessible to consciousness, preconscious contents are not yet available to consciousness but can be made available[48]. In any case, if at all, Freudian psychoanalysis provides parallels, points of contact, with Stanislavsky's theory of acting, and not historical sources of influence.

Roach regards the unconscious, to which Stanislavsky attributed "major powers of artistic creativity" as "a subconscious repository in a pre-Freudian physiological sense"[49]. The physiological sense of the subconscious is further explained by taking up Strasberg's statement about the concept of emotion memory central to the American *Method*: "The emotional thing is not Freud, as people commonly think. Theoretically and actually, it is Pavlov"[50]. Roach convincingly argues the influence of Pavlov's theories of reflex on Stanislavsky's system. For example, Pavlov saw the relationship between inner and outer world as a continuous process, a chain of interdependent learned or conditioned reflexes: learned mental reflexes are substitutes for innate physical ones. In parallel, Stanislavsky's system

defines individual units and objectives as "bits" in what will eventually, after sufficient rehearsal, become the "unbroken line of action" or "the score of the role." This line is a chain of mutually inter dependent reflex desires and reflex actions.[51]

Regarding the affective memory, it has been shown that Stanislavsky directly derived this concept from Theodule Ribot's *The Psychology of the Emotions*, translated into Russian in the 1890s, and one of the books in Stanislavsky's library[52].

A comparison of Diderot and Stanislavsky leads to the conclusion that apart from the shift of emphasis in the paradox from the actor - spectator relationship in Diderot to the actor - actor dimension in Stanislavsky, there are, as Roach points out, many parallels between the evolution of Diderot's and Stanislavsky's theories:

a) Emotion is beyond the direct reach of the will.
b) Major powers of artistic creativity are attributed to the unconscious mind.
c) the unconscious mind is interpreted as a subconscious repository in a pre-Freudian physiological sense.
d) the actor's creativity is regarded highly, but an inner model of character brought forth collectively with the playwright is conceived of.
e) Belief in long rehearsal periods to prepare a role meticulously.
f) Emphasis on the need for absorption in the stage task.
g) The role is regarded as a score or inner model of physical actions overseen by the dispassionate half of a divided consciousness.[53]

Not only the scientific theories influencing Diderot and Stanislavsky have to be considered, but also the individual ways in which the authors arrived at their theories of acting. Originally a follower of the emotional approach to acting, Diderot arrived at his views as documented in *The Paradox* after his acquaintance with the sensibility debate in science and after having seen Garrick perform. He was further influenced by his contacts with actors, and by frequently attending performances. Thus, Diderot was well informed, but still an outsider. Stanislavsky, on the other hand, arrived at his system through direct experience in acting and directing. His own experiences led him to abandon the mechanical, uninspired and ultimately frustrating way of acting he had been accustomed to for a long time, and to develop his system. This inside approach with experiences unique to it placed Stanislavsky in a position to take the same concern that guided Diderot--the risk of the actor losing self-control through (over-) indulging in an involvement with the emotions of the character--to a different end. Stanislavsky was primarily concerned with providing practical assistance to actors and directors, leading to an emphasis on practical techniques that can be applied in the day-to-day routine of rehearsal and performance in the theatre. As a result of this priority to practical matters, Stanislavsky refers to the paradoxical nature of the conscious control over simultaneously occurring phenomena of emotional involvement only in passing.

In conclusion, a model of mind of consciousness is needed to account for Stanislavsky's paradox: the actor's art of being both deeply emotionally involved while acting and yet in conscious control of acting through his ability to watch himself--a paradox that is closely related to Diderot's demand for a "disinterested onlooker" in the actor.

### c. Meyerhold

Diderot changed his views on acting from an endorsement of the actor's emotional involvement to the position documented in the *Paradox*. Stanislavsky changed his views from mechanical acting and dictatorial directing to the system outlined above. At the same time, he supported the experiments of Meyerhold, who maintained that the "truth of human relationships and behavior was best expressed not by words, but by gestures, steps, attitudes and poses"[1]. Consequently, Meyerhold placed much emphasis on the actor's physical training and discipline: he wanted an actor so "thoroughly trained that he could respond immediately, as if by reflex action, to the needs dictated by his part or by the director"[2]. To achieve this aim, Meyerhold developed an acting method called *biomechanics*. It was "a gymnastic based upon: preparation for action--pause--the action itself--pause--and its corresponding reaction"[3]. Once the actor had mastered biomechanics, "he could go beyond the needs of psychological character depiction and "grip" his audience emotionally through physiological process"[4]. According to Meyerhold, the actors were not to identify emotionally with the characters they had to portray, as in Stanislavsky's approach to acting, "but to consciously comment on the character by remaining clearly distinct from it"[5]. This concept foreshadows Brecht's views. Meyerhold's insistence on non-involvement mirrors Diderot, and is in contrast to Stanislavsky. The paradox in Meyerhold's argument, however, differs from Diderot's: Meyerhold asserted that the "correct postures and moves" which the actor achieves through mastery of biomechanics, will "lead naturally to an emotional state in the actor and, by extension, affect the audience"[6]. The paradox lies in the assumption that physical movements are not the result of emotion but their stimuli.

In developing his theory of acting, Meyerhold was influenced by his materialistic world view. The general "Zeitgeist" of the 19th century with the industrial revolution, colonialist international politics, and hunger for money had suggested materialism. It was consciously theorised by left Hegelians and some scientists[7]. In pre- and post-revolutionary Russia, Marxism, in its variety of Leninism, had strong influences on Meyerhold, claiming that all phenomena of reality are of a material nature, and all cognition like a copy or photocopy of that material reality[8].

The machine was regarded as "the representative symbol of modern life"[9], and biomechanics was devised as an acting system "as technically precise as the miracles of technology"[10]. This influence was further supported by Meyerhold's interest in Pavlov's studies of conditioned response behaviour, the origin of behaviourism. The paradox of emotions as stimulated by, resulting from physical movement, rather than themselves initially causing physical reactions, was founded on William James's and C.G. Lange's originally independent, later co-authored studies in the psychology of the emotions. They viewed emotions as "perceptions of physiological disturbances", e.g. "we do not cry because we feel sad, but we feel sad because we cry"[11]. The physiological reaction is central to emotion, but in a reversed order: in the above example, "'feeling sad' is not the cause of this reaction, but instead our experience of that reaction"[12]. Critics of the James-Lange theory have pointed out that the authors "leave largely unspecified how events and objects in our environment come to produce these physiological disturbances"[13]. The most severe criticism is that the physiological changes are so unspecific that it becomes difficult to distinguish between many different emotions and their nuances merely on the basis of unspecific physiological reactions[14]. In recent years, however, studies of voluntary facial action have shown emotion-specific changes in the autonomous nervous system[15]. In addition, stimulation of emotional states in the actor and spectator by specific movements of the actor's body is also characteristic, at least in part, of the Indian theories of acting as stated in the *Natyashastra*.

Thus, Meyerhold's view that the actor's postures and movements could arouse an emotional state in the actor which then affects the audience cannot be regarded as scientifically falsified and therefore should not automatically be discarded in further discussions of acting. On the contrary, it should be one of the phenomena of the theatre that a new model of consciousness has to explain.

### d. Strasberg

Stanislavsky's system was further developed, modified, and made popular in America mainly by Lee Strasberg. The major point of departure for Strasberg was the "magic if". For Strasberg, this concept meant a series of questions which the actor has to ask himself: "Given the particular circumstances of the play, how would you behave, what would you do, how would you feel, how would you react?"[1]. Strasberg agrees that this understanding of the "magic if" helps the actor in plays "close to the contemporary and psychological experience of the actor"[2], but fails in plays that do not fulfil that requirement, e.g. classical plays. In the recognition of the principal value of the "magic if", and in an attempt to escape its drawback, Strasberg developed the principles of motivation and substitution; regarding motivation, he credited Stanislavsky-student Vakhtangov with the initial reformulation of Stanislavsky's proposition: "The circumstances of the scene indicate that the character must behave in a particular way; what would motivate you, the actor, to behave in that particular way?"[3]. The actor should not try to imagine to be the character and derive his emotions from such an imagination. Instead of imagining to be the character, the actor should the substitution technique. Strasberg comments as follows:

> The actor is not limited to the way in which he would behave within the particular circumstances set for the character; rather, he seeks a substitute reality different from that set forth in the play that will help him to behave truthfully according to the demands of the role. It is not necessarily the way he himself would behave under the same circumstances, and thus does not limit him to his own natural behavior.[4]

To achieve this substitute emotion, the actor uses several techniques, with an emphasis on the emotion memory.

A question arises about the degree of truthfulness in acting to which such a substitution technique leads. If the actor follows Stanislavsky's line, he will, with all the training of body, voice, and mind at his disposal, attempt to "inwardly live the character"[5]. To the extent that his training and his gift allow, he will become the character, and the degree to which he is able to emotionally affect the audience will be directly dependent on his ability to live the character. The Stanislavsky actor thus is guided in his attempts to internalise the character's emotions by the causal conditions set forth in the play as leading to the emotions of the character. The actor following Strasberg, it appears, initially understands the emotions that the character is believed to be feeling. Instead of trying to inwardly live the character, he substitutes the causal conditions leading to the character's emotions as set forth in the play, by causal conditions of his own making, which are supposed to lead to the same emotions as if the causal conditions were taken from the play. The spectator is confronted with an emotion that outwardly might fit the situation of a specific scene in the play. However, what the spectator is not aware of is that the emotions do not have their origin in the sequence of causal conditions in the play, but in potentially "arbitrary", unsequenced, unrelated, individual substitutes: substitute A for emotion A, substitute B for emotion A', with A' following causally from emotion A, whereas substitute B is not necessarily related to substitute A.

Two questions result: will the spectators feel the difference between genuine and substitute emotions, and does the use of substitutes make acting easier for the actor, does it require less technique, less skill, less art, than a "through-line" of emotion?

### e. Brecht

Brecht's theory of acting has frequently been referred to as constituting the direct opposite of Stanislavsky's approach. Indeed, early in his career in the theatre Brecht wrote: "I don't let my feelings intrude in my dramatic work. It'd give a false view of the world. I aim at an extremely classical, cold, highly intellectual style of performance"[1]. Neither the actor nor the spectator should identify with the emotions of the character.

To achieve such a distance of both actor and spectator from the character, Brecht developed the concept and practice of the *alienation effect*[2]. Applied to acting, the alienation effect means that the actor "does not allow himself to become completely transformed on the stage into the character"[3]. Instead, the actor *shows* the character, he "reproduces their remarks as authentically as he can; He puts forward their way of behaving to the best of his abilities and knowledge of men"[4]. Consequently, the character's emotions have to be externalised, developed into a gesture. The actor has to find a sensible perceptible outward expression for his character's emotions, preferably some action that gives away what is going on inside him[5].

"Showing" thus becomes multi-perspectival, avoiding dogmatism. Because the actor is not emotionally involved with the character, because the actor does not identify with him, he can include a running commentary in his authentic showing of the character. The actor can "pick a definite attitude to adopt towards the character whom he portrays, [and] can show what he thinks of him (...)"[6]. Thus the spectator, not asked to identify himself with the actor/character either, can intellectually observe and criticise the character portrayed. The spectator thus reaches the ideal of a "smoking-observing" status of an "expert"[7].

While emphasising the actor's and spectator's distance to the character, Brecht wanted to avoid mechanical, stylised, or abstract acting: "he aimed for truth to life, naturalness, and close observation of actual behaviour"[8]. Actual behaviour, natural life, are characterised to a large extent by emotions. Therefore, Brecht could not do without emotions on the stage; indeed, his epic theatre did employ emotional effects. Their function, however, is not to stimulate the spectator's identification with the particular emotion, but to serve as a "technique of positive reinforcement for the intellectual message"[9].

The clue to understanding the difference in the way Brecht treated emotions in the theatre lies in his views on empathy. In psychology, empathy is defined as an individual's ability to "partially and temporarily suspend the functions that maintain one's separateness from others (usually called ego-boundaries)"[10], leading to an immediate, precognitive experience of the emotional state of another individual as one's own. According to Brecht, the aesthetic assumption that emotion can only be stimulated through empathy is crude and inaccurate. Brecht rejects empathy, because it is identification, which he wishes to avoid. Brecht maintains, however, that the "rejection of empathy is not the result of the rejection of emotions, nor does it lead to such"[11]. What Brecht aims at, then, is that the actor presents emotions without having to take recourse to empathy while performing on the stage. This, to Brecht, means doing more than just getting into the character. Yet the distanced attitude of the actor does not mean that "if he is playing passionate parts he must himself remain cold"[12]. The actor is allowed feelings, with an important qualification: "It is only that his feelings must not, at bottom, be those of the character (...)"[13]. In other words, the actor must not allow empathy, the unity of his and the character's feelings, to arise while showing those feelings, nor may the actor's "exhibiting of outer signs of emotions" lead him to become infected himself by those emotions[14].

As a result of such a way of acting, the spectator's empathy is expected not to be stimulated either, allowing the spectator's intellect to critically judge the character, including the character's distanced and empathy-free emotions. In different terms, Brecht's stance resembles Diderot's aims for an actor who is not "carried away"--subjected to empathy, in Brecht's terms. It also mirrors Stanislavsky's ideal of the actor: he inwardly lives the character, and yet there is the paradoxical second aspect of the actor's consciousness that serves as an uninvolved witness to all emotional involvement, thus safeguarding that the actor is not carried away by his emotions.

There are two or three sources for Brecht's concept of the alienation effect: one originates in Brecht's interest in Chinese theatre and will be discussed later in the context of non-Western influences (see page 77ff.). The Western sources are Russian Formalism and Hegel and Marx. In 1917 Victor Sklovskij defined the term *alienation* in the field of the arts. In a broader sense, alienation motivates the artistic process and stands behind all acts of theoretical and practical curiosity, not merely as a procedure, but as a noetic principle. As a result, the individual is enabled to recognise voluntary and forced modes of perception and experience, norms and modes of behaviour as "a pair of glasses" that has placed itself in between unmediated "seeing" and "real reality". Once those glasses have been recognised as such, one can take them off and turn them into an object (no longer only medium) of perception and reflection[15]. The object of perception is perceived in a non-expected, different context and environment.

Whereas there are opinions that the formalists were not much interested in developing an explicit theory of drama or dramaturgy, Hansen-Löve argues that the formalists considered techniques of dramatic alienation as constitutive for modern theatre to such a large extent that they preferred to concentrate on less manifest techniques of literary alienation, taking theatrical alienation as already tolerated and canonised. Hansen-Löve refers to the alienation effects in Meyerhold's stage practice: mechanisation of movements in biomechanics, and the actor distancing himself from his role[16]. The view that Russian Formalism influenced Brecht is refuted by Knopf because Brecht used the concept first in 1930, five years before his visit to Moscow--although the term he used then is *Entfremdung*, not *Verfremdung*[17].

Hilton regards Marx-Hegelian views of history as the source of Brecht's concept:

> Underlying the dynamic of history is the fact that man is alienated, either from God (Hegel) or from the fruits of his labours and from power (Marx). Alienation in the theatre is an aesthetic correlative to economic alienation, a means of showing the historical process at work behind any human action.[18]

Knopf denies that Marx's use of the word *Entfremdung* matches Brecht's concept, but points to some parallels between Hegel's theory of cognition and Brecht's concept of alienation. Hegel argued that the known is not cognised only because it is known: only such things that are not accepted by feeling or faith in an unmediated fashion can be understood. Similarly, Brecht saw the function of the alienation effect in making events and actors on the stage unfamiliar to the spectator so that the spectator might notice them[19].

The alienation effect is the major technique of Brecht's *epic theatre*, which Brecht regarded as "the only dramatic means adequate for the elucidation of the complex workings of capitalist society"[20]. Alienation increases the spectator's distance from the events on the stage. As Chaim explains, an increase of distance leads to an increase of the spectator's awareness of the fictionality of the work. This produces a "dislocation of associations"[21]. The spectator is led to view the events on the stage in a larger perspective, from the outside. The spectator applies critical judgement. Increased distance thus encourages the development of a historical perspective towards one's own time, demonstrating to the audience that events must be viewed within a particular "historical field".[22]

Here Brecht clearly shows influence from Marx. Theatre serves a function in capitalist society: it can help to make the workers aware of "historical fields", ultimately aware of their own misery in capitalism, an awareness that will lead to the formation of class-conscious proletariat, as antithesis to the dominating, ruling class of capitalists.

The assessment of Brecht's theory of acting has shown that Brecht, too, places emphasis on the actor's dual consciousness of emotionally involved and non-involved, witnessing aspects of consciousness. Brecht, however, shifts the emphasis from emotion to empathy. The question of how to define empathy and how to place this human function within the framework of consciousness has to be added to the catalogue of open issues drawn up at the end of the preceding chapters.

## f. Artaud

In their various and differing attempts to improve traditional theatre practice, Diderot, Stanislavsky, Meyerhold, Brecht and Strasberg placed major emphasis on the actor: his techniques and methods of using emotions on the stage to affect the audience. Their innovations, however, remained largely within the frame of tradition: the theatrical production of a pre-written dramatic text. Artaud insisted on the necessity of a revolution of traditional theatre. In his scathing cultural critique, Artaud regarded the theatre of his day as only one aspect of art that is generally inert and disinterested[1]. In contrast, "true culture acts through power and exaltation while the European ideal of art aims to cast us into a frame of mind distinct from the power present in its exaltation"[2].

In response to the need for a magic culture, Artaud wished to create a form of theatre that could do justice to the demands of a genuine culture: theatre should be "magical and violently egoistical, that is, self-interested"[3]. He developed the *Theatre of Cruelty*, a frequently misinterpreted concept[4]. Artaud took great pains to point out that *cruelty* was not synonymous with bloodshed. He understood the term from a "mental viewpoint", implying "strictness, diligence, unrelenting decisiveness, irreversible and absolute determination"[5]. Artaud regarded any variety of physical violence as merely one minor aspect of *cruelty*, and emphasised that *cruelty* is "very lucid, a kind of strict control and submission to necessity"[6]. *Cruelty*, finally, is for Artaud a

hungering after life, cosmic strictness, relentless necessity, in the gnostic sense of a living vortex engulfing darkness, in the sense of the inescapably necessary pain without which life could not continue.[7]

According to Artaud, this *cruelty* needed specific modes of theatre different from traditional performance practices. In particular, theatre has to look for different languages than the traditional one of dialogue to convey *cruelty*. Artaud conceptualised language that is physical, "aimed at the senses and independent of speech"[8]. This physical language, also referred to as "poetry for the senses"[9], affects primarily the senses, although Artaud pointed out that it might, at later stages, amplify its full mental effect "on all possible levels and along all lines"[10].

The effectiveness of physical language on the stage depends primarily on the actor, on the effectiveness of his acting. In his emphasis on a physical language of the theatre, Artaud compares the actor to a physical athlete, with a major difference: in the case of the actor, not actual physiological muscles are trained, but affective musculature "matching the bodily localisation of our feelings"[11]. For Stanislavsky, the solar plexus was the physiological seat of the emotions; Artaud regards the rhythm of breathing as the crucial aspect of the actor's physiological counterpart of affective musculature, maintaining that "we can be sure that every mental movement, every feeling, every leap in human affectivity has an appropriate breath"[12].

Artaud develops his argument further in demanding that together with breathing, the actor has to have a directly related belief in the soul's flowing substantiality: "To know that an emotion is substantial, subject to the plastic vicissitudes of matter, gives him [the actor] control over his passions, extending our sovereign command"[13].

The actor, then, must develop his affective musculature just as an athlete must train his physiological muscles. Such development will enable the actor to do justice to the importance placed on his acting in the performance. However, the actor must also be "a kind of neutral, pliant factor since he is vigorously denied any individual initiative"[14]. This is a paradox in Artaud's theory, still unsolved, despite Artaud's vagueness which, according to Innes, is sufficient to "allow for almost any radical or anti-traditional interpretation"[15]. The paradox of the actor's simultaneous physical presence and neutrality repeats in different terminology and on the physical level rather than the emotional, Stanislavsky's paradox within the actor, the actor's art of being both deeply emotionally involved (Artaud's physical presence) and yet still in conscious control of the acting through his ability to witness his own acting (Artaud's demand for the actor's neutrality).

According to Artaud, a sufficiently trained actor will affect the anatomy of the spectator, "first by crude means, these gradually becoming more refined"[16]. Artaud likens this process to the charming of a snake through the vibrations of music through the snake's body. Through violent physical images the audience's sensibility is to be pulverised, mesmerised, "caught in the drama as if in the vortex of higher forces"[17]. As Martin puts it, the audience is exposed, through Artaud's theatre, "to its own secret crimes and obsessions"[18]. This helps the actor to rediscover the metaphysical, mystical meaning of life. According to Auslander, "Artaud adopts the posture of a psychoanalyst in suggesting that if we can recognise and confront our dark impulses we can be free, or at least in control of them"[19]. Innes argues that confronting the spectator with violent physical images "would release repressed tendencies in an emotional purgation analogous to the classical/tragic effect of catharsis"[20]. In this process, Auslander points out, the actor experiences catharsis before the audience[21].

Stanislavsky showed non-Western, Indian influences on some of his thought. Brecht was influenced by Chinese acting in formulating his concept of the alienation effect. Artaud owes very much of his views on theatre to Balinese drama. These influences will be discussed in a separate chapter (see page 78ff.)

Artaud merges influences from Oriental theatre, Cabbala philosophy and Freudian psychology into a type of performance that, as Innes adequately indicates, "draws on areas of the mind that our intellectual western tradition represses (...)"[22]. Both Artaud's vagueness of argument, and his reference to psycho-physiological concepts that had not yet been explored in the field of theatre and thus had the ring of the "exotic", made him very influential for contemporary and later theatre theorists. Artaud's theories leave some issues open:

- How can the ancient magic effectiveness of language beyond speech be understood in terms of human consciousness?

- How, can the interrelationship of breathing and feeling, emotion, be accounted for cogently?

- How to account for the paradox of the actor's simultaneous physical presence and neutrality?

## g. Grotowski

The "paradox" is the key phrase for Diderot's theory of acting, the "system" for Stanislavsky, the "method" for Strasberg, "biomechanics" for Meyerhold and "alienation" for Brecht. Similarly, there is a heading for Grotowski's theories: "poor theatre", which he developed while he led the Polish Laboratory Theatre. Grotowski sees the "personal and scenic technique of the actor as the core of theatre art"[1]. Whereas in conventional Western theatre practice the emphasis is on the actor acquiring specific skills[2], a "proliferation of signs"[3], Grotowski developed a *via negativa* (way of negation), which "necessitates the stripping away of "how to do", a mask of technique behind which the actor conceals himself, in search of the sincerity, truth and life of an exposed core of psycho-physical impulses"[4].

According to Grotowski, the prerequisite for the actor to be able to lay bare the core of his private personality[5] is that he reaches a state of mind characterised by "passive readiness to realise an active role"[6]. In such a state of mind, the actor is able not to want anything specific; he rather "resigns from not doing it"[7].

Grotowski developed various training methods to enable his actors to reach that state of mind. The methods were mainly physical, aiming "to facilitate the activation of (...) body memory: a natural reservoir of impulses to action and expression stored within the physiological make-up of an individual, an intuitive - corporeal "intelligence"[8]. If this body memory is stimulated externally, "pure and communicable signs of an archetypal nature may be released"[9]. Ideally, the result of such a stimulation of the body memory leads to a state where the actor transcends incompleteness and the "mind-body split": the "division between thought and feeling, body and soul, consciousness and the unconscious, seeing and instinct, sex and brain then disappear"[10]. Consequently, the actor achieves totality, "a certain quality of attention, or consciousness, characterised by a full presence in, and recognition of, the moment"[11]. The actor who has attained this state is free from the "time-lapse between inner impulse and outer reaction in such a way that the impulse is already an outer expression. Impulse and expression are concurrent (...)"[12]. The process leading to such a "transcendental state of being" which parallels mystical and transpersonal states[13], has to be disciplined: undisciplined "self-penetration is no liberation, but is perceived as a form of biological chaos"[14].

An actor who has ripened to the ability of enduring the extreme tension involved in completely stripping himself emotionally, psychologically, and spiritually to "totally reveal his inner self to the audience"[15], is termed by Grotowski "holy actor". A "holy actor" has been trained through physical exercises and can produce the transcendental state of consciousness described above. Grotowski does not understand the phrase "holy actor" in a religious sense: "It is rather a metaphor defining a person who, through his art, climbs upon the stake and performs an act of self-sacrifice"[16].

Grotowski's terminology: "holy actor" for the ideal actor, the actor's activity on the stage as "self-sacrifice", as "mounting a stake", points, however, if not to religion, then to the related concept of ritual. As Kott maintains, "Grotowski stubbornly and persistently tried to turn theatre back into ritual (...)"[17]. Similarly, Bates claims that for Grotowski acting is a "ritual testing of the soul, a stretching of the limits of human communication"[18]. This aspect of Grotowski's theory is closely related to his views on the actor-spectator relationship. For Grotowski, theatre originally had a function close to that of ritual: theatre

liberated the spiritual energy of the congregation or tribe by incorporating myth and profaning or rather transcending it. The spectator thus had a renewed awareness of his personal truth in the truth of the myth, and through fright and a sense of the sacred he came to catharsis.[19]

In contemporary society, Grotowski maintained, the relation of spectators to myth is different. Therefore, instead of aiming at an identification with the myth, theatre has to confront the spectator with it. Creating a shock makes the "life-mask crack and fall away"[20].

The extreme of the actor's gift of his core to the spectator, "exposure carried to outrageous excess", returns the spectator to a "concrete mythical situation, an extreme of common human truth"[21]. As Roose-Evans puts it, "If

Brecht wanted to make the spectator think, Grotowski's aim is to disturb him on a very deep level"[22].

The confrontation with myths is closely related to Jung's concept of archetypes. At the depth of human psyche lies the collective unconscious. It is a "storehouse of latent memories of our human and prehuman ancestry. It consists of instincts and archetypes that we inherit as possibilities and that often affect our behavior"[23]. The archetypes in particular are "themes that have existed in all cultures throughout history"[24]. Jung holds that these collective memories are "universal in nature because of our common evolution and brain structure"[25]. In confronting spectators with modern versions of myth, Grotowski enlivened archetypes in their collective unconscious.

Different archetypes are not equally developed within the psyche[26]. This accounts for differences in the effect of Grotowski's work on different spectators. Gilman describes how such deep disturbance, aimed at renewing the spectator, was so forceful that

> the theater (...) has felt itself in the presence of something very like a redemption (...). Almost every moment and sound is what can only be described as "pure", without precedent or predictability, yet wholly inevitable, accurate, created, true (...) In having passed beyond all hitherto known means of expression and beyond representation, they place us in the presence of emotions and consciousness themselves, in the presence, that is to say, of a creation and not an image of one.[27]

Not every spectator responded favourably to Grotowski's approach: another critic remarked on the performance's infantilism, coarseness, delusion(s) of originality, ugliness, and nihilism[28]. Indeed, Grotowski did not present plays for mainstream audiences: he was concerned with a spectator as a spiritual seeker, who wished to improve by self-analysis through "confrontation with the performance"[29]. Grotowski tried to achieve for the spectator the same "translumination" that the actor achieves when he is fully and only present in the moment, in the state of transcendence. Grotowski's method here was to minimise, as far as possible, the distance between actor and spectator, both physically and psychologically[30]. Critic Irving Wardle's comment in his review of *The Constant Prince*, a major production of the Laboratory Theatre, points to a difficulty in this attempt: Wardle noted the "immense gap between these productions and any common experience. They start on a note of intensity and ascend from there without relief"[31]. Grotowski himself admitted "that he was impotent to influence directly the spectator's spiritual and psychic responses to the acts witness"[32].

In contrast to Diderot, Stanislavsky and Brecht, Grotowski does not deal explicitly with either the actor's or the spectator's emotions. Innes argues that Grotowski uses "archetypal ideograms (...) to awaken latent emotions in the spectator through subconscious associations"[33]. Reaching the spectator's latent emotions may indeed be one channel in which Grotowski's theatre affects the spectator. However, Grotowski's ultimate goal for both actor and spectator, the transcendental state of consciousness, or "translumination"[34] close to, if not identical with, "mystical and transpersonal states of consciousness and experience"[35], surely lies beyond the already quite subtle level of the emotions. As Kumiega points out, one characteristic of this experience is that the division between thought and feeling disappears.

Frequent skepticism among theatre theorists and practitioners towards concepts such as translumination may be rooted in Freud's and Jung's uneasiness with such concepts. In a letter to Freud, Romain Rolland commented on Freud's views on the "illusory nature of religion" in *The Future of an Illusion*. He argued that Freud had failed to analyse "spontaneous religious feelings, or religious sentiments"[36]. A few years later, Freud came back to Rolland's criticism. Freud summarised Rolland's characterisation of the religious feeling thus:

> It is a feeling which he would like to call a sensation of "eternity," a feeling of something limitless, unbounded--as it were, "oceanic". This feeling, he adds, is a purely subjective fact, not an article of faith; it brings with it no assurance of personal immortality, but it is the source of the religious energy which is seized upon by the various Churches and religious systems, directed by them into particular channels, and doubtless also exhausted by them.[37]

Whereas Rolland stated that he was never without that oceanic experience, and which he presumed to exist in millions of people, Freud could not discover this feeling in himself[38]. He intellectually traces the possibility of an oceanic experience back to the early phase of ego-feeling. Originally, the child's ego includes everything, only "later it separates off an external world from itself"[39]. The feeling in the early, unitary state can be called "oceanic". Continuation of such a feeling into adulthood can be explained with the assumption that "there are many people in whose mental life this primary ego-feeling has persisted to a greater or less degree"[40]. In the adult capable of oceanic experiences, the primary ego-feeling co-exists with the "narrower and more sharply demarcated ego-feeling of maturity (...)"[41]. An oceanic experience is thus characterised by Freud as a "regression to infantile levels of pre-individuation"[42].

C.G.Jung's model of the human mind differs from Freud's structure of Ego, Super-Ego and Id. For Jung, the levels are Ego, Personal Unconscious, Collective Unconscious, and Self. The ego is not identical with psyche or consciousness, it is one aspect of the psyche at the centre of consciousness, responsible for "our feelings of identity and continuity as human beings"[43]. The personal unconscious contains all past and forgotten experience, as well as sense impressions too weak to have become conscious. Material in the personal unconscious is accessible to consciousness in specific circumstances such as, for example, psychoanalysis. The level deepest within the psyche is the collective unconscious, inaccessible to consciousness, seat of archetypes. If the individual is placed in favourable conditions of evolution, of personal development, he can reach a state of self-realisation, where the ego is replaced by the self as the centre of consciousness[44].

The paradoxes of acting expressly formulated by, or implicit in the theories of Diderot (an emotionally not involved actor emotionally involves an audience), Stanislavsky (the same actor is both emotionally involved and distanced at the same time) and Brecht (the actor inwardly lives the character, without falling into the trap of empathy) have prepared the way for Grotowski; the paradox that resulted from such a combination, collage, of elements from various cultural sources was the insight of the creative coexistence of two elements that appear, at first sight, to be opposed and mutually exclusive: spontaneity and discipline: "what is elementary feeds what is constructed and vice versa"[45]. Grotowski insisted on his actor's physical discipline, which they gained through regular exercise. The idea that the actor can reach to the unconscious, the source of archetypes, by stimulating the body memory, goes back to the James-Lange theory of emotions and Meyerhold's application of it in his "biomechanics". Kumiega has asserted that body memory stimulates the emotions[46]. However, as argued above, Grotowski's ultimate aim is to reach beyond the emotions.

Grotowski closed the Laboratory Theatre in 1970 . According to Kott, Grotowski realised that his attempts to turn theatre back into ritual "is sacrilege, pillage of the *sacrum*" for true believers, and "for non-believers a form of cheating"[47]. In the following years, Grotowski developed paratheatrical activities. Here, he was able to fully explore his role as therapist in a process of social healing. Grotowski had aimed for his Laboratory Theatre to have a healing effect on the spectators. However, he had direct access only to the actors, and could only hope that the effect on the spectators would be according to his intention. In the setup of paratheatrical events, there was no longer a distinction between actor and audience:

> Grotowski developed a total concentration on the internal process of self-discovery in groups of the public as participants. In effect they were subjected to an extended session of psychotherapy based on the acting exercises developed by the Theatre Laboratory, (...).[48]

Grotowski's work with the Laboratory theatre in Poland owes much to non-Western aesthetics and training methods. These will be discussed later together with non-Western influences on the other theatre artists discussed in this section (see page 82ff.). The assessment of Grotowski's theory in the context of Western influences leads to the following open issues which have to be addressed part two of this study:

- How to account for experiences of the actor's "translumination" and its effect on the spectator?
- How to account for the paradox of coexistence of discipline and spontaneity in the actor?

### h. Schechner

Richard Schechner is influenced by an even larger set of theories about acting and related areas of knowledge than Artaud or Grotowski. Besides the Indian *Natyashastra* and Zeami's writings on Noh theatre, Schechner draws heavily on Victor Turner's school of anthropology. Schechner defines *drama* as a "written text, score, scenario, instruction plan, or map"[1]. The *script* is "all that can be transmitted from time to time and from place to place; the basic code of events (...)"[2]. The transmitter of the script has to know the script and he must be able to teach others, whereas the transmission of drama is independent of the transmitter's knowledge, or comprehension of the drama, even his literacy[3]. *Theatre* is "the event enacted by a specific group of performers; what the performers actually do during production. The theater is concrete and immediate. Usually, the theater is the manifestation or representation of drama and/or script"[4]. Schechner finally defines *performance* as the whole

> constellation of events, most of them passing unnoticed, that take place in/among both performance and audience from the time the first spectator enters the field of performance--the precinct where the theater takes place--to the time the spectator leaves.[5]

The different constituents of the theatre are further defined by Schechner as the domain respectively of different individuals or groups of individuals involved in the theatre process:

> The drama is the domain of the author, the composer, scenarist, shaman; the script is the domain of the teacher, guru, master; the theater is the domain of the performers; the performance is the domain of the audience.[6]

The terms "shaman" and "guru" indicate non-Western concepts.

Schechner maintains that performance is never completely original: instead, performance is characterised by "restored behavior"[7]. Performers of all kinds, not restricted to the theatre but extending to ritual and shamanism, "assume that some behaviors---organized sequences of events, scripted actions, known texts, scored movements--exist separate from the performers who "do" these behaviors"[8]. The performance, then, arises when the performer gets in touch with, remembers, or recovers these "strips of behavior".

Schechner offers two differentiations among performers: first, there are two fundamentally different modes of performing "restored behavior": either the actor is getting absorbed into the "strips of behavior", and he plays the role, even goes into a trance. Or he exists side by side with the role, characteristic of Brecht's *Verfremdungseffekt*[9]. Second, Schechner differentiates between a performance process during which the performer is "subtracted", and the opposite process during which the performer is "added to". Subtraction refers to Grotowski's concept of eliminating the obstacles and resistances from the performer's body. Schechner compares this method, which achieves "transparency", "ecstasy"[10], to the technique of the shaman in non-Western culture, and mentions Ryczart Cieslak's performance in the Laboratory Theatre's production of *The Constant Prince* as an example from Western theatre. The technique of addition implies that the performer "becomes more than s/he is when not performing"[11]. Schechner compares this approach to that of the Balinese dancer in non-Western culture, and to Stanislavsky's performance as Vershinin[12]. Schechner argues that this process leads to trance, to "the performer becoming or being possessed by another"[13].

The restoration process does not take place, according to Schechner, during the actual performance, but, in theatre, it is carried out in rehearsals; in non-theatrical performative situations, such as ritual and shamanism, the restoration work takes the form of a "transmission of behavior from master to novice"[14].

The proposition of performance as "twice-behaved", restored behaviour leads Schechner to conclude that performance is never "free and easy"[15], and therefore it never fully "belongs to" the performer. This conclusion invalidates Stanislavsky's approach to acting designed to provide the actor with techniques allowing him to make performance behaviour look "as if" it belonged to the performer"[16]. Instead, Schechner argues in favour of a performer whose art and skill lie in combining maximum spontaneity with maximum discipline[17], a paradox already familiar from Grotowski.

Schechner continues his analysis of performance by arguing that the co-existence of spontaneity and discipline, as well as any other psycho-physiological changes in the performer relating to the performance, may either be limited to the rehearsal and performance; or they may extend beyond the performance. Schechner captured this difference in his concepts of "transformation" and "transportation". If the performer goes from the "ordinary world" to the "performance world", "from one time/space reference to another, from one personality to one or more others"[18], but returns to the "ordinary world" after the performance is over, this is called transportation. In contrast, transformation performance change the performers. Transportation is characteristic of theatre performance, in the domain of theatre history, whereas transformation is characteristic of ritual, shamanistic performance, in the domain of anthropology.

Here, Schechner is influenced by Victor Turner's approach to anthropology. Turner proposes that the "roots of theatre are in social drama"[19]. He defined social dramas as "unity of a harmonic or disharmonic social process, arising in conflict situations"[20], and differentiated four phases of social dramas:

1. Breach of regular norm-governed social relations.
2. Crisis during which there is a tendency for the breach to widen.
3. Redressive action ranging from personal advice and informal mediation or arbitration to formal judicial and legal machinery, and, to resolve certain kinds of crisis or legitimate other modes of resolution, to the performance of public ritual.
4. (...) either the reintegration of the disturbed social group, or (...) the social recognition and legitimation of irreparable schism between the contrasting parties.[21]

Schechner's assumption that ritual develops into theatre when "a participating audience fragments into a collection of people who pay, who come because the show is advertised, who evaluate what they are going to see before they see it"[22] mirrors Turner's view that theatre has its roots in social drama. However, social drama as described by Turner and drama for the theatre, called "aesthetic drama" by Turner, differ. Whereas social drama, through its element of ritual, leads both performer and spectator to a transformation, a permanent change, aesthetic drama implies merely a transportation, a temporary change[23].

When it comes to the differentiation between ritual and theatre, another topic of interest to Artaud and Grotowski, Schechner shifts the emphasis towards a related pair of concepts: it is possible to lift any ritual from its "original setting" and perform it in the theatre[24];

Whether one calls a specific performance ritual or theater depends on the degree to which performance is pure efficacy or pure entertainment (...) When efficacy dominates, performances are universalistic, allegorical, ritualized, tied to a stable, established order; this kind of theatre persists for a relatively short time. When entertainment dominates, performances are class-oriented, individualized, show business, constantly adjusted to suit the tastes of a fickle audience.[25]

Turner's influence on Schechner extends beyond the broad interrelations of social versus aesthetic drama and ritual versus drama. Schechner locates the performance in an area of "betwixt and between": the performer plays a part, which is not himself, but at the same time, as he is playing the part, the portrayed character is also "not not himself". The "between" is thus applicable on the level of the performer and the part, but also between performers, between performer and script, between performers, script and environment, and finally between performers, script, environment and spectators[26]. Schechner concludes that "the larger the field of "between", of "not me (...) not not me", the more powerful the performance"[27]. The "between" is indispensable for a performance, because the performer experiences its creation as "ensemble feeling", while the spectators experience it as the sense of being "touched" or "moved"[28].

Schechner calls the "between" field "liminal space"[29], a term taken from Turner's anthropology. In the theory of ritual proposed by van Gennep, "limen" denotes a stage in the *rite de passage*, ritual initiation. In the first phase, as described by van Gennep, the ritual subjects (novices, candidates, neophytes, initiands), are separated from their previous social status. This stage is followed by a transition phase, during which the ritual subjects

> pass through a period and area of ambiguity, a sort of social limbo which has few (though sometimes these are most crucial) of the attributes of either the preceding or profane social statuses or cultural states.[30]

During the third phase, the ritual subject is returned to his/her "new, relatively stable, well-defined position in the total society"[31]. Van Gennep called the second phase, the period of transition, "margin" or "limen", ("threshold" in Latin[32]), and Turner took this concept of "limen" up and adapted it to his theory of social drama. In the post-ritualistic society, the liminal has been removed from its original ritualistic context of a *rite de passage*. Therefore, Turner calls it "liminoid", and argues that the "liminoid is not only removed from a *rite de passage* context, it is also individualized"[33]. In the context of the theatre, individualisation means that the "solitary artist *creates* the liminoid phenomena, the collectivity *experiences* collective liminal symbols"[34].

Closely related to the concept of the liminal and liminoid in Turner's anthropology are the phenomena of "communitas" and "flow", and those phenomena, in turn, play their part in Schechner's theory of the theatre. Communitas refers to a style of human interaction in which at least two individuals experience unity. Turner describes that "it has something "magical" about it. Subjectively there is in it a feeling of endless power"[35], and he asks:

> Is there any of us who has not known this moment when compatible people (...) obtain a flash of lucid mutual understanding on the existential level, when they feel that all problems, not just their problems, could be resolved, whether emotional or cognitive, if only the group

which is felt (in the first person) as "essentially us" could sustain its intersubjective illumination?[36]

Turner concludes that communitas has something of a "flow" quality as described by Csikszentmihalyi and MacAloon: merging of action and awareness; centering of attention; loss of ego; being in control of one's actions and of the environment; coherent, non-contradictory demands for action and unambiguous feedback. Finally, flow is autotelic, not needing outward goals or rewards: "To flow is to be as happy as a human can be"[37].

Turner tried to accommodate the concepts of communitas and flow with contemporary brain research and neuroscience. His emphasis in those attempts lies on the specialisation of the left and right cerebral hemispheres. The left hemisphere is responsible for speech production and linear, analytic, thought, assessment of temporal units, and sequential information processing. Spatial and temporal perception, emotion, and holistic, synthetic thought are attributed, in turn, to the right hemisphere, whose linguistic capacity is believed to be limited and the temporal capacity altogether lacking[38].

Research indicates that "the rhythmic activity of ritual, aided by sonic, visual, photic, and other kinds of "driving", may lead in time to simultaneous maximum stimulation"[39] of both hemispheres. This in turn is experienced by the participants of ritual as "positive, ineffable affect", also described by Freud's term "oceanic experience", and the Christian concept of "unio mystica", to which Turner adds, among others, the Zen term "Satori", and yogic "samadhi"[40]. In a theatrical context, Grotowski's concept of "translumination", Artaud's idea of a language beyond speech come to mind.

Schechner feels uncomfortable with Turner's attempt to "relocate and thereby resolve the "problems" of ritual action in the workings of evolution, or, more specifically, the human brain"[41]. On the other hand, Schechner admits his own attraction to such ideas, which he followed in the framework of Indian theatre and dance aesthetics. There as in Western tradition he locates the phenomenon of the actor's dual consciousness[42]. Schechner refers to Fisher's model of conscious states, who differentiates the normal "I" from ergotropic states (characterised by arousal, hyperarousal and ecstasy) and trophotropic states (ranging from tranquility and hypoarousal to Yoga *samadhi*)[43]. Schechner associates the ergotropic system with the left, and the trophotropic with the right hemisphere. He then argues that during the actor's experience of dual consciousness, the brain is functioning with three halves: "Both the ergotropic and trophotropic systems are aroused, while the "center" of the performer, the "I", stands outside observing and to some degree controlling"[44]. Schechner indicates that the neurological mechanisms of the actor's double functioning remain to be investigated[45]. Clearly, this paradox closely resembles Diderot's demand for an unmoved, disinterested onlooker within the actor[46], a concept which has been shown to re-emerge in Stanislavsky and subsequent theatre theorists.

Schechner assesses both Western and Oriental traditions of theatre, and especially the Oriental (Japanese and Indian) aesthetics lead him to place not the actor's emotions at the centre of his argument, as Diderot, Stanislavsky and Strasberg, and to a lesser extent Meyerhold and Brecht had done. It appears that the more Oriental influence makes its way into theatre theory and practice, the more the writers try to lead theatre practice and experience, both for the actor and the spectator, to an area of the mind that lies beyond the emotions. Turner wrote about this experience in terms of "flow" and "communitas"; in studies of "flow" experience in literature, the term "privileged moment" is used[47]. A common characteristic of such "peak experience"[48], the impossibility to summon it at will, presents a major problem for theatre practitioners, and explains the growing number of possible methods that have been developed help the actor achieve "flow", methods incorporating many available Western techniques of psychoanalysis, combined with Oriental meditative or physical practices. A widespread mistrust of creating theatre effect through the emotions stimulated by imagination, has led to increased emphasis on the body, placing renewed faith in contemporary forms of the James-Lange theory of emotion: the actor can stimulate his emotions through adequate manipulation of his body, which will affect his mind.

In this context, Schechner points to Ekman's research into the relationship between facial movement and emotions. Ekman studied the emotions of anger, disgust, fear, happiness, sadness, and surprise. In the experiment, he provided subjects with muscle-by-muscle instructions and coaching to produce facial configurations for those emotions. During the experiment, some of the subjects' functions, such as rate, skin conductance, finger temperature and somatic activity were monitored[49]. These are functions of the autonomic nervous system, beyond influence of the will. Ekman found that

> voluntary facial activity produced significant levels of subjective experience of the associated emotion, and that autonomic distinctions among emotions: (a) were found both between negative and positive emotions and among negative emotions, (b) were consistent between group and individual subjects' data, (c) were found in both male and female subjects), (d) were found in both specialised (actors, scientists) and nonspecialised populations, (e) were stronger when the voluntary facial configurations most closely resembled actual emotional expressions, and (f) were stronger when experience of the associated emotion was reported.[50]

Despite such findings, the relationship of the body to consciousness, however, remains vague in theories of the theatre, placing even more emphasis on the necessity of developing a model of the mind that incorporates a cogent explanation of that interaction, so as to provide a basis for comprehending what is involved in transformation, transportation, communitas, flow, and other related states of consciousness.

### i. Eugenio Barba

Barba spent some years at Grotowski's Laboratory Theatre in Poland, and continued his teacher's research into the psycho-physiological basis of acting[1]. Barba founded the Odin Teatret in Norway in 1964, moving to its permanent home in Holstebro, Denmark, in 1966. In the early 1970s, non-Scandinavians joined the group, and it has by now included members from Italy, the USA, Britain, Canada, Germany, Spain, and Argentina. The Odin Teatret became the centre for the government-funded Nordisk Teaterlaboratorium[2], inspired by Grotowski's Laboratory Theatre. Its activities reach beyond Barba's direct theatrical activities at the Odin Teatret:

> It is a major teaching center, it arranges performances for international companies in various parts of Scandinavia, it publishes and sells theatre books, it makes and rents films on the theatre, and it is the umbrella organization for several groups associated with the Odin.[3]

In 1979, the activities of the Nordisk Teaterlaboratorium culminated in the foundation the *International School of Theatre Anthropology* (ISTA), which is a most unusual school that has no classrooms or students, meets only periodically, has no curriculum, and has no graduates. Nevertheless, it is one of Europe's most important theatre research institutions.[4]

Holstebro functions as the administrative centre of ISTA; its primary work takes place, as Watson describes, at public sessions "held from time to time at the request of particular funding bodies"[5]. At these sessions, Eastern and Western master performers share their expertise with "relatively young, inexperienced" Western actors and directors. These practitioners are joined by "intellectuals including theatre scholars, anthropologists, psychologists, biologists, and critics"[6].

*Theatre anthropology* is the key concept in Barba's theatre theory and practice, and it subsumes a variety of concepts. Barba emphasises that the term "anthropology" is not used "in the sense of cultural anthropology"[7]. Rather, theatre anthropology "is a new field of study applied to the human being in a performance situation"[8]. Theatre anthropology incorporates both Occidental and Oriental theatre theory and practice and intends to provide "bits of advice" to the actor, rather than looking for universal principles or laws[9].

The actor is at the centre of theatre anthropology. Barba was inspired to set this priority by Grotowski and by his interest in the actor's *presence* on stage: "I am interested in a very elementary question: Why, when I see two actors doing the same thing, I get fascinated by one and not by the other".[10] Barba also uses the terms *body-in-life* or *bios* when analysing *presence*[11]. He distinguishes between daily behaviour, i.e. mainly unconscious "processes through which our bodies and voices absorb and reflect the culture in which we live"[12], and extra-daily behaviour, i.e. the specific codes of movement pertaining to specific performance forms, which, in their aesthetic function, differ from daily behaviour[13].

Closely related to the concept of extra-daily behaviour is the concept of the *pre-expressive*, which Barba defines as "The level [of performance] which deals with how to render the actor's energy scenically alive, that is with how the actor can become a presence which immediately attracts the spectator's attention."[14] Research has led Barba to differentiate three principles that govern the pre-expressive level of performance: "alterations in balance, the law of opposition, and (...) coherent incoherence"[15]. Whereas in daily behaviour, all movements of the body tend to follow the principle of least action, leading to a "minimum expenditure of energy for standing, sitting, and walking"[16], extra-daily behaviour of performance requires shifts in balance, which in turn lead to more energy being required for movement, for remaining still, or for retaining balance. The second principle, the law of opposition, is closely related to the alterations of balance. In both cases, daily behaviour patterns have to be distorted. In Western classical ballet the dancer maximises the opposition between body weight and gravity in "soaring feats of lightness and grace"[17]. The dancer spends much energy in the attempt to free himself from the force of gravity.

The surplus of energy needed in performance is incoherent because it "makes no sense from a practical, daily life, point of view". However, it is also understandable, and in that sense coherent, that the actor spends this much more energy in extra-daily, performative activity, because the excessive energy expenditure is a major source of the dynamic in each of the performance genres[18].

Barba suggests a sequence of development of proper (extra-daily) technique for the actor: the actor first has to distance himself from "incultured" spontaneity. He has to understand the difference between himself in daily mode of behaviour and the techniques which characterise the extra-daily mode of performance[19]. It is as if the actor has to learn all movements on the stage anew: he undergoes a process of physical acculturation[20]. However, the more conscious the actor is of his extra-daily movements, the more he becomes blocked. The actor has to aim for accultured spontaneity rather than incultured spontaneity.

In the process, Barba pinpoints a paradox at the centre of the actor's art and methodology: it is located in the actor's interaction with his role and with the audience. Barba argues that an actor does not merely present the fictional world of the play, nor does his activity end in his own experience of portraying a fictional character. For Barba, performance is a "dialectic between the two", what he calls "the anatomical theatre"[21]. In the performance, the actor portrays the fictional score, i.e. the "physical actions and vocal delivery decided upon in rehearsal and repeated in each performance"[22], and his meeting with it. This meeting will vary from performance to performance, depending on several factors:

the audience's reaction to the piece, the actor's psycho-emotional responses to events on stage as well as in the theatre, and the actor's personal associations with particular actions and/or situations in a work s/he has developed with his/her colleagues over a period of some eighteen months to two years.[23]

The relationship between (rehearsed) score and (unrehearsed, spontaneous) meeting with the score is characterised by tension. Barba maintains that it is through the convergence of these opposing forces, that our personal experiences can reach others, and be transformed into a social experience: through theatre.[24]

Here Barba's theatre aesthetics differ substantially from Grotowski's: for Grotowski, the convergence of opposing forces of score and the actor's experience was "the means by which the actor instigated a process of self-revelation that affected the spectator"[25]. This implies that the performer's catharsis leads to catharsis in the audience. For Barba, the convergence of score and the actor's experience enriches the "relationship between the performer and his/her audience directly"[26]

It is in this relationship between actor and spectator that Barba's paradox is located: the actor's "articulate actions" on the stage are perceived by the spectator as objective signs. These objective signs, however, result from subjective processes within the actor. Barba raises the question: "How can the actor be this matrix and be able, at the same time, to shape them into objective signs whose origin is in his own subjectivity?"[27]. This paradox, the simultaneity of inner subjectivity and objective outer expression and reception of that subjectivity, closely resembles the paradox of acting formulated by Diderot and taken up with different shifts of emphasis by the other theorists discussed so far. Barba's position combines the paradox in the actor--spectator relationship with the paradox in the actor himself. Indirectly, Barba also argues in favour of an actor's dual consciousness.

The externalisation of subjectivity, i.e. emotions, has to be disciplined. In Barba's theatre anthropology, discipline is closely related to training: "Training is a process of self-definition, a process of self-discipline (...)"[28]. The emphasis on training is an emphasis on the body, which in turn is in line with the general tendency among contemporary theatre theorists and artists to stress the importance of the actor's body. Training thus appears outwardly physical, but, as Barba points out, it is not the exercise in itself that counts--for example, bending or somersaults--but the individual's justification for his own work, a justification which although perhaps banal or difficult to explain through words, is physiologically perceptible, evident to the observer.[29]

What Barba appears to imply here is that the actor's physical performance as perceived by an outside observer will differ depending on the actor's mental attitude behind the physical expression.

Body technique is only one component of the "theatre's body". The second is "the organ of *u-topia*, of "non-place", residing in the actor's viscera and his right hemisphere. "It is the super-ego which the presence of a master or masters has imbued us with during the transitions from daily technique to extra-daily performance technique"[30]. This organ transforms technique and raises it "to a social and spiritual dimension"[31]. Barba describes the third organ as the "irrational and secret temperature which renders our actions incandescent"[32]. Whereas the body and the "super-ego" can be trained, the elusive third organ is "our personal destiny. If we don't have it, no one can teach it to us"[33]. A unity of the three organs of the "theatre's body", allows the actor to radiate energy, establish "presence", thus attracting the spectator's attention.

Reference to the "third organ", which remains rather elusive, is the most explicit reference to consciousness yet among the theatre theorists and artists discussed so far. Nevertheless, the reference is vague and does not lead very far. As Watson points out,

> Barba is essentially a creative artist, a poet both in the theatre and in his writings about it. This poetic quality calls for a careful reading of his ideas since he favors poetic metaphors over the more traditional intellectual approach of deductive logic to sustain his arguments.[34]

The relationship between mind and body, the phenomenon of the pre-expressive, and the three organs of the theatre's body have to be re-assessed from a cogent model of consciousness. Such a reassessment will have to address the relationship between Western and Eastern training and performance techniques, traditions, and aesthetics, too, which are so central to Barba's intercultural theories.

## j. Peter Brook

In 1942, Peter Brook (born 1925), directed his first production, Marlowe's *Doctor Faustus*. Brook continued directing in major mainstream theatre in Britain, including the Royal Shakespeare Company (RSC), as well as opera and film. Inspired by Artaud, Brook mounted a short *Theatre of Cruelty* season in 1964, and continued what Williams calls a phase of "theatre of disturbance"[1], with Genet's *The Screens*, Weiss's *The Marat/Sade*, a public reading of Weiss's *The Investigation*, about the atrocities at Auschwitz, in 1965, and in 1966, *US*, centring around the Vietnam war. Those projects all aimed, William argues, at confrontation, "comprising abrupt tonal transitions and jarring clashes of style, to create the impression of a continually shifting and mutable reality"[2]. From 1968 to 1970, Brook directed *Oedipus* at the National Theatre in London, *The Tempest* at the Théatre des Nations, and *A Midsummer Night's Dream* at the RSC. In 1968, his seminal book, *The Empty Space*, was published.

In 1970, Brook left Britain and founded the *Centre International de Re-cherche Théatrale* (C.I.R.T.; the name was changed to *Centre International de Créations Théatrales, C.I.C.T.* in 1974) in Paris, from where he has conducted his theatre research and projects since, including journeys to Africa, the USA and India, and projects including *Orghast, Conference of the Birds, The Ik, La Tragédie de Carmen, The Mahabharata*.

Commenting on Peter Brook, Jacqueline Martin argues that his ideas about acting provide a synthesis of several acting theories in the 19th and 20th centuries:

> From Stanislavsky he has learned that an actor must practice how to be insincere with sincerity--how to lie truthfully; from Brecht he has learned the value of distancing oneself from the work by stepping back and looking at the results; from Artaud he has learned that by abandoning the text and working through improvisation one can return to the roots of physical expression; (...) and from Grotowski he has learned that actors are mediumistic.[3]

Brook's main interest in the theatre is concerned with the "possibility of arriving (...) at a ritual expression of the true driving forces of our time"[4]. The different phases of Brook's career outlined above are nothing but different approaches to reach this aim. Whereas Grotowski tried to turn theatre back into ritual, Brook turns ritual into theatre[5]. Brook's ultimate aim is a "totality of theatrical expression"[6], a theatre that transcends "the surface of reality"[7]. This may be achieved by shocking the audience, as in Brook's experiments with Artaudian *theatre of cruelty*, by working with an international cast, by forays into anthropology (*Conference of the Birds*), by creating (or re-creating?) a new (ancient) language (*Orghast*), by making the elitist genre of opera accessible again (*The Tragedy of Carmen*, seen, worldwide, by at least 200,000 people[8]), by bridging the gap between theatre and storytelling (*The Mahabharata*), or the gap between theatre and science (*The Man Who*). In addition to these new approaches of "transcending the surface", while working at C.I.C..T., he directed two plays from the more traditional theatrical canon, such as *The Cherry Orchard* (1981 and 1988), and *The Tempest* (1991).

In our problem ridden society, according to Brook, transcendence is difficult to achieve; however, he maintains that despite all movement, destruction, restlessness and fashion, there are "pillars of affirmation", rare moments when during a theatre performance actors, play, and spectators merge collectively in a "total experience, a total theatre"[9]. Brook further characterises such experiences: "At these rare moments, the theatre of joy, of catharsis, of celebration, the theatre of exploration, the theatre of shared meaning, the living theatre are one"[10].

Grotowski reduced the theatre, leaving, as Brook puts it, "a solitary man playing out his ultimate drama alone"[11]. In contrast, for Brook, theatre leads "out of loneliness to the perception that is heightened because it is shared"[12]. If the theatre tries to "slavishly recapture" such experiences of sharing through imitation, however, once they are gone, theatre will become deadly[13].

Stages on the way to *total theatre* are *rough theatre* and *holy theatre*. Both "feed on deep and true aspirations in their audience, both tap infinite resources of energy, of different energies"[14]. *Rough theatre* is down-to-earth and direct; its energies are militant: anger and hatred, but also fed by lightheartedness and gaiety[15]. *Holy theatre*, Brook maintains, could also be called "theatre of the invisible-made-visible"[16]. The invisible contains all the hidden impulses of man. Brook's view mirrors Barba's position on the function of theatre: "rendering the invisible visible", implying an investigation of the process "by means of which mental energy (invisible) becomes somatic energy (physical)"[17]. Brook's understanding of the function of theatre, although using the same terms here, is different from Barba's: Brook's point of departure is the religious implication of the pair of opposites: although the invisible is visible all the time, seeing it is not automatic, but it requires certain conditions, either a mental state or a certain understanding. Meeting such conditions is not easy and it takes a long time: "In any event, to comprehend the visibility of the invisible is a life's work"[18]. Theatre that deserves to be called *holy theatre* "not only presents the invisible but also offers conditions that make its perception possible"[19]. Once *total theatre* is experienced, however, the divisions into deadly, rough and holy theatre disappear[20].

*Rough theatre, holy theatre,* and above all *total theatre* need a highly trained actor. For Brook, training first implies physical training, leading to a body that is "open, responsive, and unified in all its responses"[21]. Second is the training of the emotions, leading to the actor's "capacity to feel, appreciate and express a range of emotions from the crudest to the most refined"[22]. While the actor experiences the emotions, however, while he is sincere, he has to be detached at the same time. Brook here reflects Stanislavsky's and Brecht's paradox.

The achievement of total, transcendental theatre has remained Brook's "grail-like quest"[23] throughout his career. The actor applies his physical and emotional efforts to achieve Brook's aim of simple forms of theatre that are both understandable and simultaneously "packed with meaning"[24]. In *Orghast*, Brook had the poet Ted Hughes develop a new language, also called Orghast. The language was based on the concept of total identity between sound and meaning[25]. The intention, according to Innes, was "not only (...) to reflect the sensation of a half- barbaric world, but to affect "magically" the mental state of the listener on an instinctive level in the same way as a sound can affect the growth of plants or the patterning of iron filings"[26]. Innes points out, however, that *Orghast* worked only with intellectually sophisticated spectators, whereas a "supposedly more primitive (and therefore in theory more receptive, even more susceptible) audience on Brook's African tour, apparently found those dark primordial cries hilariously funny"[27].

Brook's production of *The Mahabharata*, both for the theatre and for film/television, has been called the apotheosis of Brook's research into theatre[28]. The title of the Indian epic implies "the great history of mankind", and the "great poem of the world"[29]. Brook attempted to arrive at universality through language in *Orghast*, and strove for the same aim in the *Mahabharata* project.

through the concept of *dharma* (duty) which he localised at the centre of the philosophy expounded in the Epic. In his view, the *Mahabharata* does not "explain the secret of *dharma*, but lets it become a living reality. It does this through dramatic situations which force *dharma* into the open"[30].

However, Brook's foray into Indian culture, using the great Indian epic of *The Mahabharata* for his theatrical purposes, has been criticised as cultural exploitation. Details of this criticism will be discussed in the larger context of interculturalism later on in this study.

## Summary

The question that led to Diderot's paradox has held its important position in the Western tradition of acting theory to the present: should the actor be emotionally involved while acting? Diderot argued in favour of non-involvement, maintaining that the actor has to have "in himself an unmoved and disinterested onlooker"[1]. According to Stanislavsky, the actor uses a concentrated mind as the major means among others to gain access to the unconscious, the source of true theatrical inspiration; however, the actor does not get carried away emotionally, he does not lose self-control, because the material brought forth from the unconscious is "weighed and determined consciously"[2]. Strasberg developed Stanislavsky's system into the "Method", with even more emphasis on the - emotions, but with less on the unconscious. Meyerhold opposed Stanislavsky's views, arguing against the actor's emotional involvement: trained by biomechanics, the actor would be able to produce physical movements that stimulated emotions which in turn 'would be transferred to the audience. Criticism of emotional involvement is most prominently voiced by Brecht, who used the actor's distance from the part as a major means to achieve an alienation effect, leading not to emotional involvement on the side of the audience, but to their intellectual stimulation to adopt a critical attitude towards the play, the characters presented on the stage. Whereas the actor shows the feelings of the character portrayed as authentically as possible, he is not involved on the level of empathy. This view mirrors both Stanislavsky and Diderot in their emphasis that the actor should not be carried away emotionally.

With Artaud, Grotowski, Schechner, Barba and Brook, the function of the emotions changes: the emotional stimulation of the audience, the transfer of emotions from actor to spectator, is less and less considered the aim of theatre performance. Instead, various means are sought to enable both actor and spectator to reach to levels of the mind beyond the intellect, beyond the emotions, variously termed "language beyond speech" (Artaud), "translumination" (Grotowski), "transformation" or "transportation" (Schechner), "communitas" and "flow" (Turner), "theatre rendering the invisible visible" (Barba) and "holy theatre" (Brook).

## 2. Western Points of Contact

So far, the theories on the actor's emotional involvement have been discussed in the framework of the theatre artists' and theorists' Western historical influences. Before addressing non-Western historical influences, further recent developments in psychology and related disciplines will be discussed. These developments did not directly influence the artists and theorists; however, our understanding of the phenomena experienced by the artists and theorists can be improved by discussing how recent theories in psychology might explain those experiences

### a. Altered states of consciousness

*Language beyond speech* (Artaud), *translumination* (Grotowski), *transformation* or *transportation* (Schechner), *communitas* and *flow* (Turner), *theatre rendering the invisible visible* (Barba) and *holy theatre* (Brook) are states of consciousness beyond the intellect and beyond the emotions; they clearly represent non-ordinary or altered states of consciousness. Traditionally, three major states of consciousness are distinguished: waking, dreaming, and sleeping. They are the "normal" states of consciousness. The term "normal" needs further explanation. What is "normal" is "defined by society and it is society's standards of perceptual normalcy that are part of an individual's personality"[1]. Normal states of consciousness, then, are what society agrees to be the norm, the ordinary. Non-ordinary states of consciousness are referred to as "altered states of consciousness" (abbreviated ASC). In one of the first attempts to account for

ASC, Ludwig describes general characteristics of ASC. They include alterations in thinking, a disturbed time sense, a loss of control, change in emotional experiences, a change of body images, perceptual distortions, changes in meaning or significance, a sense of the ineffable, a feeling of rejuvenation, and hypersuggestibility[2]. Ludwig also lists major ways of inducing ASC, and discusses the functions of ASC[3]. It is revealing that he supports seven maladaptive expressions by empirical evidence, but mentions only three adaptive expressions (healing, avenues of new knowledge and experience, social function)[4]. This emphasis on negative attributes of ASC is in line with Tart's claim that orthodox psychology regards ASC as "a temporary reorganisation of brain functioning", and holds that "our ordinary state of consciousness is generally the most adaptive and rational way the mind can be organised, and virtually all ASC are inferior or pathological", going into ASC spontaneously is a sign of mental illness, and "deliberately cultivating ASC is also a sign of psychopathology"[5]. This view, formulated in 1975, is supported by the choice of contents in an annotated bibliography on "States of Awareness" which lists articles on subjects such as depersonalisation, sleepwalking, amnesia, anaesthesia, thyroid disorders, near-death experience, deja-vu, out of body experiences and sensory deprivation[6], many of which would feature in psychopathology.

However, serious attempts can be found to account for and explain desirable and adaptive ASC. Clark constructs a map of mental states, similar to a map in geography. It "represents a large amount of information crowded into a very small space"[7]. He defines as "mind" "the whole range of mental states, i.e. of conscious states, sleeping and waking, which a person can experience"[8]. A "mental state" is defined as "the values taken by a person's set of "main" mental variables at any particular time"[9]. The main variables are "mind work, general mood: pleasant or unpleasant; Intensity of general mood and aspects of mind; on-line and off-line functions; sleeping or waking; concentration and diffusion of attention; and attention and things"[10]. Clark's incorporation of states of mental illness necessitate the inclusion of some extra variables such as "Anxiety; Obsessions; Compulsions; Phobias; Irritability; Hallucinations; Delusions; Pain; Disorientation; Anger; Fear; Guilt; Repugnance; Boredom; Depersonalisation; Derealization"[11]. However, as opposed to other researchers writing about states of consciousness, Clark also incorporates desirable, "higher" mental states in his map. For this purpose, he discusses mysticism, which "concerns an unusual kind of experience obtained other than by the senses"[12]. Clark identifies seven main ideas in the content of mystical states, and relates those to some faculties of the mind[13]:

| Seven main ideas (aspects of mind) | Faculty |
| --- | --- |
| K  Knowledge, significance | |
| U  Unity, belongingness | |
| E  Eternity, eternal now, being | Cognition |
| | |
| L  Light, exteroception | |
| B  Body sense, interoception | Perception |
| | |
| J  Joy | Emotion |
| | |
| F  Freedom | Volition |

Clark also extracts certain recurrent comments on mystical states in the writings by the mystics. They are intensity; certainty; clarity; ineffability; sudden onset; and change of personality[14]. Finally, he differentiates between an average state, a state of peak experience (expressly borrowing the term from Maslow), and the mystical state proper (which is more intensive than the peak experience, but still within the range of being describable in words)[15]. The climax of a transition from average state to peak experience to mystical experience proper is referred to as the "Void". Clark describes it as ineffable, and "a place of sudden transition"[16], and associates it with the Buddhist concept of *Nirvana*. Another "set of members of the family of mystical states", termed "Dark" in quality, are also considered by Clark. They will not be of importance to the present study, however, and are therefore not further described here.

Fischer, whose concepts of tropho- and ergotropic arousal are used by Schechner in explaining the actor's dual consciousness, developed his "cartography" of consciousness further against the conceptual background of the autopoiesis theory proposed by Maturana and Varela.

Maturana's point of departure is a radical constructivism which assumes that any perception of an object, all experience, is not the image of reality, of objects, but *a priori* its construction by the subject. An essential new aspect in this approach is the central position of the observer. Self-referral, something going on within himself, leads to those phenomena traditionally called perception and understanding. The idea behind this is that man is an autopoietic system. One characteristic of such a system is its cyclic organisation, which can be understood as self-reproduction. All information which the autopoietic system needs to maintain its circular organisation, are inherent in the circular organisation itself. For that reason an autopoietic system can be regarded as a closed system. This conclusion in turn leads to the conclusion that an autopoietic system is characterised by being self-referral: the system itself defines what will be a partner in reaction to that system. It also defines itself the modality of the import, the transformation and the export of output.

If applied to human beings, these general characteristics of autopoietic systems mean the following: the human nervous system is, anatomically, a closed system, which functions in all the regions of the body as one organ through the network of nerve cells. This organ leads all the activities of the individual nerve cells to a holistic integration. If events take place in the environment of a human being, which have any kind of effect on the human nervous system, the nervous system suffers deformations with which it has to cope. Every act of perception comprises a series of such deformations. It depends solely on the nervous system itself, what kind of deformation a certain event will constitute for the system, as what kind of event the system experiences the deformation, and what attitude the system has towards the deformation. In interpersonal relations, the deformation can be defined as the way and the intensity, effected by the partner of interaction. Because the definition of the deformation and the experiencing, the constructing of perception, are solely determined by the experiencing system, the partners of interaction have no direct influence on how they are perceived from their respective partners of interaction[17]

In this conceptual context, Fischer places his theory of states of awareness. He differentiates between the motor domain and the sensory domain of the organism. Following Maturana, Fischer states that "every change in the motor domain (M) of an organism triggers a change in activity in the sensory domain(S) and vice versa"[18]. The technical term used to express this phenomenon is "S/M closure". Every time an S/M closure is effected, it will result in "recursive reflections of the self-referential subject in the mirror of a universe that is himself"[19]. An approximate S/M ratio of 1:1 is associated with the normal state of consciousness in daily routine "construction" of outside reality. Higher S/M ratios are equivalent to a "prevalence of the subjective component"[20]. These in turn are the main feature of non-ordinary hyper-and hypo-aroused states of consciousness. Those two categories provide the major dividing pattern for Fischer's cartography, associating hypo-arousal with ergotropic aspects of the brain, and hyper-arousal with trophotropic aspects.

### b. The phenomenon of pure consciousness

The attempt to provide consciousness with a basis is found in studies of the phenomenon of pure consciousness, the mystical state proper in Clark's terminology. The term "pure consciousness" is similar to the term used by Stace to describe the extraordinary state of consciousness reported by saints and sages throughout the ages: "pure unitary consciousness"[1]. Also in the context of mysticism, Forman edited a collection of essays explicitly dealing with "Pure Consciousness Events (PCE)", defined as "wakeful though contentless (nonintentional) consciousness"[2]. Placing the PCE within Stace's framework, Forman considers them as a form of what

> W. T. Stace called "introvertive mysticism", which he distinguished from "extrovertive mysticism". In extrovertive mysticism one perceives a new relation ship--one of unity, blessedness, reality (...) --between the external world and the self. In introvertive mysticism there is no awareness of the external world per se; the experience is of the Self itself. [3]

Forman describes the current "received view" on all kinds of mystical experiences, including PCEs, as "constructivism" which argues that

> mystical experience is significantly shaped and formed by the subject's beliefs, concepts and expectations. This view, in turn, emerged as a response to the so-called perennial philosophy school. Perennialists-- notably William James, Evelyn Underhill, Joseph Maréchal, William Johnston, James Pratt, Mircea Eliade, and W. T. Stace--maintained that mystical experience represented an immediate, direct contact with a (variously defined) absolute principle. Only after that immediate contact with the "something more" according to this school, is such a direct contact *interpreted* according to the tradition's language and beliefs.[4]

In the book, Forman assembles articles that argue in favour of the existence of PCEs, by looking at Yoga, Buddhist philosophy, the writings of Meister Eckhart, and Jewish mysticism. The articles in the second part of the book argue that "constructivism has not, and cannot plausibly account for these experiences"[5].

Forman also provides two descriptions of the experience of pure consciousness. The first is from a subject just after instruction into the Transcendental Meditation technique:

> I distinctly recall the first day of instruction [in the transcendental meditation technique], my first clear experience of transcending. Following the instruction of the teacher, without knowing what to expect, I began to drift down into deeper and deeper levels of relaxation, as if I were sinking into my chair. Then, for some time, perhaps for a minute or a few minutes, I experienced a silent inner state of no thoughts; just pure awareness and nothing else; then again I became aware of my surroundings. It left me with a sense of deep ease, inner renewal, and happiness. [6]

Forman comments: "It is striking that the subject notes that he did not "know what to expect", for this tends to support the claim that one may have a PCE even without the purportedly shaping expectations"[7].

The second report demonstrates how the experiences deepen in the course of time:

> After about two years, my experience of the transcendent started to become clearer. At that time, I would settle down, it would be very quiet (...) and then I would transcend, and there would be just a sort of complete silence void of content. The whole awareness would turn in, and there would be no thought, no activity, and no perception, and yet it was somehow comforting. It was just there and I could know when I was in it. There wasn't a great "Oh, I am experiencing this". It was very natural and innocent. But I did not yet identify myself with this silent, content-free inner space. It was a self-contained entity that I transcended to and experienced.
>
> Then, with increased familiarity and contingent on the amount of rest I had, the process of transcending became more and more natural. The whole physiology was now accustomed to just slipping within, and at some point it would literally "click", and with that, the breath would almost cease, the spine would become straight, and the lungs would cease to move. There would be no weight anywhere in the body, the whole physiology was at rest. At this point I began to appreciate that this inner space was not an emptiness but simply silent consciousness without content or activity, and I began to recognise in it the essence of my own self as pure consciousness. Eventually, even the thin boundary that had previously separated individuality from unbounded pure consciousness began to dissolve. The "I" as a separate entity just started to have no meaning. The boundaries that I put on myself became like a mesh, a net; it became porous and then dissolved; only unbroken pure consciousness or existence remains. Once I let go of the veil of individuality, there is no longer "I perceiving" or "I aware". There is only that, there is nothing else there. In this state the experiencer is not experiencing as it normally does. It is there ready to experience, but the function has ceased. There is not thought, there is no activity, there is no experiencer, but the physiology after that state is incredible. It is like a power surge of complete purity.[8]

The concept of "translumination" and similar concepts by other theatre artists share several features with the state of pure consciousness, only on an advanced level characterised by a simultaneity of pure consciousness and activity--the "holy" actor, i.e. the actor who has achieved translumination, is still operating in the waking state of consciousness while at the same time experiencing qualities associated with pure consciousness.

## c. The mind-body relationship

Discussing points of contact between the theories of the actor's emotional involvement and theories of consciousness has so far helped to broaden the perspective and cleared the way for rescuing the theatre artists' experiences from the realm of unobtainable mysticism or psychopathological malfunctioning. Growing interest in physical aspects of acting has recently focused attention not only on consciousness, but especially on the relationship of consciousness (or mind) and body.

In his recent review of theories of the mind-body relationship, Hodgson concludes that the mechanistic model represents the current consensus among psychologists, philosophers, natural scientists and computer scientists[1]. De Berry uses an analogy from computer science to describe this position:

(...) the brain, like a computer, is hard-wired and (...) consciousness is totally dependent upon the existence of the brain (...) Consciousness within this model is viewed as a type of flexible software, interesting and versatile, but dependent on the mainframe circuits.[2]

Hodgson names some apparent and true dissenters, without, however, granting their views much influence in the overall consensus[3].

Among the dissident views, Velmans acknowledges the differences of dualist and reductionist theories, but finds one characteristic they share: "They assume (...) that the contents of consciousness are separate from the external physical world as perceived"[4]. Velmans argues that sensory perceptions or what he terms the "world-as-perceived" is "a construct of perceptual processing and, therefore, part of the contents of consciousness"[5]. As a consequence, Velmans proposes a reflexive model of "how consciousness relates to the brain and to the physical world":

> Whereas Dualists locate percepts *of* external events "within the mind" and Reductionists locate those percepts within the brain, the Reflexive model states that external events as-perceived are "projected" by the brain to the judged location of the initiating stimulus.[6]

Another "dissident view" can be associated with an increasing number of publications on the relevance of quantum mechanics for the mind-body relationship. Such attempts are by no means uncontroversial. Thus Lockwood cautions against enthusiasm when he writes:

> Mind and brain doubtless are quantum-mechanical, if quantum mechanics is universally applicable. And so constructing them has (...) far-reaching, not to say startling, implications. But there is nothing in any of this, taken by itself, to suggest that anything beyond classical physics and chemistry is needed, if one is to provide an account of the workings of the brain that is *functionally* adequate at the level relevant to psychology.[7]

Wolf, on the other hand, argues that there is "not the slightest shred of evidence that proves the existence of a physical world acting independently of human thought"[8]. He claims that, in parallel to quantum mechanics, "acts of observation create the sensations we call *experiences of the real world*"[9]. Wolf then describes the mind, synonymous with consciousness, as one and only one, not interfered with, and devoid of sensory experience[10]. At the same time, the mind is many: "From the one mind all minds and all experiences are projected. This means that within unity there is infinity"[11]. Jahn and Dunne argue in favour of a "quantum-mechanical model of the rudimentary consciousness-atom, consisting of an array of spherical standing waves representing probabilities-of-experience patterns in a space defined by the intensity, attitude, and of consciousness in its interaction with its personal environment"[12].

Hodgson also integrates quantum mechanics in his analysis of the mind-body problem. He accepts Popper's concept of two worlds: World 1 is physical and objective, World 2 mental or subjective:

> Matter as we know it is mind-dependent in certain respects: for its appearance, for its characteristics as we perceive them, perhaps for its existence in space, though probably not for its place in time, and probably not as its existence as code. On the approach of this book, mind or World 2 transcends the code of World 1 by "creating" matter as we know it out of

abstract code, and by determining by reason between alternative quantum possibilities to which the code gives rise.[13]

The physicist Bohm develops a new theory of the relationship between mind and matter, suggesting that it is one of participation rather than interaction. Bohm starts with the quantum mechanical insight that an electron, for example, "is regarded as an inseparable union of a particle and a field"[14]. The field is quantum mechanical in nature and can be represented in terms of a quantum potential. The electron can be thought of as moving under its own energy, but it is the quantum potential that gives the electron's motion a form. Bohm refers to this characteristic of the quantum potential as "active information", and argues that this notion suggests "a rudimentary mind-like behaviour of matter, for an essential quality of mind is just the activity of form, rather than of substance"[15]. This principle of "active information", according to Bohm, is not just accurate on the level of the electron, but at "indefinitely great levels of subtlety"[16]. The quantum potential gives rise to the movement of particles. In parallel, Bohm proposes a superquantum potential "that can give form to the unfoldment and development of this first order quantum potential"[17]. What we experience as mind, Bohm concludes, "in its movement through various levels of subtlety, will, in a natural way ultimately move the body by reaching the level of the quantum potential and of the "dance" of the particles"[18]. Bohm's model of the mind-matter relationship is based on principles of contemporary physics and can be interpreted as suggesting a quantum-mechanical common source of both mind and matter, reminiscent of Spinoza, who, according to Tallis, holds that "the original substance is neither mind or matter, the latter being attributes to the original substance rather than primary substances in themselves.[19]

In the development of theatre theory and practice from Diderot to Schechner, the body's role in acting and actor training has received increasing attention. This development is proportional to at least four factors: first, to the increase in scientific knowledge of physiological processes. The second reason for increasing interest in the body's role in performance is the growing disillusionment with numerous psychological theories which failed to provide a consensus either regarding the structure and functioning of the human psyche or the relationship of mind and body. The third reason is the growing interest in Indian dance forms which were interpreted as using and affecting mainly the body. Finally, the concept of *disponibilité*, developed by Jacques Lecoq, has to be taken into account in the context of the body-orientated performance art of improvisation.

Assessing the insights yielded by an increase in scientific knowledge of physiological processes, Pradier develops a biological theory of the body in performance. Some of the issues he addresses are (a) the *epiphanic system*, defined as "(...) the sum of physical (visual, acoustic, tactile) and physico-chemical constants pertaining to the performer that can act consciously or unconsciously on a receiver, either directly or indirectly, separately or combined"[20].

(b) Performance activity illustrating the holistic aspect of human behaviour:

the most elaborate types of behaviour always include a component of sensory and motor responses (i.e. body memory, movements involved with language activity, etc). The physiological processes of stabilisation, development, and preservation of the integrity of the central nervous system (CNS) always include a performing aspect.[21]

(c) Pradier proposes that the performing arts "correspond to an instinctive magnification of biological motions"[22]. The concept of biological motion is related to an experiment: "When a small number of lights are placed on the limbs and joints of a moving human--or animal--the motions of the lights dubbed "biological motions" (...) are sufficient to enable adult observers to perceive immediately the activity of the human"[23].

(d) Research suggests that performance "acts on the immune system of the performers"[24]. Pradier concludes that it must, in consequence, also affect the audience's immune system. In support of this hypothesis, Pradier refers to a controversial experiment carried out at Harvard University: saliva taken from spectators watching a film of Mother Theresa's healing activities in Calcutta showed a higher rate of antibodies which protect against respiratory affections (IgA)[25].

(e) The psychic exaltation of the actor, no matter whether professional or not, associated with an increase of neuro-hormones (which has yet to be verified empirically), makes it tempting for Pradier to see "a performance as a kind of neuro-hormonal reward auto-stimulation"[26].

(f) The performing arts, especially its elements of dance and mime, "have a sensory-motor stimulation function for the audience"[27]. In this context, Pradier uses the term "restoration", and he expressly puts it into the context of Schechner's use of that term: Pradier wants to

> signal a "biological restoration" as opposed to the "biological decadence" observed in daily life among most cultures. By visually and auditorily working on movement and acoustic patterns, actors/ dancers/ singers can help the audience have a stronger and more holistic and balanced alignment, a kind of embodiment.[28]

(g) Pradier presents a comprehensive list of open issues regarding possible connections of performance and biological rhythms, e.g. "Are rhythms in the performing arts also based on a neural time code (...)?"[29].

Regarding Lecoq's concept of *disponibilité*, Frost and Yarrow define improvisation as

> the skill of using bodies, space, all human resources, to generate a coherent physical expression of an idea, a situation, a character (even, perhaps, a text); to do this spontaneously, in response to the immediate stimuli of one's environment, and to do it (...) as though taken by surprise, without preconceptions.[30]

*Disponibilité*, as defined by Lecoq, "is not just a theory but an experiential condition; a way of being which can be sought and found. It sums up

> in a single term the condition improvisers aspire to: it offers a way of describing an almost intangible and nearly undefinable state of being: having at (or in) one's fingertips, and any other part of the body, the capacity to do and say what is appropriate, and to have the confidence to make the choice. Its a kind of total awareness, a sense of being at one with the context, script, if such there be, actors, audience, theatre space, oneself and one's body.[31]

*Disponibilité* is thus characterised by an experience of total presence in the present, from moment to moment. Since the body can be experienced, and such experience described in words more tangibly than an (altered state of) consciousness, and because the theories of ASC are vague and contradictory, it is no wonder that discourse in performance (theory and practice) concentrates on the body rather than the mind.

### e. A synthesis of *biomechanics* and Ekman's research: Alba-Emoting

Meyerhold had argued that the actor who has mastered biomechanics will be able to generate body postures which in turn will arouse emotions in the actor. By extension, these emotions will then affect the audience. Ekman's research showed that voluntary facial expression can arouse emotions normally associated with those facial expressions.

Susanna Bloch has developed an acting technique which proposes to unite the "method" school of acting "which asserts that the main project in acting is the creation of emotion *in the actor*" and Diderot, who asserts that "it is unnecessary, counterproductive even, for actors to worry about *feeling* emotions"[1]. For the purpose of her studies, Bloch defined emotions as "distinct and dynamic functional states of the entire organism comprising particular groups of effector systems (visceral, endocrine, muscular) *and* particular corresponding subjective states (feelings)"[2].

Laboratory research led to the conclusion that "specific emotional feelings were linked to specific patterns of breathing, facial expression, degree of muscular tension, and postural attitudes"[3]. Of the complex neuromuscular, visceral, and neuroendocrine reactions "which are activated during a natural spontaneous emotion", only those that can be voluntarily controlled and therefore reproduced were selected for further study: breathing rhythm and a "particular expressive attitude", both facial and postural[4]. Whereas Ekman studied only the emotional impact of re-creating facial expressions corresponding to specific emotions, Bloch adds breathing pattern and posture; in her view, this addition reduces the possibility that the expressions resulting from facial mimicry "may appear to the observer as artificial masks rather than re-created emotions"[5].

After establishing these three "emotional effector patterns", further experiments with "naive subjects" were carried out, showing that "if instructions for reproducing an emotional effector pattern are correctly followed, the appropriate actions will trigger the corresponding subjective experience in the performer"[6]. The effectiveness of this technique is reported to be so powerful that a specific "step-out" technique had to be developed, allowing the actor to "switch off" the emotion intentionally activated by using the ALBA EMOTING technique. The basic technique comprises six basic emotions: joy, anger, sadness, fear, eroticism, and tenderness. Once actors achieve "mastery" in reproducing these six, they can combine them in an infinite number of degrees of intensity[7]. Testing some of Bloch's techniques, Rix was impressed by the results and emphasised especially the strong potential of "the breathing patterns as a tool for emotional work"[8]. Rix, however, also raises some important questions:

> How to avoid leading students into intense emotional territory for which they are un-prepared; what to do when and if that happens; how to teach the technique so that students feel empowered rather than manipulated; how to work with students who can't reproduce breathing patterns; how (or whether) to integrate the technique into existing approaches to emotion, including memory- based ones.[9]

A model of consciousness which can accommodate all previously established requirements will also have to account for a mind-body relationship able to produce the effects demonstrated in the ALBA-EMOTING technique.

## 2. Non-Western Influences on Western Theories

### a. General non-Western influences

Stanislavsky, Brecht, Artaud, Grotowski, Schechner, Barba, and Brook derived some of their theoretical and practical inspiration from non-Western concepts of philosophy, psychology and theatre. Brecht, for example, developed his concept of the *alienation effect* not only under the influence of Russian formalism, but was also was influenced by his impressions of Chinese acting[1]. Brecht pointed out that the audience of Chinese acting was "hindered from simply identifying itself with the character in the play"[2]. In Brecht's view, this led to the spectators accepting or rejecting the character's actions and utterances consciously rather than unconsciously[3]. To achieve this consciousness in the spectators, according to Brecht, the Chinese actor expresses his awareness of being watched, i.e. he does not assume the existence of a fourth wall[4]. He limits "himself from the start to simply quoting the character played"[5], and employs self-observation as a further means of distancing the spectators[6]. The Chinese actor's self-observation is closely related to Diderot's idea of the "unmoved and disinterested onlooker"[7] and Stanislavsky's demand for an actor's dual consciousness in that the actor should be both emotionally involved and yet able to control the involvement through his ability to watch himself. The experience of dual consciousness has to be at the core of a model of consciousness able to explain the psychology of acting.

Artaud's emphasis on physical language has its origin in his admiration of Balinese theatre:

> In fact the strange thing about all these gestures (...) is the feeling of a new bodily language no longer based on words but on signs which emerges through the maze of gestures, postures (...) leaving not even the smallest area of the stage space unused.[8]

Artaud reformulated the principle of a physical language which he discovered in Balinese theatre in the context of his own views on culture. This language "develops its physical and poetic effects on all conscious levels and in all senses", and Artaud proposes that it "must lead to thought adopting deep attitudes which might be called *active metaphysics*[9]. It is the language of nature, its grammar undiscovered as yet[10]. "It poetically retraces the steps which culminated in the creation of speech"[11]. Artaud associates this "new" dimension of language with an "ancient magic effectiveness (...) whose mysterious potential is now forgotten"[12]. In aiming at a "language beyond speech", Artaud might be pointing towards a level of language that is beyond culture, and thus universal. However, since Artaud was apparently unable to transform those ideas into practical theatre, "language beyond speech" has remained just another vague concept in Artaud's theories of the theatre, which has to be accounted for in a cogent model of consciousness which this study intends to provide.

Artaud was also directly influenced by the philosophy of the Cabbala, which provided him with the concept of breathing rhythm which he adapted to the needs of the actor: the actor must understand and apply the principles of breathing: "Breathing accompanies feeling and an actor can penetrate this feeling through breathing, provided he knows how to distinguish which breathing suits which feeling"[13]. Artaud developed six main breathing combinations formed from the three components of masculine, feminine, and neuter breathing. In addition, he proposed a seventh state, "higher than breathing, uniting the revealed and the unrevealed"[14]. Again, the concept is vague. However, Bloch's research into breathing as part of her ALBA EMOTING technique suggests that Artaud's intuitions might have some validity, after all. The seventh state of breathing appears to go beyond ordinary breathing functions of the body, just as "language beyond speech" refers to a state of language beyond what is ordinarily experienced as language. Could "language beyond speech" be a form of language limited to the realm of "extra-daily behaviour" of the theatre, and could, similarly, the seventh state of breathing be restricted to aesthetic activity and experience? Both "language beyond speech" and the "seventh state of breathing" certainly point towards experiences located in a non-ordinary, altered state of consciousness.

## b. Influences of Indian philosophy

Since the major non-Western influence on theatre artists such as Grotowski, Schechner, Barba, and Brook, and the only ones in the case of Stanislavsky, comes from India, Indian philosophy and theatre aesthetics have to be taken into account when studying theories of the actor's emotional involvement. This serves several purposes: Direct influences of Indian concepts on Western theories can be highlighted, and Indian aesthetic concepts on their own may prove fruitful for the understanding of the actor's emotional involvement in the theatre.

The body of literature that makes up Indian philosophy is called "Veda", which translates as "pure knowledge"[1]. Vedic literature consists of the following texts: The four main texts are *Rig Veda, Sama Veda, Yajur Veda, Atharva Veda*. The *Upanishads, Aranyakas,* and *Brahmanas,* provide commentaries of those major texts. The *Upangas,* also known as *Darshanas,* are the six systems of Indian philosophy, comprising *Nyaya, Vaisheshika, Samkhya, Yoga, Karma Mimansa* and *Vedanta,* The first system, *Nyaya,* teaches the path of gaining knowledge. Illustrating this by using the example of the knowledge of a tree, *Nyaya* shows the way of how and where to start. The second system, *Vaisheshika,* deals with the analysis of the exterior world: it breaks up the tree into its parts, analyses its outer structure, stem, branches, leaves, metaphorically speaking. *Samkhya* analyses the subject, i.e. the deeper dimensions of the tree, e.g. the year rings. *Yoga* is the experiential science of consciousness, providing concepts of pure consciousness (*samadhi*); in the tree-illustration, *Yoga* recognises the reality of the tree in the all-pervading sap. *Karma Mimansa* emphasises the dynamics within *samadhi*, i.e. it analyses the dynamic elements present in the sap, which in turn cause the growth of the tree out of the sap. *Vedanta,* finally, the sixth system, provides the synthesis of knowledge gained by application of all the five preceding systems. It establishes that there is ultimately no difference between sap and tree. Whereas those levels, sap and tree, were experienced as separate in *Yoga*, they are experienced as unified in *Vedanta*[2]. The *Vedangas*, which correspond to the six *Upangas*, are six systems of studying the Vedic texts, i.e *Shiksha* (phonetics), *Kalpa* (rituals), *Nirukta* (semantics), *Vyakaran* (grammar), *Chhandas* (metrics) and *Jyotish* (astrology). The *Itihasa* comprises the two main epic poems, the *Ramayana* and the *Mahabharata*.

The *Upaveda* are collections of texts on specific subjects: *Ayurveda* provides the classical Indian system of medicine, *Dhanurveda* is a treatise on archery, *Stapathyaveda* deals with architecture. Finally, *Gandharvaveda* incorporates the major treatises on music theatre, the *Natyashastra*, ascribed to Bharata; the *Narada-Shiksha* by Narada, and the *Sangita--Ratnakara* by Sharngadev. All three texts of *Gandharvaveda* cover, in various scope, three aspects of music: song (*gitam*), instrumental music (*vadyam*), and dance, theatre arts (*nrittam*). The *Sangita-Ratnakara* describes in some detail the development of the human being from the unmanifest primordial sound called *nada*. In addition, this text provides a detailed description of physiology refined by meditation and music played according to the rules of *Gandharvaveda*.

Concepts of Indian philosophy which can be shown to have influenced Western theatre artists have to be examined within the framework of Vedic literature. Stanislavsky argued that the Solar Plexus, the radiating centre of *prana*, the vital energy of life, is the seat of emotion in the same way that the brain is the seat of consciousness. Stanislavsky believed that not only external, visible movements are manifest, but also "inner, invisible acts of spiritual communion"[3]. In consequence, Stanislavsky asks the actor: "In addition to the consciousness, explicit discussion and intellectual exchange of thought, can you feel a parallel exchange of currents, something you draw in through your eyes and put out again through them?"[4]. Stanislavsky termed this current of energy, derived from the Hindu concept of *prana*, "irradiation", and likened it to "an underground river, which flows continuously under the surface of both words and silence and forms an invisible bond between subject and object"[5]. According to Vedic literature, *prana* or life-energy is a direct emanation of Brahman, absolute consciousness[6]. It is located in the heart lotus, equivalent to the solar plexus[7]. Prana itself gives rise to several functions of the body: "It enables the eyes to see, the skin to feel, the mouth to speak, the food to be digested, and it performs all the functions in the body"[8]. Thus the function of *prana* appears to be related to the functioning of the body as a manifestation of consciousness more than specifically related to the emotions; a misunderstanding in Stanislavsky's sources or on his own part seems likely, associating an energy which is centred in the heart with the emotions, which are traditionally associated with the heart.

Stanislavsky described the unconscious objective as the best and most desirable, and he states: "The Hindus call such objectives the highest kind of superconsciousness"[9]. In terms of Indian philosophy, pure, contentless consciousness is called *samadhi*. In the individual process of development of consciousness, occasional glimpses of pure consciousness are called *savikalpa samadhi*. Such temporary pure consciousness is differentiated from permanent pure consciousness, or *nirvikalpa samadhi*[10]. Grotowski's concept of translumination constitutes a stage between the two: whereas the experience of pure consciousness is maintained throughout the state of translumination, it is not permanent in the sense that it will continue after the state of translumination is over. Translumination is thus more than *savikalpa samadhi* and less than *nirvikalpa samadhi*. In relation to Indian aesthetics, translumination is similar in nature to the experience of *rasa*: the experience of *rasa*, too, is originally limited to the duration of acting or spectating.

C. G. Jung, an important Western influence on Grotowski, was interested in Indian philosophy, and came across the concept of *samadhi*. Jung, however, identified it as a "trance-like or unconscious state. He believed that it is an absorption into the collective unconscious (...)"[11]. However, he rejected as "Indian philosophy overreaching itself"[12] the assumption that "the individual ego can be completely transcended and some form of universal consciousness achieved. In Jung's eyes, this was nothing more than a psychological projection of an idea which had no foundation in human experience"[13].

Instead, for Jung the mystical experience, called *samadhi* in Indian philosophy, consisted in a "replacement of the conscious ego with the more powerful numinous forces of the unconscious arising from the God or self archetype"[14]. Jung describes an experience of the source, the depth of unconsciousness as follows:

The meeting of oneself is, at first, a meeting with one's own shadow (...) a tight passage, a narrow door. (...) But one must learn to know oneself in order to know who oneself is. For what comes after the door is, surprisingly enough, a boundless expanse full of unprecedented uncertainties, with apparently no inside and no outside, no here and no there, no mine and no thine, no good and no bad. It is the world of water, where all life floats in suspension; where (...) the soul of everything living begins.[15]

Although Jung apparently experienced a state of pure consciousness, his psychological framework did not allow him to account for it in concepts such as *samadhi*, which were at odds with his own concepts of consciousness.

Grotowski saw himself in the role of a psychiatrist, facilitating the actors' and spectator' psychic improvement. Grotowski's recent public appearances have elicited the description of "guru", closing the circle to Indian influences in Grotowski's earlier stages.

The concept of "Guru" needs clarification. It dates back to the Vedic times, when the Guru was a Brahmin teacher who ensured oral tradition of Vedic hymns. He usually was a married man whose home became the home of his pupils: "Students who were qualified by birth had to be accepted and, once installed, they became the Guru's responsibility"[16]. During the minimum period of eight years of training, the students would learn the Vedic hymns by heart, and they would serve their Guru[17]. In the course of time, the concept of "Guru" broadened. Leaders of religious sects, often claiming descent from a deity, were called adi-Guru; the heads of monasteries performed the function of a Guru. The Sad-Guru, finally, is for many the "real Guru"[18]. He has reached *moksha*, liberation, and he leads others on the path to enlightenment.

In recent years, several mainly Indian spiritual movements have attracted followers and support in the West[19]. The leaders of these movements have been called "Guru", either reverentially by their followers, or critically, when the term "Guru" gets the negative connotations of mysticism, obscurity, quackery, or dogmatism[20]. Vigne points out that the roles the Sad-Guru in India and the Western psychiatrist are only marginally related. For example, most people turning to the psychoanalyst are in need of help, they are neurotic or borderline. Only few come because of intellectual curiosity or because they want to become psychoanalysts themselves. The Guru usually accepts only mentally healthy, competent, responsible people as his disciples[21]. The disciple's commitment to the Guru is for life, i.e. until the disciple has reached *moksha*, enlightenment, himself. The patient's commitment to the psychoanalyst is limited in time[22]. According to Vigne, contemporary Western skepticism towards Gurus is also due to the assumption that people who choose a Guru will be "highly emotional, without discernment, falling into the arms of anyone provided he has a white beard"[23]. In the Indian tradition, however, choosing a Guru is a very serious matter. Vigne points out that it may take years to locate him, and may take more time before one approaches him for initiation. In contrast, many people choose their psychoanalyst from the telephone book[24].

Is Grotowski a psychoanalyst, or psychotherapist, or Guru, as has been claimed? It is impossible to answer with a clear "yes" or "no". Grotowski understands his work as therapeutic, and in the theatrical framework he used archetypes to influence actors and spectators. In his paratheatrical work, techniques resemble more and more Moreno's psychodrama, although Grotowski continues to use, as with his actors in the Laboratory theatre, and as Alessandro Fersen does in his mnemodrama, mentally healthy and stable participants, not patients as in psychodrama.[25]

Calling Grotowski a Guru is not appropriate if "Guru" is used in the sense of the Sad-Guru, it only applies if "we take "Guru" in its broad sense of counsellor, or in reference to someone who looks for a way out of his problems"[26].

### c. Indian theatre aesthetics: the *Natyashastra*

Western theatre artists, especially Grotowski and Barba, and to a lesser extent Schechner and Brook, have been inspired by Indian theatre aesthetics of the *Natyashastra*, which is part of *Gandharvaveda*,

The *Natyashastra* mainly stresses the *nrittam* aspect, dance and movement of the body. From the texts of *Gandharvaveda*, it is therefore the most important for this study. In Indian aesthetics, three areas of performative activity are differentiated: *nritta*, *nritya*, and *natya*. These three are closely related to each other. The *Kathak*-dance is an example of *nritta*. It is a pure dance form, "which depends on the musical beat and in which dance steps have to be in perfect harmony with the musical beats of a percussion instrument"[1]. In *Kathak* performance, hand movements and gestures function merely as ornaments. *nritya*, with *Bharata Natya* as its most well-known contemporary representative, "is a dance form which exhibits a mental state, a mood; and, through it, attempts also to work out an incident or a small happening"[2]. Therefore, *nritya* is not limited to an emphasis on rhythmic steps, but uses the body, gestures, and facial expressions. These are no longer mere ornaments, but fully integrated and functional elements of performance. *Natya*, finally, "is a mimicry of actions and conducts of people which is rich in various emotions, and which depicts different situations"[3]. It comprises and integrates all aspects of performance, i.e. spoken dialogue, body movement and gestures, make-up and costumes, stage props "to suggest the scene of action"[4], and psycho-physical expressions of human emotions.

Both the theory of *natya* and its practical application in performance are covered in the earliest extant treatise on dramaturgy, the *Natyashastra*. The text mentions some other texts and their authors, so that it must be concluded that other sources existed prior to the *Natyashastra* itself, but no manuscripts of those earlier sources have been found so far. The authorship of the *Natyashastra* is ascribed to Bharata. However, there is no historical evidence outside the *Natyashastra* for his existence. Moreover, several critics argue, based mainly on linguistic studies of the text, that the *Natyashastra* is not a homogeneous composition of one author, but a compilation of dramatic theory and instructions for the actor of how to put the theory into practice. Critics disagree as to whether there was one original text by one author with was changed over the years, or whether the text was from the beginning a compiliatory effort of several authors. Srinivasan finds an irreducible heterogeneity in the text and argues that "we have every reason to conclude that these disparate materials are not later accretions to the *Natyashastra* known to us"[5]. A major difficulty in textual matters is that there are many manuscripts of the *Natyashastra* which differ considerably among each other as to content, numbering of stanzas and chapters, some even in ascribing the author[6]. As uncertain as the authorship of the *Natyashastra* is its date, placed between the first century B.C. and the 8th century A.D.[7].

The scope of the material covered in the *Natyashastra* is vast. There are 36 chapters, beginning with the origin of drama, and encompassing dramatic theory as well as practical instructions to the actors of how to achieve aesthetic experiences in the spectators. The term *shastra* implies a holy text, and in the *Natyashastra* itself Bharata claims that *Natya*, drama, was created by the creator, Brahman, as a fifth Veda, taking recitative from the *Rigveda*, the song from *Samaveda*, the histrionic representation from the *Yajurveda*, and the sentiments from the *Atharvaveda*[8].

For the orthodox in India thus the *Natyashastra* has the combined force and authority of a divinely revealed *shruti*, the sage-expounded *smritis*, and the broad based popular tradition of the *Puranas*.[9] It is therefore no wonder that the *Natyashastra* must still be regarded as the primary source for Indian aesthetics, and indeed all the later Indian theorists of dramaturgy expressly refer to the *Natyashastra*.

The key concept in the aesthetic theory presented in the *Natyashastra* is *rasa*. This term occurs frequently in Vedic texts, where it has various meanings:

> In *Rig Veda* the word, *rasa*, is found occurring in the sense of water (...), Soma juice (...), cow's milk (...), and flavour. The *Atharva-Veda* extends the sense to the sap of grain and the taste, the latter becoming very common. In the *Upanishads rasa* stands for the essence or quintessence and self-luminous consciousness though the sense of taste is at places conveyed (...) In Sanskrit other than the Vedic, the word, *rasa*, is used for water, milk, juice, essence, tasteful liquid, etc.[10]

The material aspect of the meaning of *rasa* is emphasised in *Ayurveda*, the ancient Indian system of holistic medicine. Here, *rasa* denotes "a certain white liquid extracted by the digestive system from the food. Its main seat is the heart"[11], and in the *Rasayanashastra*, a treatise on chemistry, which "moves round the pivot of *rasa*. Mercury, which is called *rasa*, plays here a very important part"[12]. The spiritual aspect of the meaning of *rasa* is emphasised in Shankara's commentary of the Upanishadic use of the term: "*Rasa* is here used to mean such bliss as is innate in oneself and manifests itself (...) even in the absence of external aids to happiness. It emphasises that the bliss is non-material, i.e. intrinsic, spiritual, or subjective"[13]. As such, the experience of *rasa* has been likened to the experiences of yogis by Abhinavagupta, the major commentator of Bharata's *Natyashastra*.

In the context of Indian aesthetics, *rasa* is understood as the actor's and especially the spectator's aesthetic experience. In an aesthetic context, *rasa* is translated as "sentiment". The *Natyashastra* differentiates eight sentiments: erotic, comic, pathetic, furious, heroic, terrible, odious, and marvellous[14]. Some later writers on Sanskrit poetics add one more *rasa* to this number, *santa*. The concept of *rasa* is phrased in the *Natyashastra* in form of a short statement, a *sutra*: *Vibhava- anubhava- vyabhicaribhava- samyogad rasa- nispattih*. The translation is "*Rasa* is produced (*rasa-nispattih*) from a combination (*samyogad*) of Determinants (*vibhava*), Consequents (*anubhava*) and Transitory States (*vyabhicaribhava*)"[15].

Determinants (*vibhava*) are characterised as situations that cause the emergence of *rasa*. For example, the erotic *rasa*

has two bases, union (...) and separation (...). Of these two, the Erotic Sentiment in union arises from Determinants like the pleasures of the season, the enjoyment of garlands, unguents, ornaments [the company of] beloved persons, objects [of senses], splendid mansions, going to a garden, and enjoying [oneself] there, seeing the [beloved one], hearing [his or her words], playing and dallying [with him or her]. [16]

Consequents (*anubhava*) are defined as means of histrionic representation. In the above example, the erotic *rasa* in union should be represented on the stage by "Consequents such as clever movement of eyes, eyebrows, glances, soft and delicate movement of limbs and sweet words and similar other things"[17].

The *Natyashastra* lists altogether thirty-three transitory states (*vyabhicaribhava*): discouragement, weakness, apprehension, envy, intoxication, weariness, indolence, depression, anxiety, distraction, recollection, contentment, shame, inconstancy, joy, agitation, stupor, arrogance, despair, impatience, sleep, epilepsy, dreaming, awakening, indignation, dissimulation, cruelty, assurance, sickness, insanity, death, fright, and deliberation[18]. In the example of the *rasa* of love, the *Natyashastra* states that "Transitory States in it do not include fear, indolence, cruelty and disgust"[19].

To the concern of critics, the *rasa-sutra* on its own appears not to mention all elements that work together to create *rasa*. It does not mention, that is, dominant states (*sthayibhava*) and temperamental states (*sattvikabhava*). The *Natyashastra* lists eight dominant states (*sthayibhava*): love, mirth, sorrow, anger, energy, terror, disgust, and astonishment[20]. There are eight temperamental states (*sattvikabhava*): "Paralysis, Perspiration, Horripilation, Change of Voice,

Trembling, Change of Colour, Weeping and Fainting"[21]. The text explains the relationship between *rasa* and determinants, consequents, dominant states, transitory states and the temperamental states through an analogy: just as various ingredients such as vegetables, and spices, when mixed, produce a flavour, so the combination of the "Dominant States *(sthayibhava)*, when they come together with various other States *(bhava)* attain the quality of the Sentiment (...)"[22]. All the eight sentiments, the eight dominant states, the transitory states and the temperamental states are described in the *Natyashastra* in detail with reference to the determinants, the consequents, and their relation to the sentiments.

The *Natyashastra* places much emphasis on the means of histrionic representation *(abhinaya)*. They are the techniques used by the actor to portray the consequents. "From the point of view of the playwright or the character it is *anubhava*, and from that of the actor it is *abhinaya*"[23]. Four kinds of *abhinaya* are differentiated: gestures *(angika)*, words *(vacika)*, dresses and make-up *(aharya)* and the representation of the temperament *(sattvika)*. To each of these aspects the *Natyashastra* devotes several chapters. Gestures are treated in chapters on the movements of minor limbs, hands, other limbs, dance movements, and gaits. The movements are also specifically related to the space of the stage.[24] *Vacika abhinaya*, representation through words, is covered directly in chapters on prosody, metrical patterns, dictions of play, rules of the use of languages, and modes of address and intonation; more indirectly in chapters on the construction of the plot. Other chapters provide details about costume and make-up, thus referring to *aharya abhinaya*, others about the representation of the temperaments *(sattvika abhinaya)*. The means of histrionic representation *(abhinaya)* are variously combined to give rise to four different styles of dramatic performance *(vritti)*, the verbal *(bharati)*, the grand *(sattvati)*, the graceful *(kaisiki)* and the energetic *(arabhati)*. Finally, the practice of representation in a dramatic performance is twofold: realistic *(lokadharmi)* and theatrical *(natyadharmi)*. The means of histrionic representation, *abhinaya*, belong to the category of *natyadharmi*.

Within this broad scope of material covered in the *Natyashastra*, the following information can be gathered about the actor: the actor is the agent responsible for creating an aesthetic experience, *rasa*, in the audience. He does this by his acting skills; The traditional view thus is that the majority of chapters in the *Natyashastra* represents a "how-to-do-it" manual for the actor, describing in minute detail all the different techniques of the *abhinaya*, the means of histrionic representation, especially those involving gestures (*angika abhinaya*), dress and make-up (*aharya abhinaya*), representation of the temperament (*sattvika abhinaya*), and those chapters detailing the particulars of performance-- rather than the composition, the domain of the playwright--of verbal representation (*vacika abhinaya*). The text contains repeated instructions of how to combine elements of those four performance categories to convey the emotions of the characters to the spectators, to arouse the adequate *rasa* in the spectators.

In the *Natyashastra*, the focal point of the actor's emotional involvement with the character he plays is indeed the representation of the temperament (*sattvika abhinaya*). This mode of representation has its special function in conveying the temperamental states (paralysis, perspiration, horripilation, change of voice, trembling, change of colour, weeping and fainting)[25]. In ordinary life, such states are involuntary and would be classified by contemporary Western psychology as directed "mostly by the effective motor region of our nervous system"[26]. The *Natyashastra* explains that this way of acting is accomplished by concentration of the mind. "Its nature (...) cannot be mimicked by an absentminded man"[27]. This statement appears to imply that the actor has to fully identify with the character he plays. Identification could then be understood to be equivalent to the concentration of the mind requested in the *Natyashastra* for a satisfactory performance of the temperamental states. However, the *Natyashastra* states in the same paragraph that "tears and horripilation should respectively be shown by persons who are not [actually] sorry or happy"[28]. This is a contradiction to the requirement of a concentrated mind; it is difficult to understand how the actor's mind can be so concentrated to produce "real" tears, horripilation etc. for the audience to see, without that actor's involvement in the character's emotions, those emotions shown to the spectators as the cause for the tears or horripilation.

This contradiction between involvement and non-involvement has been variously discussed by later commentators and critics of the *Natyashastra* up to the present. Abhinavagupta, for example, summarises the positions of Bhatta Lollata and Srisankuka before presenting his own view of the nature of *rasa* and the actor's role in achieving it. According to Bhatta Lollata, the aesthetic experience (...) is a matter of mere appearance occasioned by false identi-fication. It is analogous to the experience of a man who experiences fear because he errone-ously takes a rope for a snake. (...) The actor creates an illusion; he is a master of *maya*. The spectators are subject to his *maya* (...) [which] is productive of *rasa*.[29]

In creating this illusion, *maya*, the actor, according to Bhatta Lollata, is identified with the hero, and *rasa* is a characteristic of the character[30]. Srisankuka disagrees with this latter opinion. Using popular plays about Rama, hero of the Indian epic *Ramayana*, as an example, Srisankuka argues that the actor does not identify with the character, because

an actor who appears on the stage as Rama is obviously not identical with the real Rama. Nor is he "non-Rama" Since the spectators take him to be Rama, he is not different from Rama either. He cannot be said to be "similar" to Rama since the spectators do not know the real Rama. The cognition involved in the experience "enacted" Rama is unique. [31]

Abhinavagupta himself regards the actor as an instrument in conveying *rasa* to the spectators. The actor is not involved in the emotions of the character he plays. Moreover, "the moment he starts enjoying himself the emotion he is playing he ceases to be an actor and becomes a *sahridaya* [connoisseur of art]"[32] Abhinavagupta analyses the Sanskrit term for actor, *patra*, to substantiate this point. It means both "character" and "carrier-pot". The first meaning, refers to the actor proper. The latter meaning implies that the actor, just as the pot, is only the carrier of relish: "the kettle does not know the taste of the brew"[33]. Starting with the contradiction in the *Natyashastra*, we find that Bhatta Lollata appears to defend, if vaguely, an identification and involvement, whereas Srisankuka and Abhinavagupta argue against such an involvement. Among contemporary critics, Jhanji points out that "to say that the actor does not feel anything *qua* himself does not imply that he does not imaginatively reconstruct the emotive experience of the character he portrays"[34]. In support of this argument he mentions Bharata's emphasis on the *sattvika abhinaya*, the means of histrionic representation dealing with the temperamental states. He interprets these means as "internalisation of emotive experience on the part of the actor"[35]. This view presents a compromise: Jhanji accepts Abhinavagupta's idea of the actor's non-involvement. He then explains the actor's ability to get his body to function in a mode that is the domain of the involuntary nervous system by reference to "internalisation of emotive experience". However, this concept would need a thorough explanation in itself as to how it might be able to account for the phenomenon it has been used to explain.

In her study of the technique of *abhinaya* Pandya attempts to explain the actor's ability to present temperamental states with reference to the term *sattvika*, and the concept of *sattva*. Thus, she defines *sattva* as "the capability of an individual to bring into being the pleasures and pains experienced by others, making them his own"[36]. This capability applies both to the author, the actor, and the spectator. Through *sattva* the author experiences the pleasures and pains of the character he creates and is thus able to draw the character. "The actor (...) with the help of *sattva* makes theses experiences his own and presents them on the stage while the sympathetic spectators enjoy the representation through the same medium, i.e. *sattva*"[37]. Dalal's interprets *sattva* similarly. Referring to Dhanika, a later Sanskrit theorist of drama and poetry, he states that *sattva* "is a mental condition which is highly sympathetic to the joys and sorrows of the others"[38]. He adds that this mental state arises when the mind "is in a state of composure"[39]. Bhat takes both the mental and the physical aspect into account when he defines *sattvika abhinaya* as "a physical manifestation of a deep mental state"[40]. Marasinghe defines *sattva* as "a certain law (*dharma*) which governs the expression of the inner state of a person"[41].

In order to enable a cogent comparison of any Western aesthetic theory with its counterparts in Indian aesthetic theory, the latter has to be understood on the basis of the same underlying model of mind and consciousness. In particular, the following issues have to be addressed:

a. Is the actor to be emotionally involved or not while acting? The *Natyashastra* is not conclusive on this subject. In requesting the actor to be of utmost concentrated mind, it appears to suggest involvement. In stating that the temperamental states (*sattvika bhava*) should be shown by persons (i.e. actors) who are not actually feeling the emotions that cause those states, the text appears to suggest emotional non- involvement on the part of the actor.

b. How exactly does the actor achieve (process of *sattvika abhinaya*) the histrionic representation of those temperamental states (*sattvika bhava*)? The problem here is that the temperamental states belong to the domain of the autonomous nervous system. This part of the nervous system is in charge of involuntary neuro-muscular activities, commonly understood to be beyond the influence of the will. How could an actor influence this domain, independent of whether or not he is emotionally involved in the emotions of the character he is portraying.

c. A brief survey of previous attempts to clarify the problem raised in item (b) suggests that major importance will have to be placed on an adequate interpretation of the concept of *sattva* in its different occurrences in the technical terms used in the *Natyashastra* and later Indian aesthetics, such as *sattvika abhinaya* and *sattvika bhava*.

d. In this context, the frame-concept of the entire *Natyashastra, rasa*, has to be re-assessed, especially regarding the following sub-areas of interest:

i) what is the nature of the aesthetic experience called *rasa*?

ii) what importance does the number of *rasas* have on the understanding of the *rasa*-concept in general, and with reference to items (a) to (c) stated above. In detail this means an investigation of

- whether there is a difference in concept between the eight sentiments (erotic, comic, pathetic etc.), originally found in the *Natyashastra* and the ninth sentiment later added to that enumeration;

- whether there is a difference in concept between the eight or individual sentiments on the *Natyashastra* and later additions, rendered as *rasa-s*, and the eight or nine *rasa-s* and one *rasa* in the singular, on a different (possibly hierarchically higher) conceptual level.

iii) Is the spectator's aesthetic experience as described by the concept of *rasa* like, or equal to, or unlike the spiritual experience of a yogi? Is there any parallel between an actor's experience while acting with the spectator's? Is there a spiritual dimension involved in acting, parallel to the yogic practices that lead to yogic experiences?

e. Based on a thorough discussion of items (a) to (d), the meanings of the crucial terms in the *rasa-sutra, samyogad,* traditionally rendered as "combination", and *nispattih*, traditionally rendered as "produced" have to be subjected to a re-assessment.

Regarding the *Natyashastra*, Schechner argues that because it is so "full of details, of exact descriptions and specifications", it can only be a "how-to-do-it manual, collectively authored over four or five centuries"[42]. Schechner points out that some theatre "needs an audience to hear it", and some theatre needs "spectators to see it"[43]. Indian theatre, however, needs "partakers to savour it"[44]. Schechner derives this image from the main concept of the *Natyashastra*, *rasa*, which is traditionally translated as flavour, taste: "*Rasa* happens where the experience of the preparers and the partakers meets"[45]. In the context of Schechner's differentiation between transformation and transportation, both per-formers and spectators are transported, i.e. return to their ordinary state after their shared experience has passed. They are not transformed in the sense of a change continuing on after the performance[46].

Schechner also addresses the mechanism of acting: he interprets the *Nat-yashastra* to argue that the practice of proper gestures as described in the text arouses the corresponding feelings in the performer--in line with Meyerhold's views developed in his *biomechanics*, and with Ekman's research on facial movement and arousal of autonomous nervous system reactions.

Subrahmanyam argues that all forms of dance-drama that have developed in India over the centuries are based on the aesthetics of the *Natyashastra*[47]. The form that has most influenced Western theatre artists is *Kathakali*.

Grotowski had been interested in Eastern philosophy since childhood and visited India first in 1956. He was later influenced by Barba, who, when already an unofficial member of Grotowski's Laboratory Theatre, travelled to India in 1963 with "the vague agenda of finding something of value for his colleagues (...)"[48]. In India, Barba came across the dance-drama form of *Kathakali*, visited the major *Kathakali* training academy in Kerala, the Kalamandalam in Cheruthuruthy, and "was so impressed by what he saw that he wrote what was then one of the first technical descriptions of the form by a European"[49]. As a result, Grotowski introduced *Kathakali*-based exercises in his training. For Barba's later development, not only the exercises themselves proved important;

Barba was influenced considerably by the "dual ethics of intense discipline and regarding theatre as a vocation rather then merely a profession"[50].

Both Grotowski and Barba avoided merely mimicking *Kathakali* aesthetics throughout their intercultural experiments. Rather than adopt a foreign system which they understood as completely codified and thus rigid, they aimed at using some of the techniques they found in the "other" theatre aesthetics to enable further development of their Western actors along the lines they found useful.

Barba derived one of the major concepts of his theatre anthropology from the theatre aesthetics of the *Natyashastra*: the *Natyashastra* differentiates between *lokadharmi* and *natyadharmi*, realistic and theatrical forms of representation; on this basis, Barba developed his concepts of daily behaviour (equivalent, in his view, to *lokadharmi*), and extra-daily, performative behaviour (equivalent, Barba argues, to *natyadharmi*). A close look at the *Natyashastra*, however, shows that this parallel is limited. In the *Natyashastra*, both terms refer to practices of representation which can be employed in performance. The realistic style, *lokadharmi*, is defined as follows:

> If a play depends on natural behaviour [in its characters] and is simple and not articial, and has in its [plot] professions and activities of the people and has [simple acting and] no playful flourish of limbs and depends on men and women of different types, it is called realistic (*lokadharmi*).[51]

Those two verses defining *lokadharmi* are followed by twelve verses on *natyadharmi*, providing a detailed description of theatrical circumstances in which theatrical representation is appropriate. The emphasis on *natyadharmi* might lead to the conclusion that it is more important in *natya* than *lokadharmi*, and indeed all the numerous descriptions of the means of histrionic representation in the *Natyashastra*, *abhinaya*, belong to the category of *natyadharmi*. However, whatever the emphasis, *lokadharmi* is part of the actor's theatrical practice. Although it is thus possible to differentiate daily from extra-daily behaviour on the basis of the concepts of *lokadharmi* and *natyadharmi*, the important difference is that in Barba's theory, daily behaviour is outside the realm of performance; even more, it is the kind of behaviour that the performer has to *overcome* to become a good performer. In contrast, *lokadharmi* and *natyadharmi* both pertain to the performance.

Grotowski eventually became disillusioned with non-Western theatre practices, concluding that "their aesthetic is completely alien to me. I do not think we can adopt from them any techniques, or that they could inspire us directly"[52]. Further discussion of the intercultural activities of both Grotowski and Barba, especially in the light of Bharucha's critique, will have to address the question whether misunderstanding of Indian aesthetics, as in Barba's case with *lokadharmi* and *natyadharmi*, are also responsible for Grotowski's turn away from non-Western aesthetics. In this context, Brook seems to have shifted in a similar direction. Whereas at the time of producing the *Mahabharata*, he referred to it as the "great history of mankind", informed by the concept of *dharma*. During a talk in London, he characterised the Epic as an instruction manual for a young prince about the skills of being a good ruler[53].

## 4. Indian Points of Contact

The assessment of some likely direct influences of Indian philosophy and aesthetics on Western theatre artists has helped to further understand their experiences and their theories. Just as a consideration of points of contact between theatre theories and lines of Western thought clearly related if not directly influential to the theories had assisted to deepen the assessment of the Western context, a critique of points of contact with Indian philosophy and theatre aesthetics will illuminate the Indian context.

### a. Indian linguistics

Reference to Indian linguistics may assist in examining Artaud's intuition regarding a "language beyond speech". This is a "point of contact" between knowledge from different cultures, not claims of direct influence. According to Coward, linguistics and the philosophy of language, relatively recent developments in the West, "were begun by the Hindus before the advent of recorded history. Beginning with the Vedic hymns, which are at least 3000 years old, the Indian study of language has continued in an unbroken tradition right up to the present day"[1].

The main focus of Indian linguistics is on the relationship of language and consciousness--"not even restricted to human consciousness"[2]. From among many classical Indian linguists, the grammarian Bhartrihari is of special importance. He distinguishes four levels of language: *vaikhari, madhyama pashyanti,* and *para. Vaikhari* "is the most external and differentiated level", on which speech is uttered by the speaker and heard by the hearer[3]. Its temporal sequence is fully developed. *Madhyama* represents, in broad terms, the thinking level of the mind. "It is the idea or series of words as conceived by the mind after hearing or before speaking out. It may be thought of as inward speech. All parts of speech that are linguistically relevant to the sentence are present here in a latent form"[4].

The finest relative level is that of *pashyanti.* At this level "there is no distinction between the word and the meaning and there is no temporal sequence"[5]. Beyond the very subtly manifest level of *pashyanti,* Bhartrihari locates the fully unmanifest level language, *para*[6].

Bhartrihari associates the *pashyanti* level of language with the concept of *sphota.* It represents meaning as a whole, existing in the mind of the speaker as a unity. "When he utters it, he produces a sequence of different sounds so that it appears to have differentiation"[7]. The process of differentiation into sounds proceeds from the *sphota* on the *pashyanti* level of language via *madhyama* or inward thought to expressed speech on the *vaikhari* level. For the listener, the process is reversed. Although he first hears a series of sounds, he ultimately perceives the utterance as a unity--"the same *sphota* with which the speaker began"[8]. The *sphota* or meaning-whole thus has two sides to it: the word-sound (*dhvani*) and the word-meaning (*artha*)[9]. Sound and meaning are two aspects residing within the unitary *sphota,* which, according to Bhartrihari, is eternal and inherent in consciousness[10]. Meaning is thus not conveyed "from the speaker to the hearer, rather, the spoken words serve only as a stimulus to reveal or uncover the meaning which was already present in the mind of the hearer"[11].

Haney points out that the unity of name and form, of sound and meaning on the level of the *sphota* in *pashyanti* applies mainly to the Sanskrit language. He argues, however, that

because Sanskrit is considered by orthodox Indians to be the oldest documented language and probably the source of all languages, the same unity of name and form found in it must exist to some extent in other languages when experienced on sufficiently refined levels of consciousness.[12]

Artaud calls the language beyond speech, which he intuits, the language of nature. *Pashyanti* represents the subtlest manifest level of nature, and must thus be assumed to be closest to nature itself. The grammar of this language, Artaud argues, has not yet been discovered. However, in the context of Indian linguistics, experience of sufficiently refined states of consciousness, i.e. direct experience of the *pashyanti* level of language, should be able to reveal that grammar. Artaud assigns an "ancient magic effectiveness to the language beyond speech". In parallel, Abhinavagupta, the main classic commentator on Bharata's *Natyashastra*, states that it is the poetic experience of *dhvani*, the sound aspect of speech, that brings about the experience of *rasa* "as a transcendental function of suggestion removes the primordial veil of ignorance from our minds and thereby allows the bliss associated with the discovery of true meaning to be experienced"[13].

Artaud may well have sensed levels of language beyond speech actively expressed in Balinese and other Oriental forms of dance, though he associated the levels of the mind gained by the spectator through watching such performances with the intellect rather than with the emotions, let alone the even subtler level of *pashyanti*: "Thus we are led *along intellectual paths* [my emphasis] towards reconquering the signs of existence"[14]. Artaud here shows influence by contemporary science which places the intellect above the emotions and has no place for a level of the mind beyond speech. The lack in Western psychology of a model of the mind which takes levels of language beyond speech, as the *pashyanti*-level described by Bhartrihari, into account, leads to the vagueness and confusion of terminology in Artaud's argumentation.

A second area where reference to Indian linguistics providing further insight into Artaud's theories is related to Artaud's concepts of breathing: Artaud associates the seventh state beyond breathing with the Indian concept of *Sattva Guna*[15]. Jhanji translates *guna* as material quality[16]. Together with *tamas* and *rajas*, *sattva* is responsible for engendering "all the different human experiences"[17]. Jhanji further explains:

*Sattva* which refers to the freedom from all willing is the state of detachment from the pragmatic world, and it is the state of pure knowledge. *Rajas* is understood in terms of all qualities of will and all the psycho- physical activities have their origin in terms of this quality. *Tamas* refers to the state of ignorance and lack of consciousness. The entire life of an individual represents the varied combinations of these three *gunas*. Beatitude and knowledge are associated with *sattva*; greed with *rajas*, and ignorance and illusion with *tamas*.[18]

Artaud locates the concept of the seventh state beyond breathing, associated with *Sattva Guna*, in the field of metaphysics and expressly argues that the seventh level of breathing is an underlying and essential aspect of the actor[19].

The association of physical activity (in this case: breath) and emotions has already been discussed in the context of Meyerhold and Stanislavsky in relation to the James-Lange theory of the emotions, Ekman's research and Bloch's ALBA EMOTING technique. Breath has a further interesting relation to language, and here Artaud's reference to *sattva guna* gains importance. In Vedic literature, the body of texts dealing with phonetics is called *Shiksha*. It is one of the six *Vedangas*, together with *Kalpa* (rituals), *Nirukta* (semantics), *Vyakaran* (grammar), *Chhandas* (metrics) and *Jyotish* (astrology). One author of Shiksha, Panini, describes the following mechanism of language development: pure consciousness takes a direction, inspired by the intellect (*buddhi*). This tendency of direction develops towards the intention to speak. The intellect (*buddhi*) stimulates the mind (*manas*) to create such an intention of speech. The mind, in turn, stimulates the physical fire (*agni*), which in turn produces breath, vital energy (*prana*). *prana* is the stream of breath in the upward direction, on which speech is based.

Related to the four levels of language as described in the *Rig-Veda* and by Bhartrihari, *para* refers to the area of the body around the bottom of the spine, from where prana begins its ascent. *pashyanti* refers to the navel-heart area, *madhyama* to chest and throat, and *vaikhari* to the area of the head from the throat upwards[20].

The different levels of the body where prana is expressing itself are further related to different metric patterns in Sanskrit. *Para* is beyond rhythm. *Pashyanti* is associated with an 8-syllable metre (*Gayatri*), *madhyama* with an 11-syllable metre (*trishtub*), and *vaikhari* with a 12-syllable metre (*jagati*). In Vedic phonetic theory, breath is thus closely related to metre, to rhythm, in the production of language. Underlying *prana*, underlying breathing, is pure consciousness, traditionally associated with *sattva guna*[21]. In principle, therefore, Artaud's association of breathing and consciousness, emotions, is justified, even if the concepts come from different cultural traditions, combining Cabbala and Indian philosophy.

## b. The theatre aesthetics of the *Natyashastra*

Kramer has tried to compare the theatre aesthetics of the *Natyashastra* with Stanislavsky's system, acknowledging that drawing such parallels makes no claim at establishing direct influence. According to Kramer, the determinant (*vibhava*) causes a specific emotional state (*bhava*) which in turn causes a consequent (*anubhava*). This, according to Kramer, parallels Stanislavsky: "given circumstances cause emotions causes behavior"[1]. The assumptions on which Kramer bases his parallels, however, require a reassessment. The causal chain "determinants-emotional state-consequents" is not appropriate. Rather, the mechanism is as follows: in specific situations laid down in the play (determinants), the actor has to use specific means of histrionic representation (consequents) to create specific dominant emotional states (sthayibhava). Those dominant emotional states combine with transitory states (vyabhicaribhava) and temperamental states (sattvikabhava). The end product of this combination process is the aesthetic experience, *rasa*. Although Stanislavsky comes close, the parallel as argued by Kramer cannot be maintained.

Kramer links the temperamental states *sattvikabhava* to Stanislavsky's "Magic If" and "sense of truth", since "sattva" can be understood, Kramer argues, as "the mental capacity of the actor to identify himself with the character and his feelings"[2]. Similarly, the "Magic If" or "sense of truth" allows "the actor to convince himself that the circumstances are real to the character, even though, as an actor, he knows that they are not"[3]. The discussion of the concept of *sattva* has shown, however, that the concept of "sattva", whatever its exact definition, certainly refers to a state of mind that is beyond the emotions, the field of operation of the "magic If".

The comparison of aesthetic concepts, theories of acting in the *Natyashastra* and in Stanislavsky's system was inspired by Stanislavsky's apparent influence by Indian philosophy. Kramer's essay highlights the difficulties of this approach: scholarship currently lacks a consistent model of human consciousness, of the human mind, that allows a precise understanding of the assumptions of consciousness informing the aesthetics of the *Natyashastra*, and thus enables a coherent comparison with Stanislavsky's concepts.

Brecht's source of inspiration, the Chinese actor's self-observation, parallel to Diderot's unmoved and disinterested onlooker and Stanislavsky's demand for an actor's dual consciousness in that the actor should be both emotionally involved and yet able to control himself, resembles the problem (according to traditional interpretations) in the aesthetics of the *Natyashastra* regarding the actor's emotional involvement: the demand for full concentration of the emotions is regarded as an argument in favour of involvement, whereas the statement that the actor who plays sadness should not him/herself be sad is regarded as a contradiction.

Compared with some parallels between Artaud's aesthetics and the *Natyashastra*, the actor's catharsis prior to that of the actor might provide a contrast. Far from being unanimous in their interpretation of the *Natyashastra* in this respect, some commentators as prominent as Abhinavagupta have argued that the actor himself should, while acting, not relish the aesthetic experience, *rasa*, which was for the audience alone[4].

Artaud thus also has points of contact with the *Natyashastra*, which appears to show the same paradox of the actor's simultaneous emotional involvement and non-involvement. Artaud's simultaneous denial of the actor's individual initiative limits the parallel, because both Stanislavsky and the *Natyashastra* definitely demand individual initiative from the actor.


## 5. Interculturalism and Postmodernism

### a. Western positions on interculturalism

The review of theories of the actor's emotional involvement in acting has demonstrated that Western theatre artists and theorists are increasingly influenced by general psychological or philosophical, and more specific aesthetical concepts of non-Western cultures, notably India. In Stanislavsky's case, direct influences are slight. Artaud was mainly inspired by his interpretation of Balinese dance, criticised as factually faulty[1]. Grotowski experimented with non-

Western techniques of influencing the actors but abandoned them in the end. Schechner welcomes interculturalism, but does not, fully discuss the implications of latent exploitation of the non-Western culture by Western theatre artists. Brook strives for a universal language of the theatre, often combining Western and non-Western techniques and theatre aesthetics; in view of this monumental aim, he would regard the issues of cultural exploitation as petty questions of political correctness[2].

Barba, on the other hand, expressly addresses the controversy of cultural exploitation: his theatre anthropology incorporates both Occidental and Oriental theatre theory and practice. The Oriental element in this, Barba argues, "cannot be copied or transplanted. It can only serve as a stimulus, a point of departure"[3]. Barba thus safeguards himself against the accusation of cultural exploitation, imperialism, and colonialism in the line of Orientalism as described by Said. Said defines "Orientalism" as "a style of thought based upon an ontological and epistemological distinction made between "the Orient" and (most of the time) "the Occident""[4]. The relationship between Occident and Orient, Said argues, is one "of power, of domination, of varying degrees of a complex hegemony"[5]. Reduced to its simplest form,

the argument (...) was clear, it was precise, it was easy to grasp. There are Westerners, and there are Orientals. The former dominate, the latter must be dominated, which usually means having their land occupied, their internal affairs rigidly controlled, their blood and treasure put at the disposal of one or another Western power.[6]

If Western theatre artists take up material from Indian cultural traditions in general, and dance-drama forms in particular, they have to face the issue of whether they are guilty of "a continuation of colonialism, a further exploitation of other cultures"[7]. Barba has written on this issue. He holds that the relationship of Western and Eastern traditions of theatre is characterised by mutual reduction, imitation and exchange:

We in the West have often envied the Orientals their theatrical knowledge, which transmits the actor's living work of art from one generation to another; they have envied our theatre's capacity for confronting new themes, the way in which it keeps up with the times, and its flexibility that allows for personal interpretations of traditional texts which often have the energy of a formal and ideological conquest.[8]

Western attitudes to Oriental theatre, according to Barba, are informed by ethnocentrism which relegates the experiences implied in Oriental drama to the realm of the useless. However, the same "distortion of perception idealises, and then flattens, the multiplicity of Oriental theatre, or venerates it as sanctuaries"[9]. In the attempt to avoid both traps, Barba requires the actor to define his own professional identity, a process that implies "discovering one's own centre in the tradition of traditions"[10].

*Tradition of traditions* is a vague concept, possibly open to the performer's experience, but difficult to express in words. *Tradition of traditions* does not refer to any isolated tradition of an individual performer or an individual form of dance/drama, but to a common pool of traditions, close to the concept of the collective unconscious in Jung's psychology. The collective element is reminiscent of Turner's concept of *communitas*, also characterised by a shared experience. However, attempting to describe a shared experience of *tradition of traditions* is essential in view of the even larger extent of vagueness associated with the term *tradition* itself, for example in the context of contemporary "traditional", "classical" Indian dance forms such as Bharata Natyam, Odissi, or Kathak. The history of Indian dance usually describes that dance was originally confined to the temple and presented by *devadasis* (female temple dancers). In the course of time, the dance and the female dancers were associated with *nautch girls* or prostitutes, and eventually all dance was forbidden by the state[11]. In the case of Bharata Natyam, the south Indian dance form, a revival is associated with three factors:

(1) the name of the dance form was changed from *sadir* to *bharata natyam* in 1932; (2) Rukmini Devi, an upper- class brahmin, learned the dance form, thereby investing it with dignity, and established a dance school called Kalakshetra (Academy for Fine Arts) for the transmission of traditional knowledge; and (3) the great dancer Balasaraswati, whose artistry depended to a large extent on her ancestral connection to the *devadasi* tradition, spread the fame of *bharata natyam* to the far corners of the globe.[12]

Thus Bharata Natyam as it existed in the 1930s, and which is today frequently referred to as being the classical, traditional way of dancing in that particular style, is already innovative and "new" compared to the predecessors in temple dance[13]. Vatsyayan demands that the double implication of the term "classical" as referring to a historical period or the quality of a work of art[14] is taken into account. Erdman comments that the term "classical" is a Western concept that both Westerners and Westernised Indians try to apply to an Indian phenomenon[15]. Both these views make the issue of how to define what is "classical", "traditional" in contemporary Indian dance even more complex.

Already the two original innovators of Bharatanatyam in this century, Balasaraswati and Rukmini Devi represent, according to Meduri, "a dialectic of style. (...) If Balasaraswati focused on inner feeling, on surrender to the medium that led effortlessly to the concentration of the Yogic mind, Rukmini Devi approached the same goal through body control, mind and awareness"[16]. Meduri argues that Rukmini Devi focused on form because she anticipated the secularisation "that is the most singular feature of Indian dance today"[17]. The aims of Kalakshetra, to "educate public opinion and develop good taste through concerts, public lectures, demonstrations, exhibitions and publications"[18], in line with the original aims of the *Natyashastra*, led directly, Meduri claims, to the "notes and extensive explanations that accompany a dance recital today"[19]. Meduri concludes that "Without the intellectual awareness, we might have lost forever a meaningful cultural experience. Yet because of it we have lost something of the spirit of Balasaraswati, that inner spiritual exuberance or fullness"[20].

The difficulties Indian dancers and scholars articulate in their paper presentations, publications, and also in their "innovative" choreography (Kathak, the North Indian dance style, in jeans, or Bharatanatyam choreographed not on subjects taken from the Vedic epics *Mahabharata* and *Ramayana*, or Hindu religion, but on topics of contemporary life --e.g. the dancer's dilemma between tradition and innovation[21]) accentuate the ambiguity of *tradition*.

To avoid the difficulties arising from such an ambiguous concept as *tradition*, Barba tries to fathom his own practical experiences and those of his performers by using the new, if vague, concept of *tradition of traditions*, which concurrently unites West and non-West. *Tradition of traditions* thus shares the transcendental quality of *translumination*, *communitas*, *flow*, *language beyond speech* and *total theatre*, key concepts for Grotowski, Turner/ Schechner, Artaud and Brook.

Theatre artists, then, directly or indirectly tackle the issue of interculturalism by referring the ideal intercultural theatre experience to an a-historical, universal realm beyond petty exploitation, where all performers and spectators are one anyway. This is in line with Pavis' view that theatre scholars would like to place the "historical contradictions" of interculturalism "in brackets"[22]. Indeed, perspectives on interculturalism in the theatre have been mainly descriptive, providing categories of interculturalism (Carlson[23]) or functional models (Pavis[24]). Such perspectives have also argued mainly from the Western point of view. As a result, the first critique of interculturalism from a non-Western critic, Rustom Bharucha, was widely noted.

### b. Bharucha's critique of interculturalism

In his critique of interculturalism, Bharucha's main argument, reshaped in various contexts, is that "a valid theory of interculturalism can be initiated only through a respect for individual histories out of which a "world" can be imagined in which the colliding visions of theatre can meet"[1].

As an Indian trained in the West, Bharucha is mainly interested in forms of interculturalism that involve Western theatre artists taking up philosophy, theatre aesthetics and other aspects of India. He discusses in particular Artaud, Grotowski, Schechner, Barba and Peter Brook, and concludes that none of these artists "has turned to India out of the faintest concern for its present socio-cultural tradition. Rather, they have been drawn almost exclusively to our "traditional" sources"[2]. *condition*

Bharucha calls Artaud "one of the most inspired mythologisers of the *oriental theatre*"[3], who was not interested at all in historicity. Bharucha follows Sontag and situates Artaud's "almost frantic need to absorb non-western cultures", associated with a "pathological need to escape the strictures of "Logical Europe" (...)"[4] in Artaud's history of mental illness, although Bharucha warns against dismissing all of Artaud's writings as "mystical" or "cosmic"[5].

Bharucha sets Artaud's mythological, a-historical attitude to Artaud's own construct of "oriental theatre" against Grotowski's pragmatic approach: Grotowski used Indian techniques such as Hatha Yoga and training methods of Kathakali with his actors at the Laboratory Theatre, where one of Grotowski's earliest productions was that of the Indian classic *Shakuntala*. Bharucha emphasises that Grotowski did not seek a "celebration of stereotypes evoking the exotic Orient", but that the production was instead a "deliberate mischievous, parodic and artful debunking of Oriental icons"[6]. The self-consciousness of the project, according to Bharucha, prevented Grotowski's version of an "ancient Indian fable from becoming disrespectful"[7]. Grotowski became increasingly sceptical about the usefulness of "borrowing performative conventions from the East"[8], to the extent of admitting that "the aesthetic of "oriental theatre" was completely alien to him: I do not think we can adopt from them any technique or that they could inspire us directly"[9]. Whereas the hand-and-finger positions, *mudras*, key elements in Indian theatre aesthetics, are timeless,

> understood and accepted by Indian performers (and spectators) from performance to performance, a sign (as defined by Grotowski) relates very specifically to a moment in a particular performance which the actor had "scored".[10]

Moreover, whereas signs in Indian theatre are understood to be fixed, Grotowski's signs aim at immediacy and spontaneity, "coalescing to produce a living form possessing its own logic"[11].

Bharucha especially points to Grotowski's disillusionment with Yoga: Grotowski stopped using Yoga practices for his actors when he "realised that it produced an "introverted concentration" that was harmful to his actors"[12]. Bharucha argues that the highest state of Yoga is "an equipoise of the mind and being when all expressions and feelings are obliterated"[13]. The question whether such a state of consciousness is necessarily harmful to an actor will have to addressed by a model of consciousness able to explain the psychology of acting.

Whereas Bharucha almost excuses Artaud's faulty interculturalism with reference to Artaud's mental problems, Bharucha does not find any similar excuses for the faults he finds in Richard Schechner's approach to interculturalism. According to Bharucha, Schechner's performance theory, enclosing views on "ethology (*sic?*), anthropology, kinesics, animal behaviour, trance, and more recently, the left and right function of the brain"[14], reveals Schechner's eclectic interests and modes of perception. Bharucha finds the "seeming randomness"[15] of Schechner's thought to be in line with a remark by Schechner: "I want to reveal myself as a set of disconnected thoughts, which is the way I am. I want to celebrate my fragmentation"[16]. Bharucha regards this attitude as characteristic of the "post-modern consciousness"[17]. Schechner argues that for the self "to see itself and become involved with that reflection or doubling as if it were an other is a postmodern experience"[18]. Bharucha agrees with Schechner's proposition that confrontation with "the other" can deepen our grasp of who we ourselves are. He sees a difficulty, however, "when the Other is not an other but a projection of one's ego. Then all one has is a glorification of the self and a cooption of other cultures in the name of representation"[19].

This criticism goes hand in hand with another of Schechner's problems, according to Bharucha, in dealing with interculturalism: it is that Schechner

presumes to present "other" cultures by placing them in his own "map" of post-modern performance. Instead of questioning the validity of this "map" to the individual contexts of other cultures, he upholds its universal applicability through links like sociobiology, computer languages and multinational corporations.[20]

Bharucha also highlights the methodological problem posed through Schechner's use of interviews, especially the assumed use of an interpreter, and the fact that Schechner has "rewritten the transcripts--the sentences flow with an almost unreal clarity and attention to grammatical detail"[21]. Finally, Bharucha draws attention to "cultural tourism", very much supported by Schechner: the implications of changing traditional rituals for tourist purposes. In this context, Bharucha accuses Schechner of failing to analyse or even acknowledge the "social and human turmoil resulting from this exposure of "traditional performance" to the "international market"[22].

Bharucha argues that throughout his performance theory, Schechner follows a dehistoricizing tendency, a criticism echoed by Zarrilli's critique of Barba's "version of the "oriental" actor", which is considered to be

completely devoid of socio-cultural contexts. There is little sense of the processual labours of a particular performer's movements towards specific acts of embodiment. Nor does Barba acknowledge that even in those traditions where he finds his inspiration there are a great number of performers who fail to achieve the high level of "presencing" with which Barba is so fascinated. Nor is there any attempt to articulate precisely how the native performer perceives what Barba receives as presence.[23]

Bharucha finds it difficult to accept Barba's separation of the expressive from the pre-expressive (a state of being which precedes the expression of the actor), mainly because of his own inability to "see any performance on an exclusively pre-expressive level"[24]. The result of forcefully separating expressivity and pre-expressivity "can only result in aridity, a reduction of a particular state of being to a tortured set of techniques (...)"[25].

Bharucha's most vehement and most widely read critique is levelled against Brook's *Mahabharata*. He accuses Brook of having taken a text that is one of the most significant in Indian culture and "decontextualised it from its history in order to sell it to audiences in the West"[26]. Bharucha does not wish to suggest that Western theatre artists should be banned from touching sacred Indian texts. However, he wishes to assert

> that *The Mahabharata* must be seen on as many levels as possible in the Indian context, so that its meaning (or rather multiple levels of meaning) can have some bearing on the lives of the Indian people for whom the *Mahabharata* was written, and who continue to derive their strength from it.[27]

According to Bharucha, Brook's *Mahabharata* fails on this account. References to Hindu philosophy are scattered and lack perspective; a larger, cosmic context is not provided, rendering many incidents in the play arbitrary, without inner stringent motivation. The impression that characters act merely in response to their feelings is enhanced by a lack of reference to the caste system.

It is important to note that Brook's *Mahabharata*, in Bharucha's view, fails with a non-Indian audience--Indians themselves, steeped in the knowledge of the *Mahabharata* from early childhood, can watch the Indian television serials of the *Ramayana*, "synthetic, tacky, sticky, in the worst tradition of Hindi films" and transform "this representation into a deeply spiritual experience"[28]. Bharucha does not provide any evidence, however, for this transformation of television kitsch to spiritual experience.

The question arises, then, whether Bharucha provides any illuminating insights into the "proper" use of Indian traditions like the *Natyashastra*, or whether he is merely setting up a nationalist mystique against a multicultural or orientalist one? Following his critique of Western practices of interculturalism, Bharucha describes his own practical involvement in intercultural theatre: together with a German director, Manuel Lutgenhorst, he staged a play by the German contemporary dramatist Franz Xaver Kroetz, *Request Concert*, in three cities in India, Calcutta, Bombay and Madras. The play is without words and shows day-to day activities of a lonely woman, culminating in her suicide. For each production, a different actress was chosen, and the frame of the activities was adapted to the customs of the city. The aim was to "create individual productions of Kroetz's play that would be rooted in the indigenous cultural context of Asian cities"[29]. In this way, the differences "embodied in the productions" will help to "illuminate the specificities of particular cultures"[30]. Realising and accepting those differences is vital for obtaining a "deeper understanding of the relationships between cultures"[31]. Ultimately, truly respected differences "can help us to understand what we have in common"[32].

In retrospect, Bharucha argues that it was the very "foreignness" of the German text which "illuminated what is normally taken for granted in India"[33]. In what way, however, is this practice of interculturalism (the adaptation of a German play for Indian purposes), different from Brook's adaptation of Indian material, the *Mahabharata*, so heavily criticised by Bharucha? Is it that the German play, because it has been written by one of many German playwrights, is inferior, open to adaptation, whereas *The Mahabharata* as the major epic of India is superior and must not be touched for adaptation purposes? Bharucha does not appear to be making the political statement that it is fine to take material for adaptation from colonialists, whereas the colonialists must not take Indian material for similar adaptations. His argumentation is on an aesthetic level, where it needs further elaboration.

### c. Postmodernism

According to Birringer, "there is very little discussion about what "postmodern theatre" might be" among "actors, directors, and writers"[1], and he notices the same reluctance "among drama critics and scholars who continue to write about a world of texts and performances that seems largely untouched by the debates on the politics of postmodernism or on the technological transformation of late modern culture"[2].

From among the few critics who do discuss postmodernism in the context of theatre, Fischer-Lichte points to Brook's collage technique as relevant for discussion of his theatre under the heading of postmodernism. Bharucha discusses Schechner's wish to celebrate his own "fragmentation", evident in Schechner's "eclectic interests and modes of perception", the "seeming randomness" of Schechner's thoughts, and regards that attitude as characteristic of "post-modern consciousness"[3]. Indeed, more and more theatre artists draw their inspiration from an increasing number of intercultural sources, and they put their source material to practice in different ways. If interpreted as fragmentation, as an active endorsement of intended and precise pluralism, then it is a postmodernist aspect of theatre.

Drawing on a wide, intercultural range of source material can be considered postmodern also because it is a strikingly postmodern intertextual activity. Intertextuality can be regarded as a superimposed concept for methods of more or less conscious, and to some extent concrete references in the text (including the performance text) to individual pre-texts, groups of pre-texts, or underlying codes and complexes of meaning[4]. These methods are already established individually in literary criticism under such terms as source study, influence, quotation, allusion, parody, travesty, imitation, translation, and adaptation[5]. Two extreme concepts of intertextuality with different points of departure can be differentiated: the global model of post-structuralism regards every text as part of a global intertext. In contrast, structuralist and hermeneutic models argue in favour of a more conscious, intended, and marked reference between a text and a pre-text or groups of pre-texts[6]. Broich and Pfister propose a model if intertextuality that mediates between the two positions: specific criteria for intertextuality can be defined and their intensity evaluated in quality and quantity from case to case. Those criteria are: referentiality, communicativity, autoreflexivity, structure, selectivity, dialogue, density and number of intertextual references, and number and range of pre-texts[7]. Detailed analyses of intercultural performances on the basis of those criteria is likely to yield high levels of intertextuality.

George highlights *ambiguity* as a postmodern characteristic of performance. He argues that postmodernism "finds the world hyphenated, elliptical; reversing all established hierarchies and questioning the reduction behind them, deconstruction finds the world doubled, ironic, decentered"[8]. George then asks: "Beyond roles, masks and other "duplicities", was it not always this which performance already proclaimed: "I am-biguous"?"[9]. George extends this argument to the reception process: all spectators (as, indeed, performers) "are always negotiating between at least two worlds"[10], i.e., the real world of the spectator's life as a spectator in the audience, and the fictional world presented on the stage. Such negotiation leads to doubts. In a non-theatrical context, such doubts would in turn lead to "existential anguish". In the theatre, however, the doubts are "restricted to the realm of the possible", and therefore, they can be "enjoyed, relished"[11]. This pleasure, an ambiguous phenomenon, has been analysed in Western culture in terms of psycho-analysis, conceptualised as a "form of retarded climax and therefore ascribed, like all ambiguous phenomena, to the realm of the abnormal"[12]. Because postmodernism does not fear contradiction, because it recognises contradiction as the existential base, ambiguity of performance, in the performative and the receptive aspects, could be an essential feature of a postmodern performance theory. George concludes as follows:

> The predominance in post-modern and deconstructionist discourse of terms such as play, game, contradiction, process, performance, suggests that we may be entering an age in which there *are only* media (semiosis, assumptions, paradigms, models) and no ontology, only experiences (and no Self except the one like an actor's career made up of the parts we enact and rewrite), a world in which difference is primordial (no ur-whole) and time endless. For such an age, performance is the ideal medium and model and ambiguity is its life.[13]

In describing postmodernism, George uses the term "decentered", a reference to Jacques Lacan's theory. Lacan holds that psychoanalysis reveals a split between "the self, the innermost part of the psyche, and the subject of conscious discourse, behaviour and culture"[14]. This division creates a hidden structure inside the subject---the unconscious. The conditions of human existence, according to Lacan, imply that man is "essentially a being by and for the other"[15]. The common ground on which individuals "assert themselves, oppose each other and find themselves again"[16] is the symbolic. To become an individual, accession to the symbolic is necessary. However, such accession is balanced with "the division of the subject"; in the symbolic, "the subject can be no more than represented or translated"[17],

Proposing a decentered self, a split between the self and the subject of discourse, is a postmodern phenomenon. If performances represent the fragmentary, in opposition to "unitary ambitions"[18], they thus represent what Lacan's postmodern discourse has discovered: the decentered self, the split between self and subject of behaviour and culture.

Regarding performances as postmodern when they show fragmentation of sources and ambiguity together with a high degree of intertextuality is in line with critics like Crohn-Schmitt, or George[19], who research the parallels of contemporary quantum mechanics and the theatre. Crohn-Schmitt distinguishes between Aristotelian theatre and the "important segment of contemporary theater variously referred to as antitheater, postmodern theater, or simply, new theater"[20], maintaining that new theatre violates "not only Aristotelian aesthetic principles but also the view of reality that they imply, thus profoundly disturbing many audience members"[21]. From 20th century quantum physics, Crohn-Schmitt infers that "the idea of a single true account of reality is challenged"[22], and together with it the role of the individual:

> Because there is no correspondence between mind and nature, human beings cannot find their unique, essential purpose and pleasure in knowing; like the rest of nature, they have no ulterior purpose. They have no more importance in nature than any other part.[23]

Crohn-Schmitt quotes John Cage's view that art must teach us "to accept our purposelessness"[24]. In her opinion, contemporary artists do not feel depressed by the fact that neither the self nor the perceived world are "discrete, inviolable, and constant"[25]. Their excitement with the exploration of this newly discovered world view mirrors the optimistic, even euphoric mode of postmodernism.

Birringer, however, has quite a different view of postmodernism. He links postmodernism strongly with technological advances and deplores that in "today's mass market of overproduced images and ubiquitous information circuitries, the imaginary has trouble surviving, since reality seems already always replaced by its simulations"[26]. Rather than accept the fragmented impression of reality conveyed by our senses, especially sight, Birringer argues, theatre should enable a "radical and unfashionable vision"[27]; without forgetting "the limits and frames of the conditions of its theatricality", performance practices should be developed that "think of themselves as "acts from under and above" (...)---acts that need the limits of the theatre in order to be able to imagine different realities, under and above our normal ways of seeing"[28].

Birringer's quest for "acts from above and under", non-ordinary modes of perception, fits in with the insight that many contemporary theatre artists share a common interest in Eastern, especially Indian, theatre practices, mixed with religion and philosophy. What inspires their "turn to the East" are Eastern assumptions about states of consciousness beyond the intellect, beyond the emotions, parallel to Birringer's "under and above our normal ways of seeing"[29].

Such states of consciousness are experienced by the theatre artists, induced by all kinds of techniques, both Western and Eastern. Their attempts, however, to understand or even systematically reproduce those experiences are often enough frustrated: altered states of consciousness are met with skepticism in Western psychology, and the few attempts in the West to account for ASC are limited in scope and explanatory value. As the brief survey of Indian aesthetics, based on the *Natyashastra*, has shown, although altered states of consciousness feature more prominently in Indian philosophy, their understanding is far from clear. This makes it difficult for some Western theatre artists like Grotowski to use Eastern theatre techniques efficiently.

The search for states of consciousness beyond the intellect, beyond the emotions, ultimately, then, the search for "pure consciousness" together with all aspects of the waking state of consciousness, is where theatre artists, postmodern in their intercultural, intertextual activities, part with postmodernism: Crohn-Schmitt points out that "at the most elemental level, the description of nature necessarily becomes the description of experienced phenomena, not a representation of something more fundamental, an independent physical reality"[30].

There is, thus, no overarching universality underlying all phenomena of the world. The denial of a universal basis for creation, arrived at by application of quantum physics to human life, is the basis for pluralism. Crohn-Schmitt's argument is thus in line with postmodernism's critique of any position that opposes in principle the pluralism characteristic of postmodernism. The emphasis of postmodern philosophers on pluralism arose as a countermovement against metanarratives, grand narratives, such as "dialectics of the Spirit, the hermeneutics of meaning, the emancipation of the rational and working subject or the creation of wealth"[31]: according to postmodernist philosopher Lyotard, the postmodern condition is one in which the grand narratives of modernity formulated in the 18th century by philosophers of the Enlightenment "have lost all their credibility"[32].

The theatre artists' search for pure consciousness is nothing but a search for a new grand narrative. In this sense, theatre artists, whose endorsement of pluralism is a postmodern aspect of their work, ultimately do not share the distrust of grand narratives. However, they follow different grand narratives than Hegel or Marx: as shown by the fact that the more the artists are influenced by Western, and especially Eastern aesthetics and psychology, the more they aim for experiences in both actors and spectators that go beyond the senses, beyond the intellect, and even beyond the emotions, although the latter are mainly used to reach for the area of the mind called, with reference to Freud, Jung and other Western psychologists, the subconscious or unconscious. Through activation of the unconscious level of the mind, they hope to stimulate the experiences of communitas, of flow, of unification of binary opposites. They are, in other words, searching for an overarching totality, but not in the expressed fields of science, art, morality, or law, as the 18th century philosophers of the Enlightenment, but in a field beyond expression, in the field of consciousness.

## 6. Towards a Model of Consciousness

The exploration of the relationship of Western theories of the actor's emotional involvement and

- theories of altered states of consciousness, the phenomenon of pure consciousness, the mind-body relationship, and *Alba-Emoting* (Western points of contact),
- direct non-Western influences, especially the influences of Indian philosophy and Indian theatre aesthetics (*Natyashastra*), and
- Vedic linguistics and the *Natyashastra* (Indian points of contact).

have served to accentuate the shift of emphasis among theatre artists and theorists away from a dominant concern with the emotional stimulation of the audience and the transfer of emotions from actor to spectator towards levels of the mind beyond the intellect and beyond the emotions. For each of the artists discussed, as well as for the Indian theory represented in the *Natyashastra*, open questions remain, focusing on issues of consciousness.

Levels of mind beyond the intellect and the emotions are not mere speculations, but subject to direct experience by the theatre artists, actors and spectators. The experiences are vaguely conceptualised as *flow*, as *communitas*, *universality*, *unity of opposites*, and they are not limited to the field of theatre. Western literature provides many descriptions of "privileged moments"[1]. Yarrow's study of this phenomenon led to a list of eight major characteristics of "privileged moments":

1. suspension or extreme refinement of physical activity.
2. suspension of judgment (indifference, neutrality);
3. extension of perceptual boundaries (including sensitivity to language);
4. consciousness of being conscious (meta-awareness);
5. sense of unity or wholeness (self plus work/world; all aspects of work; organic understanding);
6. modification of evaluation of self;
7. potential for creating form (readiness for voluntary acts; awareness of multiple possibilities; spontaneity);
8. conjunction of distance and involvement.[2].

Yarrow points out that it is not necessary for all those characteristics "to be experienced every time"[3]. Characteristics 1-4 are most likely for a "momentary condition of potential liberation"[4]. Characteristics 5-8 will be more evident in a "more continuous situation in which an increasing ability for active perception/creation of wholes or *Gestalts* occurs against a background of silence and alertness"[5]. Yarrow terms the momentary condition "case A", the more permanent condition "case B", and argues that repeated exposure to experiences of (A) are likely preconditions for the more permanent nature of the experiences in case B. Yarrow concludes that to account for such experiences, a model of the mind will have to be developed that meets specific criteria. Yarrow's list can be adopted and enlarged for the purpose of this study. A model of the mind has to meet the following requirements:

1. It should cogently locate, define and describe feeling, intellect and the heart in its psychological significance, imagination, empathy, sensibility, on a "map" of mind or consciousness;

2. It should explain the experiences of *dual consciousness, translumination, communitas*, and *flow*;

3. It should relate these experiences to others already known;

4. It should account for consciousness as a dynamic phenomenon or process of shifting between different states;

5. It should account for language beyond speech;

6. It should offer a perspective on the possibility of a universal language of the theatre;

7. It should address the paradoxical coexistence of discipline and spontaneity;

8. It should deal with consciousness in psycho-physiological terms and not just as a philosophical concept, thus providing a model of the relationship between mind and body necessary

a) to explain the interaction of breathing and feeling,

b) to contextualise Meyerhold's biomechanics and Ekman's and Bloch's studies that appear to corroborate the effect of physical behaviour on the experience of emotions;

9. It should enable insights concerning the larger issues of interculturalism and postmodernism;

10. It should lay the foundation for a coherent interpretation of Indian aesthetics as found in the *Natyashastra*;

11. It should address the interaction of actor and audience in all the issues listed so far;

12. It should take into account relevant aspects of other models (psychological, mystical, philosophical, literary-theoretical.

# THE ACTOR'S EMOTIONAL INVOLVEMENT FROM THE PERSPECTIVE OF VEDIC PSYCHOLOGY

## 1. Vedic Psychology's Model of Consciousness

### a. Vedic Science and the "turn to the East"

In 1977, Cox drew attention to the fact that since the beginning of the nineteenth century Western intellectuals, when "disillusioned with the limits of science or the Enlightenment" have "almost always looked for the Orient for a fresh transfusion of magic or mysticism"[1]. Cox points out, however, that *Orientalism* is no longer a concern only for intellectuals, but in what he calls *neo-Orientalism* has taken hold of far wider ranges of the public. In particular, Cox focuses on the increased interest in Oriental forms of spirituality, arguing that most of the movements he looked into

> have altered the Oriental original (...) profoundly (...). Their leaders have stirred in such generous portions of the occult, of Christian images and vocabulary, and of Western organisational patterns, that trying to understand them in relation to an older "mother tradition" can ultimately be quite misleading.[2]

Eastern spirituality is of major importance in the New Age movement, whose development coincides with Cox's and Said's publications. It is a very polyvalent and complex movement, but nevertheless focused on one aim: to create a new conception of the world, acknowledging the interdependence of all phenomena in the universe[3]. A close analysis of this movement, which is also known under such names as "The Turning Point" (taken from an influential book by Capra[4]), or "Aquarian Conspiracy" (taken from a survey of the movement by Marilyn Ferguson[5]), reveals several terms that are of basic importance to the New Age movement. They will be briefly summarised to provide an understanding of the range of the movement's assumptions[6].

*New Age*. Humanity is facing a turning point in its cultural development, leading to a better, more complete and fulfilling life and world. The dimension of this turning point is almost inconceivable, and happens only once in thousands of years. The term "New Age" is used in a variety of differing contexts: in a superficial and often commercial way (One can buy New Age shoes, wear New Age clothes etc.); to describe all kinds of exotic, esoteric and occult teachings and practices; as a metaphor for change in social, economic and technological contexts; finally, as a spiritual event, as the birth of a new consciousness, a new awareness and a new experience of life.

*Paradigm*. Representatives of the New Age movement claim that the onset of the New Age is to be regarded as a change in paradigm, transferring Kuhn's definition of that term from the field of science to all areas of life in general. Any change of paradigm is, at first, met with harsh criticism.

*Holistic*. The machine can be regarded as the symbol of the old paradigm, and the organism is that of the new one. It harmonises the opposites of man and woman, culture and nature, mind and matter, intuition and ratio, mysticism and science, mind and body, man and God. The holistic paradigm aims at man being one with the universal Self, as well as with other humans and all mankind. It is a synthesis of all contradictions.

*New Consciousness*, which not only thinks holistically, but also experiences a holistic reality.

*Development of Consciousness* is necessary to experience reality holistically, especially the development of the intuitive qualities often associated with the right hemisphere.

*Self-Realisation* is a process that begins with man's longing for a true, fulfilled and holistic way of living, and means the quest for realising ones own possibilities, for realising one's own authentic self.

*Spirituality* refers both to a general basic orientation with all its corresponding attitudes, value-preferences and ways of life as well as basic assumptions of a spiritual conception of the world.

*Self-Organisation*. Theories first developed to account for phenomena studied in the natural sciences have been applied to the social and individual dimensions, emphasising values such as creativity, flexibility, autonomy, self-realization, common goals, decentralisation, independence, pluralism.

In the late seventies, then, there was both an increased interest in Oriental philosophy, in the popular domain of the New Age movement, and an accentuated critical awareness towards *Orientalism* in its historical and contemporary forms, raised by scholars such as Said and Cox. In the eighties, theatre artists became more aware of the implications of *Orientalism* in their intercultural work: Schechner developed his theatre anthropology, selecting concepts from various theatrical traditions, East and West. Barba devised his ideas of *Eurasian theatre*, aware of the dangers of *Orientalism* in theatre practice. Peter Brook's intercultural production of *The Mahabharata* for stage and film led to an extensive discussion of potentially exploitative implications of intercultural theatre practice, giving voice to those possibly most immediately concerned: non-Western, "Oriental" theatre artists and critics[7]. Rustom Bharucha's critique of the shortcomings of Western intercultural theatre practice led him to the conclusion that it was necessary to come to terms with his own, Indian, (theatrical) identity first, in an intracultural rather than intercultural context[8].

In 1958, five years after the death of his master, Brahmananda Saraswati, in 1953, Maharishi Mahesh Yogi began his world-wide activities of teaching Transcendental Meditation. TM was originally presented in Indian philosophical discourse as a method for gaining enlightenment, for developing higher states of consciousness. The media, however, were alerted by comparatively superficial effects such as an improvement of insomnia, ignoring or expressing doubt about Indian philosophy. In consequence, Maharishi Mahesh Yogi changed the marketing strategies towards scientific research on the TM technique, with the first publication by Wallace in *Science* in 1970[9], based on his PhD thesis. Since then, more than 500 studies have been conducted, most of them also published[10]. In 1980, while continuing the scientific marketing strategy, Maharishi Mahesh Yogi started to turn his attention to the Indian tradition from which the TM-technique originates in the first place. During the eighties, scientists at Maharishi International University, USA, discussed with Maharishi Mahesh Yogi parallels between their disciplines and concepts and knowledge found in Vedic literature. Findings of this major research project have been published in the journal *Modern Science and Vedic Science* since 1987, with articles on psychology, physics, literature, literary theory, physiology, sociology, computer science, education, art, mathematics, biology, agriculture, and economics. In addition to a study of parallels between Western and Vedic concepts of knowledge, Maharishi Mahesh Yogi places substantial emphasis on elucidating Vedic concepts in their own right, as in his reassessment of *Ayurveda*, *Jyotish* or *Stapathyaveda* (Vedic medicine, astrology and architecture respectively).

Maharishi Mahesh Yogi has termed the reassessment of Vedic literature in comparison with Western traditions of knowledge *Vedic Science*. Within the framework of a general "turn to the East", Vedic Science can be understood as Maharishi Mahesh Yogi's development from Indian discourse in 1958 via a science oriented discourse throughout the sixties and seventies to a determined return to the Indian discourse since the beginning of the eighties and still continuing today. On a different scale, this pattern resembles Bharucha's period of Western training at Yale, his comparisons of Western and Indian concepts of theatre in the context of interculturalism, and his tenacious return to, and demand for, intracultural theatre practice as far as India is concerned.

Within the framework of Vedic Science, Vedic Psychology is concerned with the structure and functioning of the human mind. To be able to critically assess the implications of Vedic Psychology's model of consciousness for the actor's emotional involvement, it is essential to locate Vedic Science and Psychology in their relation to Vedic literature, defined as the corpus of canonical texts of Indian philosophy.

## b. Vedic Science in the context of Vedic literature

Western scholars often refer to concepts of Indian philosophy as "speculation"[1]. The orthodox conviction, however, is that Vedic literature was not composed by individual "authors", but cognised on the level of consciousness by the seer (*rishi*) as "an eternal, impersonal truth"[2]. As Coward describes,

> The *rishi's* initial vision is said to be of the Veda as one, as a whole, the entirety of *Brahman*. This is represented in the *Mandukya-Upanishad* by the mantra AUM, which includes within itself the three levels of ordinary consciousness--waking, dreaming, and deep sleep--yet also reaches out beyond to the transcendent where the sound itself comes to an end.[3]

Maharishi Mahesh Yogi has contributed to the understanding of the rishi's cognition process. Whereas Vedic Science as formulated by Maharishi Mahesh Yogi mainly provides a synthesis of knowledge covered in Vedic literature, in this area it offers a new view of the interaction of the various constituents of Vedic literature, linking this interaction with the process of creation as found, for example, in *Samkhya*. Maharishi Mahesh Yogi takes up the paradox of unity in diversity at the basis of creation. *Brahman*, the absolute, unmanifest level of creation, which can be experienced by human consciousness as *atman*, the individual Self, or pure consciousness, is not merely flat, unchanging, without dynamics, but has simultaneously an infinite dynamism within it. The Sanskrit term for the unity aspect is *samhita*. Vedic Psychology views the processes of creation on the universal level as the activities of a "cosmic psyche", closely parallelled by the individual human psyche. In particular, the cosmic intellect, *buddhi*, causes the unity of *samhita* to express a diversity within itself. Originally, that diversity takes the form of an interaction of three elements in unity. The elements are *rishi, devata,* and *chhandas*. *Rishi* here is not the in-dividual seer of Vedic literature, but an abstract principle of consciousness: the knower, experiencer, observer, or subject. *Devata* corresponds to process of knowing, experiencing, observing, or subject-object relationship. *Chhandas* corresponds to the known, the experienced, the observed, or the object. The three components of unity (*samhita*), subject, subject-object relationship and object (*rishi, devata* and *chhandas*) interact with the unity and among each other. The nature of that interaction is self-referral[4]. The interaction of *samhita* and *rishi, devata* and *chhandas* begins on the absolute, unmanifest level. The interaction, even though unmanifest, creates a vibration. The varieties in vibra-tion resulting from the different interactions (*samhita-rishi; samhita-devata; samhita-chhandas; rishi-samhita; devata-samhita; chhandas-samhita; rishi-devata; devata-chhandas; chhandas-rishi* etc.) bring forth the different sets of Vedic literature. The interactions have a direction. The *samhita* of *rishi, devata* and *chhandas* leads to the knowledge contained cognised by the Vedic seers, rishis, as the *Rig-Veda*. The following table shows the interactions and the resulting parts of Vedic literature[5].

| Aspect | Directed Towards | Resulting Vedic Literature |
|---|---|---|
| Rishi | Samhita | Samaveda |
| Devata | Samhita | Yajurveda |
| Chhandas | Samhita | Atharvaveda |
| Samhita | Rishi | Upanishads |
| Samhita | Chhandas | Brahmanas |

| Aspect | Directed Towards | Resulting Vedic Literature |
|---|---|---|
| *The six Vedangas* | | |
| Rishi | Chhandas | Shiksha (phonetics) |
| Chhandas | Devata | Kalpa (rituals) |
| Devata | Rishi | Nirukta (semantics) |
| Rishi | Devata | Vyakaran (grammar) |
| Devata | Chhandas | Chhandas (metrics) |
| Chhandas | Rishi | Jyotish (astrology) |
| | | |
| *The six Upangas* | | |
| Shiksha | Samhita | Nyaya |
| Kalpa | Samhita | Vaisheshika |
| Nirukta | Samhita | Samkhya |
| Vyakaran | Samhita | Yoga |
| Chhandas | Samhita | Karma Mimansa |
| Jyotish | Samhita | Vedanta |

All transformations of the *rishi* aspect of the *samhita* are shown in the *Itihasa*, the epics of *Ramayana* and *Mahabharata*. All transformations of the *devata* aspect are portrayed in the *Puranas*, and all aspects of the *chhandas* aspect in the *Smritis*.

In the process of creation from the *Rig-Veda-samhita* to the *Itihasa*, *Smriti*, and *Puranas*, the primordial sound caused by the interaction of *rishi*, *devata* and *chhandas* in the unity, *samhita*, has become more and more expressed, and it transforms into the first traces of matter. In this transformation, *rishi* assumes the value of *vata*, *devata* that of *pitta*, and *chhandas* that of *kapha*. Their balance, corresponding to the unity of *samhita*, is responsible for *Ayurveda*, the Vedic discipline of medicine. A dominance of the material correlate of *rishi*, *vata*, gives rise to Gandharvaveda, the body of texts on song, music and art; a dominance of the material correlate of *devata*, *pitta*, causes the creation of *Dhanurveda*, the treatise on archery, behaviour in general, and politics. Finally, a dominance of the material correlate of *chhandas*, *kapha*, expresses itself in the *Stapathyaveda*, a treatise on architecture.

The cosmic psyche, whose interactions give rise to the entire body of Vedic literature, proceeds to develop the material correlates of *rishi, devata*, and *chhandas*, i.e., *vata, pitta* and *kapha*, to take even more manifest forms of expression, including the human body. Vedic Science thus proposes that the body is a manifestation of consciousness. In terms of the relationship between mind and matter, this view is in the tradition of subjective monism. According to Vedic Science, the interaction of *rishi, devata* and *chhandas* within the absolute, within the unity, *samhita*, brings forth, on the unmanifest level, the body of Vedic literature. The interaction ultimately leads to manifestation. Following *samkhya*, Vedic Science describes that the cosmic mind (*manas*) is connected with the manifest world of objects by the ten senses (*indriyas*), five senses of perception (*gyanendriya*), i.e. hearing, touch, seeing, taste, and smell, and five organs of action (*karmendriya*), i.e. language, ability to take hold of, ability to walk, discharge, procreation. Subtle matter arises in the next stage of development: the *tanmatras* constitute

the five basic realities, or essences, of the objects of the five senses of perception. They express themselves in the five elements which go to make up the objects of the senses, and which provide the material basis of the entire objective universe. Thus the essence of sound (*shabda tanmatra*) expresses itself in space, the essence of touch (*sparsha tanmatra*) in air, the essence of form (*rupa tanmatra*) in fire, the essence of taste (*rasa tanmatra*) in water, and the essence of smell (*gandha tanmatra*) in earth.[6]

The elements that constitute material creation are called *mahabhutas*, and they are space (*akasha*), air (*vayu*), fire (*tejas*), water (*apas*) and earth (*prithivi*). Whereas cosmic ego (*ahamkara*), cosmic intellect (*buddhi*), and cosmic mind (*manas*) are characterised by three governing principles, the three gunas, *sattva, rajas* and *tamas*, the elements (*mahabhutas*) have 20 different characteristics or *gunas*.

From the five elements, all matter is formed. *Ayurveda* describes how this manifestation continues in the human body. *Ayurveda* corresponds to the Western discipline of medicine; it describes three places "sandwiched between mind and body, where thought turns into matter; it is occupied by three operating principles called *doshas*"[7]. The three *doshas* are *vata*, in control of movement; *pitta*, in control of metabolism; and *kapha*, in control of structure. *Vata* arises from the combination of space (*akasha*) and air (*vayu*). *Pitta* is associated with fire (*tejas*) and water (*apas*), and *kapha* has its origin in water (*apas*) and earth (*prithivi*). Hagelin has associated the five *tanmatras* with the five spin types discussed in quantum field theory[8]. Each main *dosha* consists of five sub-*doshas*, each located in different parts of the body. The following table gives a survey[9]:

| Dosha | Subdosha | Location of Subdosha |
|-------|----------|----------------------|
| Vata | Prana | brain, head, chest |
| | Udana | throat and lungs |
| | Samana | stomach and intestines |
| | Apana | colon, lower abdomen |
| | Vyana | throughout the body via the nervous system, skin, and circulatory system |
| Pitta | Pachaka | stomach and small intestine |
| | Ranjaka | red blood cells, liver, spleen |
| | Sadhaka | heart |
| | Alochaka | eyes |
| | Bhrajaka | skin |
| Kapha | Kledaka | stomach |
| | Avalambaka | chest, lungs, lower back |
| | Bhodaka | tongue |
| | Tarpaka | sinus cavities, head, spinal fluid |
| | Shleshaka | joints |

The next level of concreteness is cell metabolism, dominated by the [13] forms of digestive fire, *agni*. Their activity leads to tissues, or *dhatus, rasa, rakta, mamasa, meda, ashthi, majja*, and *shukra*. Some sources place *ojas* as the first of these, as the most expressed, or as the last, the most subtle. Vedic Science holds that *ojas* pervades all *dhatus*. From the tissues (*dhatus*), all further levels of the body naturally follow, anatomy, functional systems etc.[10].

## c. Pure consciousness and the structure of the mind

Having established Maharishi Mahesh Yogi's Vedic Science in the contexts of the "turn to the East" and Vedic literature, we can proceed to discuss the model of consciousness proposed by Vedic Psychology. First, a hierarchical model of the structure of the mind will be introduced, followed by theories concerning higher stages of human development.

Several theatre artists theorise or report the experience of states of consciousness beyond the intellect and beyond the emotions, variously called *translumination, language beyond speech, communitas,* etc. The phenomenon of *pure consciousness* has been studied in contemporary Western psychology (Forman) and in surveys of mysticism (Stace).

The theory and practice of Vedic Psychology maintains that the human nervous system enables the direct experience of pure consciousness at the basis of creation as the *samhita* of *rishi, devata* and *chhandas.* In asserting this possibility, Vedic Psychology is in line with the mystics and those who, like Forman, accept their experiences as real and natural. Unlike the mystics, Vedic Psychology holds that through mental techniques which can be learnt easily, everyone can have this experience, not only a few isolated individuals.

Some characteristics of pure consciousness as described by the mystics or as researched by Western scientists have already been discussed. Vedic Psychology's definition of pure consciousness allows further parallels to be drawn. According to Vedic Psychology, pure consciousness is self-referral, or self-reflexive. This level of consciousness is "fully awake to itself. (...) there is nothing else to be aware of but awareness itself. (...) All the forms and phenomena in the universe arise from the self-referral manifestations of the field of pure consciousness"[1]. This theory recalls Velmans' reflexive model of the mind-body relationship. Whereas Velmans regards the world as-perceived as the result of the perceptual processing and as such a phenomenon of reflexive consciousness, Vedic Psychology goes even further in proposing that both mind and matter arise from a basic field which can be experienced as pure consciousness.

Self-referral is also the principle at the basis of many of the latest insights in quantum mechanics. At the beginning of the seventies, quantum field theories had their difficulties in explaining the phenomena they could observe in particle accelerators. The problem was based in the assumption that the respective basic fields (electro-magnetic, strong and weak interactions, gravity) had so many and so complex interactions that it was difficult to clearly describe the relationships of those interactions. The discovery of the spontaneous symmetry breaking, which shows deeply hidden symmetries of nature on fundamental space-time scales, made it possible to unify electro-magnetic and weak interaction forces to an electroweak field. This unification is possible by regarding both fields as parts of the same mathematical symmetry group. Thus the interactions of the two become self-referral. Theories of "grand unification" unify--according to the same principle--weak, strong and electromagnetic forces and particles. A further principle of symmetry, called supersymmetry, allows the unification of fields with opposed spin. By incorporating all other forces into gravity, a unified field theory is now expressed. Today, quantum field theorists work on the most elegant formulation of this unified field theory. All these developments, which took place during the last fifteen years, are based on regarding the different basic forces more and more as self-referral phenomena of a unified field[2]. Vedic Psychology identifies this field within the human being as the field of pure consciousness.

Hagelin has explored "striking parallels between unified field theories of physics and the field of pure consciousness" as described by Vedic Psychology:

> One of his arguments for asserting that the unified field is the source of consciousness as well as of physics involves demonstrating that at the scale of super-unification, nature displays attributes characteristic of pure consciousness: self-referral, self- sufficiency, and infinite dynamism.[3]

This view goes in the direction of Tallis' model based on Spinoza: it assumes an original substance, the unified field, or "Cosmic Psyche". Consciousness and matter are, however, not so much attributes of the unified field, as in Tallis' model, but expressions or manifestations of it.

In proposing pure consciousness to be at the basis of all creation, expressed consciousness as well as expressed matter, Vedic Psychology is also in accord with Bohm's implication that "in some sense a rudimentary mind-like quality is present even at the level of particle physics"[4]. Vedic Psychology provides a theory of the processes of manifestation from within the field of pure consciousness to expressed consciousness and matter[5]. Within the scope of this study, it will suffice to indicate that the process suggested is very close to Bohm's view that "that which we experience as mind, in its movement through various levels of subtlety, will, in a natural way ultimately move the body by reaching the level of the quantum potential and of the "dance" of the particles"[6].

A final interesting parallel between Vedic Psychology and Bohm's theory is Bohm's statement that even far distant particles can affect each other on the quantum mechanical level through the quantum potential[7]. Vedic Psychology proposes that pure consciousness is a common field that links all individuals. This hypothesis, as many others in Vedic Psychology, is testable:

> In ten trials, EEG was concurrently measured from pairs of subjects, one practicing Transcendental Meditation and the TM-Sidhi-technique of "Yogic Flying" (YFg)-- said to en-liven the proposed field of consciousness-- and the other performing a computer task. (...) analysis indicated that coherence changes in the (...) band sensitive to TM and YFg, consist-ently led coherence changes in the other subject's (...) band. A clear relationship was seen among subjective reports, coherence patterns, and strength of intervention effects.[8]

These data support a field model of consciousness.

Pure consciousness as described by Vedic Psychology is not only related to modern Western theories of consciousness, but also resembles the description of "pure unitary consciousness", a term coined by Stace in his survey of mysticism. Gelderloos and Beto argue that the characteristics of pure con-sciousness as defined by Vedic Psychology are similar to the characteristics of "pure unitary consciousness" as described by Stace[9].

> EGO QUALITY: refers to the experience of loss of self while consciousness is never-theless maintained. The loss of self is commonly experienced as an absorption into something greater than the mere empirical ego.[10]

Vedic Psychology differentiates between self, the individual ego, the core of personality, and Self, or pure consciousness. When pure consciousness is expe-rienced, the self "is not lost; it rather becomes expanded toward a higher dignity (...)"[11].

> UNIFYING QUALITY: refers to the experience of the multiplicity of objects of perception as nevertheless united. Everything is in fact perceived as "One".[12]

Pure consciousness is experienced as one field of consciousness underlying all manifestations. Pure consciousness is beyond any perception. Therefore, Vedic Psychology holds that the perception of unity in diversity is not characteristic of the experience of pure consciousness on its own. Rather, only when the unity of pure consciousness "becomes carried over into the field of diversity" will the resulting experience be that of perceiving "the multiplicity of objects of perception as nevertheless united"[13].

INNER SUBJECTIVE QUALITY: refers to the perception of an inner subjectivity to all things, even those usually experienced in purely material forms.[14]

Pure consciousness is regarded as inner subjectivity. After it has been experienced on the transcendental level, i.e. in its pure form without any contents, it is afterwards sequentially experienced "in more and more expressed levels of consciousness, feelings, thinking, senses"[15].

TEMPORAL/SPATIAL QUALITY: refers to the temporal spatial parameters of the experience. Essentially both time and space are modified with the extreme being one of an experience that is both "timeless" and "spaceless".[16]

Pure consciousness is experienced as being beyond time and space. In parallel to the unified field described in quantum physics, it is timeless, unbounded, omnipresent and source of all diversification.

NOETIC QUALITY: refers to the experience as a of valid knowledge. Emphasis is on a nonrational, intuitive, insightful experience that is nevertheless recognised as not merely subjective.[17]

Vedic Psychology takes up a concept developed by Patanjali in his definition of *samadhi* (pure consciousness) in his *Yoga Sutras*. This implies that a fully developed person can function from a level of consciousness termed *ritam bhara pragya*, "the level that knows only the truth"[18]. It is a level just this side of pure consciousness, on the finest level of manifestation. Knowledge gained on this level is gained "directly, without the intermediacy of *indriyas* [senses] or *manas* [mind]"[19].

INEFFABILITY: refers to the impossibility of expressing the experience in conventional language . The experience simply cannot be put into words due to the nature of the experience itself and not to the linguistic capacity of the subject.[20]

Vedic Psychology fully agrees with this finding: "although pure consciousness can be experienced daily, it cannot be expressed in words, it is beyond speech and thoughts"[21].

POSITIVE AFFECT: refers to the positive affect quality of the experience. Typically the experience is of joy or blissful happiness.[22]

Vedic Psychology classifies affect as an expressed form of consciousness. Because pure consciousness is unexpressed, it cannot be "appreciated by emotion"[23]. The experience of pure consciousness is nonetheless later described in terms of "bliss or ultimate contentment"[24].

RELIGIOUS QUALITY: refers to the intrinsic sacredness of the experience. This includes feelings of mystery, awe, and reverence that may nevertheless be experienced independently of traditional religious language.[25]

Vedic Psychology explains that "for many people an experience of the highest magnificence like the experience of the Absolute is appreciated with awe and reverence"[26]. Such an experience is then likely to be described and interpreted in religious terms. Vedic Psychology appreciates the religious quality of the experience. In agreement with Stace's assumption that the religious quality "may be experienced independently of traditional religious language", Vedic Psychology "highlights the universal nature of the experience of pure consciousness, emphasizing the scientifically verifiable reality of the Vedic perspective"[27].

So far, the concept of pure consciousness has been explained within the frame of Vedic Psychology, and its relationship to contemporary theories of the relationship between mind and matter has been discussed, taking into consideration theories of mysticism as well as self-reflexivity or self-referral and quantum mechanics. Scientific research into the Transcendental Meditation and its advanced techniques--said to enliven the field of pure consciousness---have led to conclude that pure or transcendental consciousness represents a fourth main state of consciousness besides waking, dreaming, and sleeping[28].

Vedic Psychology proposes pure consciousness as the basis of more expressed levels of awareness, and a hierarchical structure of the mind, defined as the "overall multilevel functioning of consciousness"[29]. On levels characterised by increasing concreteness, activity, diversity, and decreasing subtlety, the field of pure consciousness gives rise to the individual ego, the level of feelings, emotion and intuition, the intellect, the mind, desires, and the senses. This sequence of structures of the mind corresponds to traditional Vedic literature, particularly *samkhya* and *yoga*[30], where *ahamkara* (ego), *buddhi* (intellect), *manas* (mind), *akasha* (space, the object of the sense of hearing), *vayu* (air, the object of the tactile sense), *tejas* (fire, the object of the sense of sight), *apas* (water, the object of the sense of taste), and *prithivi* (earth, the object of the sense of smell) are differentiated[31]. In addition, Vedic Psychology locates emotion, feeling and intuition between the levels of ego (*ahamkara*) and intellect (*buddhi*).

In principle, each subtler level can "observe and monitor the more expressed levels"[32], with the level of pure consciousness, being at the basis of all expressions of the mind, informing all levels of the mind. This principle is in line with Bohm's theory of the relationship between mind and matter when he claims that thoughts can be regarded as a series of

> more and more closely woven nets. Each can "catch" a certain context of corresponding "fineness". The finer nets cannot only show up the details of form and structure of what is "caught" in the coarser nets; they can also hold within them a further context that is implied in the latter.[33]

In Vedic Psychology, the ego is further defined as the inner value of the experiencer, the most immediate expression of the field of pure consciousness. The concept of ego is thus different from those of Freud, Jung or other Western psychologists. The hierarchy of levels of mind represents a synthesis of the six *upangas*, the systems of Indian philosophy. The ego features prominently in *Samkhya*, where it represents the principle responsible for the individuation of *mahat*, the first state of evolution "where the previously undifferentiated primal substance, *prakriti*, begins to move towards manifestation, begins to take a specific direction"[34]. The principle of *ahamkara* thus refers both to the cosmic as well as the individual human level.

The emotions, feelings and intuition are closely related to the ego. The intellect, *buddhi*, again both cosmic and individual, is characterised by its discriminating abilities, and it is this quality of discrimination that the intellect takes up from the field of pure consciousness, which "is capable of discriminating both knower and known" within its own self-referral structure[35]. It should be noted that the term "mind" in Vedic Psychology refers both to "the whole range of mental activity and structure, in contrast to pure consciousness on the one hand or the body on the other"[36] and to "the specific level of thinking within that overall structure"[37]. The function of the mind (*manas*) on the individual level, is to consider possibilities and their relationships, and it "also serves the functions of memory and thought"[38]. Desire also originates in a particular characteristic of the field of pure consciousness, its desire to know itself. It connects the mind and the senses with the environment: "Desire may be understood as motivating the flow of attention and thus, in daily experience, connecting the mind with the environment through the senses"[39].

## d. Higher stages of human development

Vedic Psychology does not stop at describing the interrelationship of the elements of consciousness and pure consciousness as their source. In answer to the question "What are the highest possible forms of human development?"[1], Vedic Psychology proposes that it is possible not only to have occasional experiences of higher states of consciousness as described by the mystics, or called "peak experiences" by Maslow, but to systematically develop such more advanced states of consciousness as phenomena of permanent daily experience. Although Vedic Psychology regards the Vedantic experience of "*aham Brahmasmi*", "I am that, thou art that, all this is that"[2] as the highest stage of development, it also charts the development to that level implied by the other *upangas*.

The exploration of adulthood has only recently attracted "significant attention from developmental psychologists"[3]. Focal point of the emerging theories is the relationship of proposed models of higher stages of human development to the seminal theory of cognitive development advanced by Jean Piaget. He differentiated distinct developmental stages, leading to an endpoint termed "formal operations":

> For him [Piaget], formal operations is the culmination of cognitive development: there is no further development of the organisational form of thought beyond this stage; remaining changes are in terms of increased competence with formal operations and their more comprehensive application in the accumulation of greater knowledge.[4]

The developmental stage of formal operations is normally attained, according to Piaget, during the teen years. It thus belongs to "preadult development, even though full facility in this mode of thinking may not develop until adulthood--or may never develop"[5].

Alexander holds that assessing the possibilities of adult development beyond Piaget's stage of formal operations, involves three related issues:

> Does development towards the endpoint proceed through qualitatively distinct stages? What mechanisms underlie this development? What major areas get developed (e.g., cognition and affect), and how do they interrelate?[6]

Alexander differentiates non-hierarchical and hierarchical theories, theories of advanced moral development, and theories of consciousness and self-development[7]. The concepts of adult development proposed by Vedic Psychology fall into the last category.

Based on the proposition to regard pure consciousness as a fourth state of consciousness next to the commonly known and experienced ones--waking, dreaming, and sleeping--Vedic Psychology describes three further stages of consciousness development. Termed "cosmic consciousness", a fifth state of consciousness is characterised by the coexistence of waking, or dreaming, or sleeping, and pure consciousness. In cosmic consciousness, the level of pure consciousness, which is never overshadowed in daily experience by the activities and experiences of the individual psyche, becomes a "stable internal frame of reference from which changing phases of sleep, dreaming, and waking life are silently *witnessed* or observed"[8]. Just as the states of waking, dreaming, sleeping, and of pure consciousness can be researched with reference to different, and state-specific subjective experiences as well as equally different and state-specific patterns of bodily functions such as EEG activity, eye movement, metabolic rate, breathing patterns, Galvanic skin response, and concentrations of various hormones in the blood, which are open to psychophysiological empirical studies, cosmic consciousness, too, has its state-specific patterns of subjective experience and psychophysiological variables. The *Bhagavad-Gita*, an important part of the *Mahabharata*, describes the experience of an individual who has gained the state of cosmic consciousness like this: "He who sees that all work, everywhere, is only the work of nature; and that the spirit watches his work--he sees the truth"[9].

The following is a description of witnessing dreaming:

> Often during dreaming I am awake inside, in a very peaceful, blissful state. Dreams come and go, thoughts about the dreams come and go, but I remain in a deeply peaceful state, completely separate from the dreams and the thoughts. My body is asleep and inert, breathing goes on regularly and mechanically, and inside I am just aware that I am.[10]

This double nature of experience, pure consciousness witnessing the activities of waking, dreaming, and sleeping, is not equivalent to an uncomfortable dissociation or split personality, as evident, for example, in Thoreau's description in *Walden* of occasionally *witnessing* his own thoughts and feelings:

> I only know myself as a human entity; the scene, so to speak, of thoughts and affections; and am sensible of a certain doubleness by which I can stand as remote from myself as from another. However intense my experience, I am conscious of the presence and criticism of part of me, which, as it were, is not a part me, but spectator, sharing no experience, but taking note of it: and that is no more I than is you. When the play (...) of life is over, the spectator goes his way. It was a kind of fiction, a work of imagination only, as far as he was concerned.[11]

The following lines of the modern Hispanic poet Juan Ramon Jimenez demonstrate his recognition of the "witnessing" Self to be his essential nature:

I am not I
    I am this one
Who goes by my side unseen by me;
Whom I, at times, go to visit,
And whom I, at times, forget.
He who keeps silent, serene, when I speak,
He who forgives, sweet, when I hate,
He who takes a walk where I am not,
He who will remain standing when I die.[12]

Referring to a contemporary woman athlete, Billie Jean King, Alexander points out that "witnessing" as an experience characteristic of cosmic consciousness is not limited to quiet moments. King experienced "witnessing" during a tennis match and describes it in relation to "its value for spontaneous right action and personal fulfilment":

I can almost feel it coming. It usually happens on one of those days when everything is just right. (...) It almost seems as though I'm able to transport myself beyond the turmoil of the court to some place of total peace and calm. Perfect shots extend into perfect matches. (...) I appreciate what my opponent is doing in a detached abstract way. Like an observer in the next room. (...) It is a perfect combination of [intense] action taking place in an atmosphere of total tranquility. When it happens I want to stop the match and grab the microphone and shout that's what it's all about, because it is. It's not the big prize I'm going to win at the end of the match or anything else. It's just having done something that's totally pure and having experienced the perfect emotion.[13]

A number of psychophysiological studies have shown a significant correlation between the enhanced frequency of reported experiences of higher stages of consciousness and physiological variables. The variables studied include, among others, periods of virtual respiratory suspension, increased alpha and theta EEG coherence; increased capacity for absorption; self-actualisation; internal locus of control; decreased symptoms of stress; improved ability on measures on fluid intelligence, creativity, perceptual and motor skills[14].

The next stage of development, according to Vedic Psychology, is called "refined cosmic consciousness". In cosmic consciousness, the field of pure consciousness is permanently experienced together with waking, or dreaming, or sleeping. This level of functioning is maintained in refined cosmic consciousness and "combined with the maximum value of perception of the environment. Perception and feeling reach their most sublime level"[15].

The British poet Kathleen Raine reports her experience of seeing a hyacinth, suggestive of an experience of refined cosmic consciousness as predicted by Vedic Psychology:

I dared scarcely to breathe, held in a kind of fine attention in which I could sense the very flow of life in the cells. I was not perceiving the flower but living it. I was aware of the life of the plant as a slow flow or circulation or a vital current of liquid light of the utmost purity. I could apprehend as a simple essence formal structure and dynamic process. This dynamic form was, as it seemed, of a spiritual not a material order; or of a finer matter, or of matter itself perceived as spirit. There was nothing emotional about this experience which was, on the contrary, an almost mathematical apprehension of a complex and organised whole, apprehended as whole, this whole was living; and as such inspired by a sense of immaculate holiness. (. ..) By "living" I do not mean that which distinguishes animal from plant or plant from mineral, but rather a quality possessed by all these in their different degrees.[16]

The philosopher Fichte describes the experience of refined perception like this:

> (...) and the universe appears before my eyes clothed in a more glorious form. The dead inert mass which only filled up space, has vanished: and in its place there flows onward, with the rushing music of mighty waves, an endless stream of life and power and action, which issues from the original Source of all life.[17]

The final level of human development according to Vedic Psychology is called "unity consciousness". In this state of consciousness, "the highest value of self-referral is experienced"[18]. The field of pure consciousness is directly perceived as located at every point in creation, and thus "every point in creation is raised to the (...) status" of pure consciousness[19]. "The gap between the relative and absolute aspects of life (...) is fully eliminated"[20]. The experiencer experiences himself and his entire environment in terms of his own nature, which he experiences to be pure consciousness. The *Bhagavad-Gita* describes unity consciousness thus: "The yogi who is united in identity with the all-pervading, infinite Consciousness, and sees unity everywhere, beholds the Self present in all beings, and all beings as assumed in the Self"[21]. Maharishi Mahesh Yogi translates:

He whose self is established in
Yoga, whose vision everywhere is
even, sees the Self in all beings,
and all beings in the Self.[22]

The *Yoga-Vasishta* describes unity consciousness similarly:

> I salute the self! Salutations to myself--the undivided consciousness, the jewel of all the seen and unseen worlds (...) you have been gained. (...) What ever there is in the universe is the one self. In the past, the present and in the future, here, there and everywhere (...) The self is the eternal existence. I, the self, alone am.[23]

Descriptions of unity consciousness are also found in the Upanishads: "I am that [Brahman]. Thou art that. All this [universe] is nothing but that."[24], or "All this is Brahman alone. There is none other than Brahman and that is I"[25].

Gustave Flaubert "describes a transient experience that suggests this state in the 1849-1858 version of his novel *The Temptation of St. Anthony*"

> It is true, often I have felt that something bigger than myself was fusing with my being: bit by bit I went off into the greenery of the pastures and into the current of the rivers that I

watched go by; and I no longer knew where my soul was, it was so diffuse, universal, spread out. (...) Your mind itself finally lost the notion of particularity which kept it on the alert. It was like an immense harmony engulfing your soul with marvellous palpitations, and you felt in its plenitude an inexpressible comprehension of the unrevealed wholeness of things; the interval between you and the object, like an abyss closing, grew narrower and narrower, until the difference vanished, because you both were bathed in infinity; you penetrated each other equally, and a subtle current passed from you into matter while the life of the elements slowly pervaded you, rising like a sap: one degree more, and you would have become nature, or nature become you (...) immortality, boundlessness, infinity. I have all that, I am that! I feel myself to be Substance, I am Thought! (...) I understand, I see, I breathe, in the midst of plenitude (...) how calm I am![26]

## 2. The Actor's Emotions and Vedic Psychology

### a. The Paradox

The theories of the actor's emotional involvement during acting discussed in the first part of this study have one important element in common: they take their cause in close observation, often paired with direct experience, of mental processes believed or experienced to take place during acting. Diderot observed many actors, found those who were emotionally not involved more convincing, matched this finding with concepts of psychology and physiology known to him, and arrived at the paradox of the emotionally uninvolved actor able to stimulate emotions in the audience. Stanislavsky started from his own experience as an actor, and matched his experience with pre-Freudian psychology and notions of Indian philosophy to arrive at his paradox: the actor has to be both deeply emotionally involved and yet in conscious control of acting by watching himself. The phenomenon of *dual consciousness* is also characteristic of Artaud's paradox of the actor's simultaneous physical presence and neutrality.

Different experiences, all relating to consciousness, however, are pivotal for Meyerhold, Strasberg, Brecht, Grotowski, Schechner, Barba and Brook. Meyerhold's emphasis is on the ability of the body to induce emotional states, a concept successfully developed further in *Alba Emoting*. Strasberg has mainly developed the focus on the emotion memory aspect in Stanislavsky's theories; Brecht argued against the actor's empathy with the role, rather than against emotion. Grotowski's aim in his theatre practice was to achieve a state of *translumination* for actor and spectator alike. Schechner takes up Turner's concepts of *communitas* and *flow*, Barba's paradox, the simultaneity of inner subjectivity and objective outer expression, again asks the question of the relationship between consciousness and outward reality; Brook, finally, aims for a universal language of the theatre, for total theatre beyond the holy, the rough and the dead theatre.

The first part of this study has demonstrated that the theatre artists and theorists were influenced by concepts of knowledge (philosophy, psychology) that were historically at their disposal. The same phenomenon-- acting--has thus been described in different discourses. The difference of discourse, however, does not alter the fact that the subject of discussion--the actor's functioning during acting--remains unchanged. Although individual differences among theatre artists and theorists, influenced by their historical conditioning, give rise to different terminology, all their experiences and their subsequent theorising are related to the crucial concept of consciousness. In many cases, the theories, the descriptions of experiences of non-ordinary states of consciousness have been characterised as paradoxes, i.e. as somehow beyond established means and paths of explanation offered by orthodox science.

The historical development of the theatre artists' theories of the actor's emotional involvement while acting, which has been documented in the first part of the study, cannot be denied. Illuminating that development, however, did not solve the paradoxes, although it helped to accentuate them.

Vedic Science offers an opportunity to explain the actors' consciousness-related experiences from its model of the mind. Diderot's theory of the emotional stimulation of the spectators through an emotionally uninvolved actor is paradoxical on the level of an ordinary waking state of consciousness as described by Vedic Psychology. On this level of consciousness, the Self as the basis of the mind is not open to direct experience. It is overshadowed by the (sensory) objects of experience. The Self identifies with the objects of sensory perception, or with the emotions and feelings. In such a state, detachment from one's own experiences and actions is difficult, and ordinarily considered as undesirable, a symptom of mental disturbance. Roach refers to the actor's ability to detach himself from his body as a "highly unusual, even freakish capacity"[1]. Related "out-of-body-experiences" are delegated to the domain of "popular psychology"[2].

According to Vedic psychology, in the state of cosmic consciousness the Self is by definition experienced as separate from the manifest levels of the mind (ego, feelings, mind, intellect, senses). This liberated Self could be associated with Diderot's "disinterested onlooker" whom the actor must have in himself[3]. The Self is fully developed in cosmic consciousness, and the actor's development towards that stage is characterised by his increasing ability to perform with growing realisation of the Self. This growth will be experienced both in time quantity, as well as in quality, i.e., depth. Initially, the experience of "witnessing", characteristic of cosmic consciousness, will be experienced for short periods during a performance, the length of experience will increase, and ultimately the experience of the Self will be maintained throughout activity, no longer limited to acting on stage. Simultaneously, the functioning of the expressed levels of the mind will be improved, so that the actor can meet Diderot's demand for penetration, an intellectual quality. Moreover, the actor's ability to observe nature as source for imitation will be enhanced by heightened sensory functioning.

A passage from Ronald Harwood's contemporary play *The Dresser* can illustrate the idea of *witnessing* one's activities from the perspective of pure consciousness in a theatrical context. The main character in the play is called "Sir". He is an old actor in the actor-manager tradition, allegedly based on Sir Donald Wolfit, whose dresser Ronald Harwood was at one time in his career. The play shows one day in Sir's life: he plays Lear at a provincial theatre, during the Second World War. He describes the following experience to his wife:

> Speaking "Reason not the need", I was suddenly detached from myself. My thoughts flew. And I was observing from a great height. Go on, you bastard, I seemed to be saying or hearing. Go on, you've more to give, don't hold back, more, more, more. And I was watching Lear. Each word he spoke was fresh invented. I had no knowledge of what came next, what fate awaited him. The agony was in the moment of acting created. I saw an old man, and the old man was me. And I knew there was more to come. But what? Bliss, partial recovery, more pain and death. All this I knew I had yet to see. Outside myself, do you understand? Outside myself.[4]

This fictional account of *witnessing* activity, characteristic of cosmic consciousness, has its parallels in real-life experiences. The actor Ray Reinhardt reports:

> There are two stages of having the audience in your hand. The first one is the one in which you bring them along, you make them laugh through sheer skill--they laughed at that,

now watch me top it with this one. But, there's a step beyond that which I experienced, but only two or three times. It is the most--how can you use words like satisfying? It's more ultimate than ultimate: I seemed to be part of a presence that stood behind myself and was able to observe, not with my eyes, but with my total being, myself and the audience. It was a wonderful thing of leaving not only the character, but also this person who calls himself Ray Reinhardt. In a way, I was no longer acting actively, although things were happening: my arms moved independently, there was no effort required; my body was loose and very light. It was the closest I've ever come in a waking state to a mystical experience.[5]

At least two aspects of this report are striking: it shows an infrequent, but clear experience suggestive of witnessing during activity. The experience itself is described as highly satisfying, and, at the same time, improving the performance.

Dual consciousness also appears to be important to representatives of contemporary Indian dancers who stand in the most direct tradition of the *Natyashastra*. Thus, Padmanathan Nair, a renowned Kathakali dancer told Richard Schechner in 1976: "A good actor is one who understands the character very well, thus becoming the character itself. [...But] we should not forget ourselves while acting. While acting, half of the actor is the role he does and half will be himself"[6]. It is not clear either from Nair's formulation or from the context whether Nair has a glimpse of cosmic consciousness in mind here, or just an intellectual type of dual consciousness.

Diderot claims that the actor should not feel while acting. Understanding this claim from the perspective of Vedic Psychology leads to a modification of Diderot's assumptions. The "disinterested onlooker", identified as the Self, does indeed not feel in the sense that once a person has risen to cosmic consciousness, the Self is no longer overshadowed by any experience. Because the Self, the essence of the actor's consciousness, is not involved, the actor can afford to be involved on the manifest level of the emotions and feelings. In permanent cosmic consciousness, the emotions are developed to the fullest possible degree, thus allowing the actor deep penetration of the character's emotions as set out by the dramatist, and the actor's fully developed intellect will allow a "rendering of the outward signs of feeling"[7] that, together with the emotions actually felt, will provide maximum effect on the audience. Approximations of that ideal mark performances on the path to the state of cosmic consciousness.

The actor's development of consciousness entails the development of the Self as a "disinterested onlooker", witnessing, and not overshadowed by any experience of the senses, the mind, the intellect, the emotions or the ego. Proposing the "disinterested onlooker" to be the Self implies that the actor need not be emotionally uninvolved on the expressed level of the mind relating to the emotions. On the contrary, the actor in cosmic consciousness, always witnessing the actions of the expressed levels of the mind including the emotions, is fully able to feel and portray the emotions the character is believed to be feeling.

How does an actor functioning in the way described, influence the audience? In performance the actor approaching cosmic consciousness functions more and more with the full potential of all levels of his mind (in the wide sense), i.e. senses, mind (in the restricted, functional sense) intellect, emotions, ego, and transcendental Self. The actor affects the individual spectator on all those levels. An actor not involved on the level of the Self, but emotionally involved to the degree of his development of consciousness, affects the spectator on the level of pure consciousness, the Self, because pure consciousness is a field that connects all individuals. In addition, the actor affects the spectator on each level of mind, to the degree that the actor has developed those distinct levels of his mind. In parallel, the spectator's development of the distinct levels of the mind determines the amount to which he can be affected by the actor. For example, a spectator whose intellect is more developed than the emotions will respond more to intellectual stimuli from text and performance. Differences in response of different spectators to the same production of a play, or to the same actor, then, have their cause in the differences in the actor's and spectator's degree of development of the distinct levels of the mind.

The proposed solution to Diderot's paradox from the perspective of Vedic Psychology also applies to Stanislavsky. Whereas Diderot proposed unemotional acting stimulating emotions in the spectator, Stanislavsky described the actor's art of being both deeply emotionally involved while acting and yet in conscious control of acting through watching himself. Vedic Psychology would argue that the actor's deep emotional involvement is facilitated through the actor's development of consciousness. This development goes along with the growing ability to experience the Self as a witnessing agency of consciousness together with the witnessed objects of (sensory) perception, together, that is, with any activity.

Brecht required the actor to feel the emotions of the character without empathy, i.e. without being involved with the emotions. Brecht hoped to achieve this aim by emphasising the intellect through which the actor should work, and the spectator's intellect which should be stimulated. According to Vedic Psychology, complete noninvolvement is possible only when the Self is experienced as independent of, and witnessing all activities of the mind. In such a state, cosmic consciousness, neither emotional involvement nor empathy will overshadow the actor's experience of his/her Self. As a result, the actor's performance will affect the spectator on all levels of the mind. This does not imply that all levels of the spectator's mind are necessarily influenced equally. Different dramatists will have different aims for their plays, intending to affect primarily the spectator's emotions, or his/her intellect, or leading to the experience of the Self. The actor in cosmic consciousness, having by definition developed the full capacity of the intellect and the emotions, will be able, if he/she and/or the director should choose, to do full justice to the dramatist's intentions as to which level of the mind to influence most.

The concept of "dual consciousness" re-appears in Artaud's paradox of the actor's simultaneous physical presence and neutrality. However, the paradox undergoes a significant shift: Diderot argued for the emotional stimulation of the spectator through an emotionally uninvolved actor, Stanislavsky for the dual consciousness in the actor who is simultaneously emotionally involved and in conscious control, and Brecht shifted the emphasis from emotion to empathy. Although the three theorists do not neglect the physical/physiological aspect of emotions, their paradoxes are still more in the domain of psychology than physiology. Artaud emphasises physical presence, along with a physical language, in which he hoped to realise his vision of language beyond speech. From the perspective of Vedic psychology, an actor in cosmic consciousness will have developed fully not only his consciousness, but also his physiology--a perfectly functioning physiology is the prerequisite for the mind's ability to reflect pure consciousness on the individual level. With the unity of mind and body fully developed, the actor will have maximum possible presence on stage. The closer the non-enlightened actor approaches the state of cosmic consciousness, the closer will his presence rise to its full potential. Artaud's reference to the actor's neutrality can be explained, with reference to Vedic Psychology, in two ways: first, it applies to the "neutral" feature of pure, contentless consciousness, the "witnessing" function of consciousness which features in the explanation of "dual consciousness" for Diderot's, Stanislavsky's and Brecht's theories. Second, "neutral" refers, on a more practical level, to the actor's ability, growing on the path to and perfected in the state of cosmic consciousness, to adopt any shade of intensity on the stage, depending on the circumstances and requirements of the given production.

Grotowski aims for a state of consciousness and body where the actor transcends incompleteness and the mind-body-split, where he achieves totality, full presence, where he becomes a *holy actor*. Such *translumination* is clearly an experience of not only cosmic consciousness, characterised by a separation of Self and activity, but an experience of unity consciousness as defined by Vedic psychology: knower and known are experienced as a unity, the striking duality of Self and expressed levels of consciousness, characteristic of cosmic consciousness, disappears. For the duration of the experience of cosmic consciousness or unity consciousness, all action, performative or other, is fully spontaneous, there is no longer a time-lapse between inner impulse and outer action. At the same time, all activity in those states of consciousness will be fully disciplined in the sense that there will be no entropy, no waste of energy, actions will lead to the intended result following the principle of least action. Barba's concept of *incoherent coherence* is thus rendered obsolete. The coexistence of spontaneity and discipline is characteristic of higher states of consciousness.

The model of consciousness proposed by Vedic psychology also helps to makes sense of Turner's concepts of *communitas* and *flow* which influence Schechner's performance theory. *Communitas* is the style of human interaction in which at least two individuals experience unity. Although Turner rhetorically asks "Is there any of us who has not known this moment..."[8], thus implying that it is a common experience, *communitas* is the experience of a non-ordinary state of consciousness, an ASC. In the context of Vedic psychology, it is a short, temporary experience of unity consciousness, where the dualism between Self and witnessed activity of waking, or dreaming, or sleeping, characteristic of cosmic consciousness, is united in the experience of all-pervading unity between the Self and the expressions of the Self. Such a state of consciousness has "something of a flow quality", as Turner puts it, which shows all the features listed by Csikszentmihalyi and MacAloon[9], and resembling Yarrow's and Jephcott's compilation of characteristics of "privileged moments" in literature. In leading the actor and the spectator to ultimately permanent higher stages of consciousness, theatre has a transformative function and goes well beyond *transportation* in Schechner's definition of those terms.

In Barba's theories, the claim for a co-existence, in the actor, of inner subjectivity and its objective outer expression and subsequent subjective reception by the spectator is problematic. Vedic Psychology can assist in understanding the implications. In cosmic consciousness, the Self is fully developed, and all aspects of the body are fully developed. Thus inner subjectivity can be expressed objectively in the sense that it neither overshadows the Self, nor is subjective to the extent that it is incommunicable, incomprehensible to a spectator. On the contrary, acting from a state of cosmic consciousness will enable the actor to shape his fully developed subjectivity in such a way as to allow the spectator maximum benefit, taking the individual spectators' state of consciousness into account and tuning his performance to the level of consciousness of the spectators. The actor's subjectivity thus becomes the focal point of acting, because it initially decides the objective outer expression. The actor's subjectivity, through the means of objective expression, concurrent with subjectivity, without time lapse, has a direct impact on the spectator's subjectivity.

### b. The *Natyashastra* from the perspective of Vedic Science

#### i. The position of the *Natyashastra* in Vedic literature

The *Natyashastra* is part of *Gandharva-Veda*. *Gandharvas* are divine musicians, and *Gandharva-Veda* is defined as music in accord with natural law[1]. Maharishi Mahesh Yogi explains the etymological association of *Gandharv* and the first word of *Rig-Veda*, *Agnim*, or *A-GaN-Im* (the "a" in "ga" is not pronounced). *Gan* means the same as GNIM, with *Agnim* translated as fire, light, primordial impulse of life. The primordial syllable *A* contains the tonality of all sounds; therefore, it is at the beginning of the *Veda* and at the beginning of most alphabets. *GNIM* represents the inner dynamism of *A*, or all possible transformation mechanisms of all sounds and linguistic forms of expression[2].

In the context of the system of Vedic literature proposed by Vedic Science, *Gandharva-Veda* arises from a domination of the cosmic *vata* principle, which in turn originates from, or represents, the *rishi*-value of unity (*samhita*[3]).

There are three major treatises on *Gandharva-Veda*: the *Natyashastra*, ascribed to Bharata; the *Narada-Shiksha* by Narada, and the *Sangita-Ratnakara* by Sharngadev. The *Sangita-Ratnakara* describes in some detail the development of the human being from the unmanifest primordial sound called *nada*. In addition, the *Sangita-Ratnakara* provides a detailed description of physiology refined by meditation and *Gandharva-Veda* music, which goes beyond the material covered in the *Ayurvedic* texts[4]. The *Natyashastra* represents the value of *rishi* among the three texts of *Gandharva-Veda*, *Narada-Shiksha* corresponds to the *devata* element, and the *Sangita-Ratnakara* is associated with *chhandas*[5].

All three texts of *Gandharva-Veda* cover, in various scope, three aspects of music: song (*gitam*), instrumental music (*vadyam*) and dance, theatre arts (*nrittam*). The unity of *gitam*, *vadyam* and *nrittam* forms a unity which corresponds to the unity of *samhita*, with song (*gitam*) representing the *rishi*, *vadyam* the *devata* and *nrittam* the *chhandas* element[6].

The *Natyashastra* mainly stresses the *nrittam* aspect, dance and movement of the body. It provides a very detailed enumeration of different positions of the head, the eyeballs, eyelids, eyebrows, the nose, the cheeks, the lower lip, the chin, the mouth, the neck; seventeen different gestures of the hands are differentiated, single or combined; further gestures of the breast, the sides, the belly, the waist, the thigh, the shank, and the feet are described on their own and in combinations, specifying for each single movement or combination in which situation prescribed by a play such movements should be used, and, in some cases, what their predicted effect on the audience will be. For example, the first two of thirteen gestures of the head are *Akampita* and *Kampita*. The *Natyashastra* specifies as follows:

19. Akampita: Moving the head slowly up and down is called the Akampita.
Kampita: When the movements in the Akampita head are quick and copious the same is called Kampita.
20. (Uses): The Akampita head is to be applied in giving a hint, questioning, addressing in an ordinary way (lit. naturally), and giving an order.
21. The kampita head is applicable (lit. desired) in anger, argument, understanding, asserting, threatening, sickness and intolerance.[7]

According to the *Gandharva-Veda*, dance originally symbolises the subtle, rhythmical dynamics of transformations from one note to the other, a manifest expression of unmanifest processes in *samhita* on which the entire creation is based. Primordial sounds are qualities of consciousness. Thus the expressed values of consciousness, the individual dance movements, each represent a specific quality of consciousness[8]. A performer who has full command of consciousness, i.e., who has established at least cosmic consciousness, will automatically, without time-lapse between impulse and expression, use the gesture, or combination of gestures that is the manifest equivalent of the quality of consciousness required in a given situation of performance dictated by the contents of performance and the outer conditions of performance, e.g. performance space and audience. Thus the description of *angika abhinaya*, gestural means of histrionic representation, is a description from an enlightened consciousness of what a fully developed actor will spontaneously, and with full discipline of mind and body, do to create a specific effect on the spectator in a given theatrical situation. The inner dynamics of the primordial sound of *nada* begins to vibrate in every cell, gaining such strength that it finally takes hold of the entire body and causes it to dance[9]. The art of dancing was developed into the art of theatre. The intention of this development was, as described in the *Natyashastra*, to enable people who had lost touch with their unmanifest source to gain familiarity with Vedic truths.

ii. The aesthetic experience: *rasa*

Theatre, in the sense of dance-drama, functions not only on the level of symbolism of theatrical action, but also through language (*vacika abhinaya*), costume and make-up (*aharya*) and representation of the temperament (*sattvika-abhinaya*). Costume and make-up will function mainly through the sense of sight, affecting the emotions. The symbolic nature of theatre affects mainly the intellect. Gestures (*angika abhinaya*), function through the sense of sight, and language (*vacika abhinaya*) through the sense of hearing. Both gestures and language arise from the level of pure consciousness, and will ultimately affect the spectator on that very same level of pure consciousness. The fully developed actor, then, achieves his effects on the spectator by stimulating the spectator's senses, his intellect, the emotions, and both through stimulating all these, and unmediated, the actor reaches to the spectator's Self, pure consciousness, which is the ultimate target of his art and skill. In meditation, the aim might be to reach the experience of pure consciousness on its own. However, as Vedic psychology shows, the ultimate aim of meditation is not pure consciousness on its own, but the coexistence of pure consciousness with waking, or dreaming, or sleeping, a state called cosmic consciousness, which develops further to refined cosmic consciousness and ultimately unity consciousness. What theatre in the Vedic sense aspires to is to provide the spectators with experiences of at least cosmic consciousness, initially only lasting for a short time, eventually longer. Repeated exposure to Vedic theatre will train the mind to naturally experience pure consciousness together with sensory impressions.

One of the characteristics of pure consciousness, or *sat chit ananda*, absolute (*sat*) bliss (*ananda*) consciousness (*chit*) is bliss. Any experience of pure consciousness will have that quality. Thus the specific experience in the theatre, an aesthetic experience, if it allows the spectator's mind to reach pure consciousness, will suffuse the impressions gained by the senses with the underlying quality of bliss. Neither the sensory impressions nor the bliss, however, will overshadow the Self: when the spectator experiences temporary cosmic consciousness while watching a play, his Self is separate from the sensory impressions, and bliss is a quality of the Self itself. In cases of temporary experiences of unity consciousness through the stimuli of the performance, the spectator will experience the events acted on the stage, the actors, and even the fellow-spectators, as expressions of the same pure consciousness that also forms his own basis. There is an experience of unity, all in terms of the Self, which is not overshadowed.

The nature of the aesthetic experience, *rasa*, is thus the experience of pure consciousness together with performance-specific theatrical contents of the mind (in the broad definition of Vedic psychology). Through repeated exposure to the experience of pure consciousness, brought about by the art of the actor in the theatre, the spectator's consciousness is trained to uphold pure consciousness for longer periods of time, ultimately indefinite, not only in subsequent theatrical performances, but also in daily life outside the theatre. The *Natyashastra's* claim of its original purpose, to restore the golden age which had given way to the silver one, thus becomes more than a rhetorical claim for usefulness.

*Rasa* has been re-defined from the spectator's perspective as a combination of blissful pure consciousness and the specific impressions on the mind provided by a theatrical performance. Abhinavagupta held that the actor does not experience *rasa* himself. From the point of view of Vedic Psychology, this assumption needs a re-assessment. What affects the spectator are the actor's means of histrionic representation, gestures, words, representation of temperament and costume and make-up. For the enlightened actor, gestures and words, it has been shown, will proceed spontaneously from his pure consciousness, transforming itself without time-lapse into objective expression, which is then subjectively experienced by the spectator, affecting his senses, intellect, emotions, and through those his pure consciousness. Pure consciousness has been discovered to be a field that connects all individuals. If the actor, then, operates from the level of pure consciousness, he will affect the spectator not only on the expressed levels of the mind, but also directly on the level of pure consciousness. The enlightened actor has the continuous experience of the bliss characteristic of pure consciousness. If he produces from within that pure consciousness the expressed means of histrionic representation, he combines bliss with expressions of *abhinaya*, which make up the experience of *rasa*. Thus the actor establishes *rasa* within himself in the process of stimulating the experience of *rasa* in the spectator.

In Bharata's *Natyashastra*, eight *rasas* are mentioned, the erotic, comic, pathetic, furious, heroic, terrible, odious, and marvellous[10]. A ninth *rasa* is added to this list by later theorists. Abhinavagupta describes it as follows:

Now *santa*, which has sama for its *sthayibhava*, and which leads to *moksha*, arises from *vibhavas* such as knowledge of the truth, detachment, purity of mind etc. It should be acted out by the *anubhava* such as *yama* and *niyama*, meditation on the Self, concentration of the mind on the self (*dharana*), devotion (*upasana*), compassion towards all creatures, and the wearing of religious paraphernalia (*lingagrahana*). Its *vyabhicaribhavas* are disgust with the world (*nirveda*), remembrance, firmness of mind, purity in all the four stages of life (*asrama*), rigidity (of the body) (*stambha*), horripilation etc. The following Aryas and Slokas exist on this subject: *Santa Rasa* has been taught as a means to the highest happiness (*naihsreyasa*). It arises from a desire to secure the liberation of the Self and leads to knowledge of the truth. *Santa Rasa* should be known as that which brings happiness and welfare to all beings and which is accompanied by the stabilization (*samsthita*) in the Self that results from the curbing of the organs of perception and the organs of physical activity. *Santa Rasa* is that state wherein one feels the same towards all creatures, wherein there is no pain, no happiness, no hatred and no envy. *Santa* is one's natural state of mind (*prakrti*). Other emotions such as love etc. are deformations of that original state. The deformations arise out of this natural state of the mind and in the end again merge back into it. The emotions arise out of *santa* depending on their particular respective causes. And when the specific causes cease to function, they all merge back into *santa*. Those who know dramaturgy see nine *Rasas* along with their characteristics in this manner.[11]

*Santa* is called "one's natural state", which is termed *prakriti*. This refers to *samkhya* philosophy, where *prakriti* is a major principle of creation. *Prakriti* is primordial nature, everything arises from it[12]. The three *gunas, sattva, rajas,* and *tamas,* the creating, stimulating and restricting powers, are in balance on the level of *prakriti,* so that no structures can come into existence. *Prakriti* is faced by the other major principle, *purusha.* In other Vedic texts, this principle is referred to as *atman,* Self. It is characterised as eternal, pure, conscious, liberated, and self-sufficient[13], without action[14] and a witness[15]. The principles of *purusha* and *prakriti* function both on the cosmic and on the individual human levels. *Purusha* is experienced as pure consciousness, and *prakriti* represents the dynamism within *purusha,* within pure consciousness, a dynamism that will eventually lead to all possible manifestation.

The characteristics of *santa rasa* match with the descriptions of pure consciousness as contentless: the individual experiencing *santa rasa* feels "the same", i.e. nothing, "towards all creatures". There is no pain, no happiness, no hatred, and no envy. The effects that experiencing *santa rasa* bring to the spectator are "happiness and welfare", "highest happiness", "stabilization of the Self". The ingredients leading to the experience of *santa rasa* are also related to the process of gaining liberation: (*moksha*): the dominant emotion (*sthayibhava*), the determinants (*vibhava*), the consequents (*anubhava*), and the transitory states (*vyabhicaribhava*).

*Santa rasa* is called the natural state of the mind, in the sense that it is the basis of all other states. Seen from the perspective of Vedic Psychology, *santa rasa* is equivalent to the experience of pure consciousness evoked in actor and spectator through theatre; the other eight *rasas* represent the influence of the expressed stimuli of theatre, leading to an aesthetic experience dominated by love, mirth, sorrow, anger, energy, terror, disgust, and astonishment[16]. The fully developed actor is best able to create *santa rasa* and a specific expressed *rasa* in the spectator. Again the assumption applies that the actor, too, not only the spectator, experiences *rasa*.

These considerations necessitate a re-assessment of the *rasa-sutra: Vibhava-anubhava-vyabhicaribhava-samyogad rasa-nispattih.* The translation provided by Ghosh is: "*Rasa* is produced (*rasa-nispattih*) from a combination (*samyogad*) of Determinants (*vibhava*), Consequents (*anubhava*) and Transitory

States (*vyabhicaribhava*)"[17]. Ghosh translates the term *vibhava* from the expressed context of the theatrical situation as "determinant", given situations found in the playtext in which specific means of histrionic representation have to be used. In view of the fact that *santa rasa* is pure consciousness, and taking into consideration that *vibhava* also means "pure consciousness"[18], the use of the term *vibhava* in the context of the *Natyashastra* refers to situations structured as possibilities in the dynamism of pure consciousness. Such latent situations, present as potentialities on the level of pure consciousness, take their shape in the theatrical context as *anubhava*. Ghosh again renders this term on the expressed level, as "consequent", means of histrionic representation doing justice to the "Determinants". *Anubhava* also means the experience of multitude after arising from pure consciousness[19]. In other words, the potentialities of *vibhava* are experienced by the actor and in turn by the spectator as taking a specific shape in the theatrical context. Manifestation progresses further by "adding the ingredient" of *vyabhicaribhava*, translated by Gosh as "transitory states [of emotion]". Indeed, *vyabhicaribhava* means the spreading, the expression of that experience of multitude[20] implied by *anubhava*. *Samyogad* has been translated by Ghosh as "combination", taking recourse to the illustration provided by the *Natyashastra* itself, which compares the functioning of the different elements in creating *rasa* to adding diverse ingredients to cook delicious food. *Samyogad*, however, means not so much a combination, an adding together, but implies a unity[21]. Only when a unity of pure consciousness (*vibhava*), the experience of the multitude after coming out of pure consciousness (*anubhava*) and the spreading, or expression of that experience form a unity will *rasa* be produced in actor and spectator alike.

To summarise: *rasa* is an aesthetic experience for both actor and spectator, consisting in the coexistence of pure consciousness with aesthetic, theatre/performance-specific contents, sensory impressions, stimuli for the mind, the intellect, and the emotions. As time is non-existent on the level of pure consciousness, the basis of theatrical activity in the case of the enlightened actor, creation of *rasa* in the actor will be simultaneous with the stimuli creating *rasa* in the spectator being emitted by the actor. The time-lapse between the onset of those stimuli and their taking effect in the consciousness of the spectator, and the degree to which they take effect, depend on the "openness" of the spectator's consciousness. Repeated exposure to such experiences will train the spectator in responding to *rasa*-inducing stimuli faster, and to a larger degree. In due course, experiences of pure consciousness together with other (i.e. not necessarily aesthetic) contents of the expressed mind will be the natural consequence of the training process.

### iii. The enlightened actor

Any person has reached *enlightenment* when he or she is permanently established in at least cosmic consciousness. Statements about the modes of activity of an enlightened person are currently difficult because the majority of the population use between 10 to 20% of their mental potential, whereas enlightenment is characterised by use of one's full mental potential. The possibilities inherent in a range of between 80% and 90% are difficult to gauge. The following remarks about the enlightened actor are conclusions from current understanding of *enlightenment*, termed cosmic, refined cosmic and unity consciousness, respectively, as defined in Vedic Psychology, in conjunction with the *Natyashastra*.

The enlightened actor will not be emotionally involved while he acts. In cosmic consciousness, his Self will be separate from the activities of the waking state of consciousness; the actor will witness his activity of acting. In unity consciousness, the Self and its expressions are experienced as one. The fully concentrated mind, demanded of the actor by the *Natyashastra*, is a mind in which the Self is in such a non-involved state, while the expressed aspects of the mind are fully developed, and thus capable of full concentration. This concentration pertains to the senses, the mind, the intellect, the emotions, and the ego. The actor's concentration extends even to the autonomous nervous system commonly assumed to be beyond intentional control by the will. From cosmic consciousness onwards, the actor can voluntarily induce the symptoms (*sattvika abhinaya*) required to portray temperamental states (*sattvika bhava*).

Such full concentration will enable the actor to fully comprehend, understand, and feel the emotions the character is supposed to be feeling. Thus he may fully appreciate the dramatist's intentions, but he may also go even beyond those intentions. This implies that the work and its meaning are not established and fixed *sub specie eternitatis*. As Orme-Johnson points out, the creative process of writing means that the writer's mind takes recourse to pure consciousness and expresses the dynamic values latent in that unmanifest field of consciousness. From this infinite reservoir the individual writer will make a selection-- consciously or unconsciously. The selection is governed by the historical conditions influencing the writer.

Vedic psychology holds that knowledge is different in different states of consciousness. Different spectators will react differently to the same play, depending on their state of consciousness. This concept is not even highly philosophical: if the spectator is tired after a long day in the office, he will appreciate the play differently from a well-relaxed spectator, determined by the difference of alertness in his mind, in turn interdependent with the state of the nervous system- -tired or fresh. All possible reactions of all possible spectators latently exist in the field of pure consciousness, a field that connects all individuals. Thus if the actor gains access to that level in his own mind, he will be able to use a large variety of ways of rendering the different dimensions of meaning associated with a particular role in a particular play. He can choose from that reservoir to suit the historically specific needs of specific spectators at a specific performance, and to vary the chosen elements of rendering in the next performance.

The preceding discussion has centred on the enlightened actor, arguing that the *Natyashastra* is primarily a description of what the fully developed actor naturally, automatically, spontaneously does to create specific aesthetic experiences in the audience. Two aspects of the concept of enlightenment need further explanation. First, what makes an actor an actor: from among a shoemaker and an actor who have both reached cosmic consciousness, the actor would be the better actor. The concept of *dharma*, central to Peter Brook's interpretation of the *Mahabharata*[22], is essential in this issue. On a general level, *dharma* is "that invincible power of nature which upholds existence. It maintains evolution and forms the very basis of cosmic life. It supports all that is helpful for evolution and discourages all that is opposed to it"[23].

On the personal level, one meaning of *dharma* is "allotted duty", "that which it is natural for one to do, that for which one was born"[24]. *Dharma* can also be associated with law, justice, customary morality, reflective morality, duty and conscience[25]. According to Kakar, *dharma* refers to the ground-plan of any person's life, as the individual's life-cycle, *ashramadharma*, and, most important, the individual's "own particular life-task, his *svadharma*"[26]. According to the

*Bhagavad-Gita*, each individual has "his own inborn nature, *svabhava*, and to make it effective in his life is his duty, *svadharma*"[27]. This individual life-task is not absolute, but embedded in the individual's historical condition:

> Hindu philosophy and ethics teach that "right action" for an individual depends on *de-sa*, the culture in which he is born; and *kala*, the period of historical time in which he lives; on *srama*, the efforts required of him at different stages of life; and on *gunas*, the innate psycho-biological traits which are the heritage of an individual's previous lives.[28]

In the course of time, Kakar argues, *svadharma* came to mean "traditional action (...) in the sense that an individual's occupational activity and social acts are right or "good" if they conform to the traditional pattern prevalent in his kinship and caste group"[29].

It is important to note that the concept of *dharma* functions on two levels, similar to those of the *Natyashastra*: originally, *dharma* describes how nature functions. This applies to the level of enlightenment, where such functioning in accordance with the laws of nature, of the cosmos, is automatic, spontaneous, fully life-supporting for all concerned, and not subject to manipulation or misuse. The descriptive function of *dharma* corresponds to the level of the *Natyashastra* on which it can be regarded as a description of what the enlightened actor will do automatically, spontaneously, to create specific effects in specific audiences. The second function of the *Natyashastra* is to serve as a teaching manual for the actor to reach enlightenment. *Dharma* also functions on such a level, laying down rules intended to serve as guidance for non-enlightened people on their path to enlightenment. Such rules originate from enlightenment. However, applied rules of *dharma* vary according to the historical and cultural circumstances of the times in which they were written down. For example, in Vedic times (2500 BC to 500BC), women enjoyed equal status to men, participating fully in religious and social activities[30]. At a later stage, documented in the *Manusmritis*, a major text in the canon of *dharmashastra*, holy texts on *dharma*, the role of women in society had changed considerably[31]. Thus, as soon as *dharma* becomes open to individual, culture-bound interpretation, it becomes open to manipulation and misuse. Someone might, for example, wish to maintain his status of power by convincingly suggesting to others that their *dharma* is to be in a position of comparatively less power. Once open to ignorance, *dharma* as a concept may be misused. As a cosmic, universally applicable force or pattern of nature's functioning, however, *dharma* is not changed by such misuse. On a relative level, open to misuse, there may well be clashes between what someone is told to be his duty, and that same person's "real" *dharma*, vocation in life. If *dharma* has its own way, in an enlightened society, duty and vocation will be the same. As this chapter deals with the enlightened actor, for him, then, allotted duty and vocation are the same.

The precondition or characteristic of enlightenment is that the individual follows his *dharma*, his allotted duty, because only then will evolution take place. Consequently, the person who has gained enlightenment will fully live his *dharma*. Thus by definition the enlightened actor is an individual whose *dharma*, purpose in life is to be an actor; he will thus be a better actor than the enlightened shoe-maker, whose *dharma*, purpose in life, is to be a shoe-maker.

The second question is whether there will be a difference in the acting of two actors who are enlightened. Yes, there will be. According to Kuppuswami, "the ruling idea in ancient Indian thought is unity in diversity, not uniformity"[32]. Although the basis of creation, pure consciousness, is the same and links all individuals, and thus all actors, the infinite dynamism, the potential for infinite possibilities that characterise this field causes the infinite variety of manifest creation, including the variety among human beings. Thus people will not become more alike on their path to enlightenment. On the contrary, each person will develop the full potential of his individuality. This applies to every person in ever profession. It follows that two actors who have gained enlightenment will have fully developed individual personalities, characteristics, traits etc.

iv. Training the actor

Now that the concept of a fully developed actor has been described, the question arises: what about the actor who is not enlightened? A person whose *dharma* it is to be an actor will find the learning and training process for the art and skills of acting easier and more enjoyable, no matter whether his training is based on the *Natyashastra* or on Western principles.

The actor trained in the tradition of the *Natyashastra*, as is the case in all contemporary dance forms in India[33], such as *Bharata Natyam* or *Kathak*, will learn the different means of histrionic representation derived from the *Nat-*

*yashastra*. Those gestures etc. directly originate in pure consciousness, they are the most immediate physical expressions of the dynamics of transformation from one primordial sound to another. Using them, the actor stimulates the experience of *rasa* in the spectator. The means of representation, in turn, have an effect on the actor's physiology, and because physiology is a manifestation of consciousness, the means of representation have an effect on the mind, on consciousness as well. Thus the not enlightened actor develops his physiology to be able to sustain the experience of pure consciousness, to gain enlightenment, through the means of histrionic representation as described in the *Natyashastra*.

As such, acting technique could be compared to yogic techniques which also aim at developing the human mental potential. Traditionally, *yoga* is associated with physical exercises or meditation practices based on concentration of the mind[34]. Vedic psychology acknowledges both these aspects; it emphasises, however, that *yoga* not only refers to techniques to reach higher levels of development, but that it also refers to the aim to be achieved by the various techniques (the terms "pure" consciousness and "transcendental" consciousness are used synonymously):

> Yoga begins when the mind gains transcendental consciousness; Yoga achieves maturity when this transcendental (...) consciousness (...) has gained ground in the mind to such an extent that, in whatever state the mind finds itself, whether waking or sleeping, it remains established in the state of Being.[35]

Understood as a set of techniques for the development of consciousness, *yoga* makes use of the intimate relationship of mind and body. The physical exercises referred to as Hatha Yoga train the physical nervous system, and thereby "condition the mind to gain the state of transcendental [pure] consciousness and eventually to gain cosmic consciousness"[36]. Mental meditation techniques train the mind and thus condition the nervous system to be able to reach and maintain pure and cosmic consciousness[37]. The physical means of histrionic representation described in the *Natyashastra* work in a manner equivalent to that of Hatha Yoga: through physical exercise, the actor's nervous system is trained in a specific way to give rise to higher states of consciousness. It is only in such higher states of consciousness that the actor will be able to efficiently and fully represent the temperamental states (*sattvika bhava*).

To understand how the techniques of histrionic representation described in the *Natyashastra* function to raise the level of the actor's and the spectator's consciousness, it is necessary to remember, first of all, that although the *Natyashastra* and later works on Sanskrit dramaturgy devote much space to the description of the physical techniques, they emphasise the representation of the temperamental states as being most important in the creation of an aesthetic experience for the spectator[38]. The actor, through a specific mode of acting (*sattvika abhinaya*) portrays the temperamental states (*sattvika bhava*). The meaning of *sat* is "eternal, absolute". In Sanskrit, pure consciousness is referred to as *Sat-Chit-Ananda*, eternal or absolute (*sat*) bliss (*ananda*) consciousness (*chit*). This is the meaning of *sat* within the unmanifest, transcendental field of life, which is beyond the level of the senses, the mind, the intellect, the feelings and emotions, and the ego. It is a quality of the unmanifest Self, at the basis of all manifestations. On the level of manifestations, the term *sat* is found in the term *sattva*. This is one of the three *gunas*, elementary forces of nature, the others being *rajas* and *tamas*. According to Vedic Psychology,

the entire creation consists of the interplay of the three gunas (...) born of prakriti or Nature. The process of evolution is carried on by these three gunas. Evolution means creation and its progressive development, and at its basis lies activity. Activity needs rajo-guna to create a spur, and it needs sato- guna and tamo-guna to uphold the direction of the movement. The nature of tamo-guna is to check or retard, but it should not be thought that when the movement is upwards, tamo-guna is absent. For any process to continue, there have to be steps in that process, and each stage, however small in time and space, needs a force to maintain it and another force to develop it into a new shape. The force that develops it into a new shape is sato-guna, while tamo-guna is that which checks or retards the process in order to maintain the state already produced so that it may form the basis for the next stage.[39]

On the relative level, the proportion of the three gunas, *sattva*, *rajas* and *tamas*, can vary. A pre-dominance of *tamas* will lead to stagnation and suffering, and a pre-dominance of *sattva* leads to "increasing happiness and is eventually transformed into bliss-consciousness"[40]. Thus it is evident that on the relative level of life, among the three *gunas*, *sattva* is closest to the eternal quality, *sat*, of pure consciousness. By performing in a state of consciousness in which the level of *sattva* dominates the levels of *rajas* and *tamas*, the actor gradually, by continued practice, rises more and more in the *sattva* quality until he is able to maintain pure consciousness while acting, initially only for short periods of time, but eventually as a permanent phenomenon. This is the state of cosmic consciousness. Acting simultaneously stimulates the same processes in the spectator.

How does the actor manage to saturate his mind with the quality of *sattva*? Vedic literature describes three aspects of *yoga*, unity: the body has to be free of restricting impediments, the mind focused, and the spirit liberated. To achieve the state of *yoga* for body, mind and spirit, three methods are prescribed: physical exercises, *asanas*, often the only association with *yoga*, create *yoga* in the body; breathing exercises, *pranayama*, lead to a focused mind, and meditation produces a liberated spirit. All three methods are applied together, and together they lead to the state of *yoga*. The gestural means of histrionic representation, *angika abhinaya*, function in parallel to *yoga asanas*, conditioning the body to sustain the experience of *sattva*. Control of breath is also crucial in performance, both in the West and in India. As Zarrilli points out in his studies of *Kathakali*, breath, associated with energy, is of vital importance in making "otherwise mechanical facial configurations", in which are "encoded the message *pleasure/ erotic* or *fury*", "live with presence"[41]. Accurate control of breath, life-force, is also at the centre of the actor-spectator relationship:

> In all such precise psychophysical moments, the "character" is being created--not in the personality of the actor but as an embodied and projected/energised living form between actor and audience. These Asian forms assume no "suspension of disbelief", rather the actor and spectator co-create the figure embodied in the actor as "other". The "power of presence" manifest in this stage other, while embodied in this particular actor in this particular moment, is not limited to that ego. That dynamic figure exists between audience and actor, transcending both, pointing beyond itself.[42]

Acting according to the guidelines of the *Natyashastra*, then, always employs techniques parallel in effect to *asanas* and *pranayama*, conditioning the body and the mind to sustain experiences of higher states of consciousness.

v. Summary: The purpose of theatre

The *Natyashastra* has a twofold function: it serves as a description of what an enlightened actor spontaneously does on the stage to create a specific effect on the spectator. The *Natyashastra* also serves as a manual of how the not enlightened actor may develop to higher states of consciousness using his art and skills as the means to achieve the goal, perfection in acting and in life as a whole.

The purpose of theatre, on that basis, is also twofold: the first refers to both actor and spectator: the actor creates the experience of *rasa* in the spectator. The degree of success of that function depends on both the actor's and the spectator's levels of consciousness. The second function of theatre relates to the actor himself: theatre provides the not enlightened actor with techniques of developing enlightenment. Even if both actor and spectator are enlightened, the logical conclusion of the spiritual development of actor and spectator, performance does not become superfluous. True, it has fulfilled its primary purpose of development of consciousness. But creation, life, activity, dynamism, do not stop once that level has been achieved. All the actor's activity originating from a state of enlightenment, activity in full command of an infinite potential of possibilities, will be enhanced in effect by the reverberations in the consciousness of the spectator. The effect is one of enjoying that variety of expression: the actor's skill and art are enjoyed by the spectator, and the actor in turn enjoys the spectator's full appreciation of what the actor has to offer. It is a play and interplay and exchange of fullness, of unity, currently grasped in concepts such as *communitas* or *peak experience*.

## 3. Interculturalism and Postmodernism

The preceding assessment of Western and Indian theories of the actor's emotional involvement allows new insights on the issue of interculturalism. Bharucha's critique of Western theatre artists' interculturalism will again provide the focal point of the inquiry.

### a. Artaud and language beyond speech: universality

Bharucha criticises most of Artaud's writings on the theatre as a-historical and mystical; two areas where Bharucha grants Artaud some validity are first that the actor's breathing "is related intensely to the emphasis of the external movement", and second, Artaud's speculations "on the points of localisation in an actor's body that can be used to project particular emotions (...)"[1] Bharucha admits that Artaud's assumptions bear much similarity to traditional Indian performer training[2]. However, Bharucha qualifies this concession: he maintains that Artaud's ideas are speculations, even if visionary.

An examination of points of contact between Western theories of the theatre and Vedic literature has shown that another of Artaud's speculations, language beyond speech, is an established concept of Vedic linguistics. Such a language could well qualify as a universal language of the theatre. In order to test in principle the possibility of a universal language of the theatre, Fischer-Lichte suggests several levels of theoretical discourse. The first implies the question as to what could be communicated in such a universal language of the theatre. Modern semiotics could provide answers, as could recourse to old treatises on drama, i.e. Aristotle, *Poetics*, the Indian *Natyashastra*, or Zeami Motokiyo's poetics of the Japanese Noh. Although different, they agree in pointing not towards a cognitive, but psychological-emotional aspect of the reception process. Fischer-Lichte asks whether this psychological-emotional level could be the aim and contents of a universal language of the theatre.

The second level deals with the specific conditions which would enable a universal language of the theatre. It has to be established whether cultural determination of every-day use of the body can be transferred to aesthetic use of the body. If not, universal language of theatre need not be dependent on intercultural performances but every culture could develop a universal language of the theatre.

Finally, Fischer-Lichte argues, the function of such a universal language of the theatre should be discussed. In Third-World countries, intercultural theatre with major reference to the culture's own theatre dominates. This dominance is related to the countries' attempts to establish their own cultures. Collage techniques, merging different cultures, is in opposition to such an attempt, and might have to be discussed in the context of postmodernism and cultural imperialism[3].

If the reassessment of Artaud's intuition of a language beyond speech from the perspective of Vedic Psychology is applied to the framework of the theatre, the following picture emerges: if the actor has established pure consciousness permanently, i.e. when he has reached the state of cosmic consciousness, he will have direct access to the unmanifest level of language, *para* as described in *Rig Veda*, the level of language beyond (expressed) speech. As a result, he will also have access to the more expressed levels of language, described by Bhartrihari, i.e. *pashyanti*, *madhyama* and *vaikhari*. He will thus be able to understand a different speaker's utterance without distortion, and will himself be able to use the means of language (verbal *and* non-verbal) to maximum effect on his audience. His level of efficiency will depend, however, on the listeners' openness of consciousness to those subtle levels. Still, an actor communicating from the level of pure consciousness will be more effective than an actor whose consciousness is not established in cosmic consciousness and who performs mainly from the level of *vaikhari*, with only occasional and probably unsystematic access to the awareness of subtler levels of language.

If theatre, therefore, is able to reach beyond the performer's and the spectator's intellect, even beyond their emotions, if theatre is able stimulate the co-existence of pure consciousness with the waking state of consciousness, i.e. cosmic consciousness, then theatre will have reached the level of language which is universal. It is a level of consciousness, moreover, which is universal in every respect, not limited to language.

Once it has been established that theatre can allow actors and spectators to access the universal level of pure consciousness, it has to be asked whether in addition to universality as the goal of theatre, the relative, expressed languages of the theatre, verbal, gestural, costume, make-up etc., and their combination, can also be universal, i.e. independent of culture and history. Here Fischer-Lichte's question becomes relevant, whether aesthetic activity, as opposed to everyday activity, could be independent of cultural determination.

Vedic theory of music, *Gandharvaveda*, proposes that the primordial sound, *nada*, is at the basis of all creation, including consciousness, and that the dancer's/ actor's body starts moving in the rhythms and movements of nature when all cells of his/her body begin to resonate with that primordial sound[4]. Thus sound is directly transformed into movement of the body. It could well be argued--as a working hypothesis for further studies--that if the composer composes, (or the choreographer choreographs, or the dancer dances, the actor acts) in a state of cosmic consciousness, the result (the composition, choreography, dancing or acting activity) will be fuelled by impulses emanating directly from the universal level of pure consciousness, unmediated by culture or history. Such impulses will then reach the spectator and enable his mind to reach the same underlying, universal level of consciousness from which the aesthetic impulses originated. Creative activity will be culturally and historically mediated when such activity does not originate from cosmic consciousness characterised by a simultaneity of pure consciousness and activity, but if it originates from ordinary waking state of consciousness which has no systematic, only ephemeral, "coincidental" experience of pure, or cosmic consciousness (e.g., Grotowski's *translumination*, or Brook's *total theatre*).

To return to the three levels of discourse on a universal language of the theatre proposed by Fischer-Lichte: a universal language of the theatre would lead to the experience of pure consciousness. Such an experience would be enabled by techniques of using expressed language of the theatre able to lead the actor's and spectator's mind to pure consciousness. The function of a universal language of the theatre aims at a level of consciousness beyond history and culture, and thus, perhaps, beyond postmodern fragmentation or cultural imperialism.

### b. Grotowski's disenchantment with Indian philosophy and theatre aesthetics

Bharucha emphasises that although Grotowski was influenced by non-Western theatre aesthetics, he maintained his own position throughout. For example, Grotowski defines the sign as relating very specifically to a moment in a particular performance which the actor had scored. In contrast, the timeless *mudras* of the Indian performer are understood and accepted by Indian performers and spectators from performance to performance. This difference, formulated by Grotowski, led him to abandon the idea that Indian theatre techniques might be adopted or serve as inspiration.

*Mudras* are first described in the *Natyashastra*. The *mudras* are not isolated means of histrionic representation: in specific situations in a given play, specific means of histrionic representation have to be used to create a specific emotional and aesthetic experience in the spectators. The *Natyashastra* functions on two levels: it is both a description of what a "perfect" actor, an actor who has reached a state of enlightenment, or *moksha*, liberation, will automatically, spontaneously do to create a specific emotion, a specific aesthetic experience in a specific audience. For an actor who is not yet "perfect", the techniques described in the *Natyashastra* are a means to achieve perfection, enlightenment, *moksha*, parallel to reaching this state through yoga or meditation practices.

Thus, though the *mudras* and other means of histrionic representation are apparently fixed codes, laid down and described as such in the text of the *Natyashastra*, they originate in the very moment they are created by the enlightened actor. Grotowski's and Bharucha's argument that Indian signs are fixed thus loses its ground.

Bharucha has commented favourably on Grotowski's disillusionment with yoga as leading to introverted concentration harmful to the actor. There are techniques that are meant for people who have consciously chosen the way of life of a monk, in a monastery. Renouncing the world, they hope to gain enlightenment. However, this is not the only path to the same goal: there are also methods specifically for the individuals who have to deal with everyday activities; in this case, the meditative practices do not draw the person's mind inwards with the result of such individuals becoming incapable of ordinary day-to-day activities. Rather, the techniques are geared to produce deep physical relaxation together with refined states of consciousness during the meditation, allowing the mind to access levels of consciousness otherwise not open to experience. Such subtler levels of the mind reverberate with energy, which is taken out into the activity after meditation. Thus, meditative practices intended for householders as opposed to monks will support the householder's activity. Indeed, activity is an integral part of the development to enlightenment: in alternating meditative experience of *samadhi* with ordinary activity, the nervous system is trained to maintain a state where pure consciousness can co-exist together with the ordinary state of consciousness[5]. Such co-existence is not an intellectual understanding, but a profound holistic experience, is the aim of both the monk and the householder. What differs are the paths adopted by the different types of individuals to obtain that state of liberation.

When Grotowski found that the practices he used tended to block his actors from activity, then it must be assumed that he used practices intended for monks, rather than techniques which would indeed support the actor's activities, thus providing the service that Grotowski had hoped to gain from having his actors train in those methods.

Moreover, the understanding of techniques, whether intended for monks or householders, is deficient. Frequently the understanding is that enlightenment is gained by practicing detachment of the senses, concentration of the mind. In the specific context of Patanjali's *yoga*-philosophy, the eight limbs of yoga were understood as representing different practices to gain the ultimate stage of *samadhi*, pure consciousness. The procedure was interpreted as starting with the practice of *yama*, five qualities of observance (truthfulness, non-violence, non-covetousness, celibacy, and non-acceptance of others' possessions); yoga was then thought to continue with the practice of *niyama*, the five rules of life (i.e. purification, contentment, austerity, study, and devotion to God). The next stages in the path to *samadhi* is said to be *asana*, the sphere of body posture, then *prana* (individual breath), *pratyahara* (turning away of the senses from their objects); *dharana* (steadiness of mind); *dhyana* (meditation), all are said to lead to the experience of *samadhi*, the goal of yoga practice. Vedic Psychology argues that cause and effect have been confused in traditional interpretations:

> Samadhi cannot be gained by practice of yama, niyama, and so on. Proficiency in the virtues can only be gained by repeated experience of samadhi. (...) each limb is designed to create the state of Yoga [unity] in the sphere of life to which it relates. With the continuous practice of all these limbs, or means, simultaneously, the state of Yoga grows simultaneously in all eight spheres of life, eventually to become permanent.[6]

It is not the impossibility of using non-Western methods for achieving specific purposes that led to Grotowski's decision not to use yogic techniques any more, but a lack of understanding of the numerous methods available in India today.

### c. The historical dimension

Although Bharucha emphasises the necessity of historical contextualisation of interculturalism, his view is not limited to the boundaries set by history or a historical view of the world. Bharucha argues that "Western performance theories (...) for all their assimilation of non-western material, fail to confront (and, at times, acknowledge) a sense of the divine, without which no traditional art of India can be adequately understood"[7]. Bharucha also acknowledges that his reading of *Krishnattam*, a series of plays about Krishna, "eventually culminates in an acceptance of love that transcends the mediations of "rationality and scholarship"[8]. However, historical perspectives intervened in his experience of *Krishnattam*. Bharucha believes that A transcendental level beyond history, beyond time and space, does exist, and all theatre rightly aims for an experience of that level, but the means to achieve this level have to be historical, within, and that means aware of, time and space[9]. The level on which theatre is practically made is historical, conditioned by the individual histories of individual performers. The aim may be universality, but that is "located" on a level beyond the physical activities of the theatre, a level to which the physical activities, however, should lead.

The means of histrionic representation provided in the *Natyashastra*, understood from the perspective of Vedic Psychology, could be the key for the combination of historical awareness and transcendental, universal aim: pure consciousness, in analogy with the unified field described in quantum physics, is the source of all manifestations, thus including theatre. It is universal. Originating from a transcendental realm of universality in human consciousness, the means of histrionic representation take shape according to the specific historical conditions in a specific, historically defined performance situation.

Bharucha's claim for historical awareness is thus justified on the level of practical theatre. It does not, however, include the transcendental aim of theatre, which Bharucha found in the specific form of *Krishnattam* but which appears to be his aim for theatre in general.

### d. Postmodernism

In aiming at experiences of *rasa, language beyond speech, translumination, total theatre, the invisible made visible,* or *tradition of traditions,* 20th century theatre artists are in search for experiences of pure consciousness together with the ordinary waking state of consciousness. They try to express, explain and recapture this experience through the various bodies of knowledge available to them, including Western psychology, Cabbala, and non-Western concepts. In looking for a level of consciousness which is beyond the intellect, beyond the emotions, which is indeed a field of consciousness underlying every individual, and which is universal, the theatre artists are indeed striving for an overarching hierarchy, one of the focal points of postmodern criticism.

Against the background of this overarching characteristic of pure consciousness, the interpretation of one of the key elements of the postmodern condition, *fragmentation,* is subjected to a striking shift of emphasis. Without a universal background in pure consciousness, fragmentation is frightening, prone to ambiguity, and art may acquire the function of helping the audiences to overcome such anxieties, helping the spectators to come to terms with the purposelessness of life, a view which is supported by a certain interpretation of quantum physics.[10]. If pure consciousness is accepted as an underlying level of human existence, then the Vedantic principle of *unity in diversity* applies. Diversity is seen as manifestations of unity, in the sense of a playful expression (Sanskrit concept of *lila*). In this view, Intertextuality becomes a playful, conscious activity. Vedic Psychology's model of creation, i.e. all creation emanating from the various directions of interaction of *rishi*, *devata* and *chhandas* in / and the wholeness of *samhita*, makes further sense of the principle of unity in diversity by explaining that diversity is an inherent aspect of unity.

The Vedic discipline of phonetics, *Shiksha*, is the first of the six *Vedangas*, and results from the interaction of *rishi* and *chhandas*. *Shiksha* argues that the Sanskrit alphabet provides a guide to the formation of language. On the unmanifest, not yet expressed level of pure consciousness, the short [a] is pure sound, not yet formed. The *buddhi* (intellect) quality of pure consciousness, on the unmanifest level, recognises within the [a] sound the double nature of the sound: a continuous fluctuation between fullness of pure consciousness and the limited point value of the sound [a]. This duality is, at the same time, a unity, just as the diversity of *rishi*, *devata* and *chhandas* exists within the unity of the *samhita*. Unmanifest intellect recognises the unity value of duality. This results in bliss, expressed by a long [a:]. Prior to the insight of unity within duality, consciousness "wonders" at the duality and the desire arises to return to unity. This desire is expressed by the short [i]. Increase of that desire leads to the long [i]. Thus [i:] does not develop in the same way as [a:]: it does not result from the unification of two elements, but from a quantitative increase.

Pure consciousness creates something, because only after having created something can it re-cognise something. The "opening of the eyes" is expressed in [u]. If consciousness, still on the unmanifest level, cognises something, that is in a sense a development of ignorance--as if c had forgotten that consciousness is its own object. All further developments of the alphabet represent further developments of pure consciousness expressing itself to ultimately return to the unity of the final letter of the alphabet, [.], *bindu*. The same unmanifest *buddhi* that is at the source of the unmanifest processes leading to the alphabet, stimulates the mind (*manas*) to stimulate the physical fire (*Agni*). *Agni* in turn produces vital energy (*prana*), the stream of breath that allows the language preformed on the unmanifest level of pure consciousness to take shape in actual speech in its manifest forms of *pashyanti, madhyama* and *vaikhari*[11].

It is thus possible to make sense of the apparent paradox of unity in diversity. How does this interpretation fare in view of apparently contradictory views of quantum mechanics which has been used to highlight the fragmentary nature of life? The fragmentary aspect is accurate when expressed levels of matter are concerned. The ground state theorised in quantum physics is the unified field. Detailed studies, mainly on the basis of empirical data and experience reports of subjects practicing the Transcendental Meditation and advanced techniques, quantum physicist Hagelin proposed to regard the unified field theorised in physics and pure consciousness experienced during meditation, as identical[12].

The postmodern concept of the *decentered self*, theorised by Lacan, also undergoes a shift when viewed from the perspective of Vedic Psychology. According to Lacan, the self is the innermost part of the psyche[13]. But this self cannot be expressed directly: it is decentered because it can only be represented or translated to function on the level of symbolic discourse. Vedic Psychology's model of the mind is different. The innermost part of human psyche, according to Vedic Psychology, is the Self, pure consciousness. As long as someone has not reached the higher stage of development, cosmic consciousness, the Self is overshadowed by the impressions of the senses, and in this sense the term "decentered" might be used. However, in cosmic consciousness, the Self is independent of the sensory impressions, witnessing mental and physical activity. All the more expressed levels of the mind, ego, intuition and feeling, intellect, mind, desire, and senses, are fully developed, and thus fully able to express whatever is latently available on the level of the Self. There is, therefore, no longer a split between Self (*self* in Lacan) and (symbolic) expressions of it in conscious discourse, behaviour and culture. The Self, which contains, in seed form, as it were, all forms of expression, can express itself fully without mediation, representation or translation.

Previous overarching hierarchies which are at the centre of postmodern criticism lack the possibility of being directly experienced: they are limited to the intellectual discourse of philosophers. Today, however, many techniques are available that enable anyone to directly experience pure consciousness and to grow in such experiences until higher stages of human development are reached. As argued before, the means of histrionic representation detailed in the *Natyashastra* can serve as one such set of techniques, meditation may be another.

# CONCLUSION

The model of consciousness proposed by Vedic Psychology provides a cogent description of hierarchically structured levels of the mind, ranging from the most concrete level of the senses to the most abstract level of pure consciousness or Self, via desire, the mind, the intellect, the emotions and feelings, and the ego. Vedic Psychology also proposes three higher stages of human development, cosmic, refined cosmic, and unity consciousness, characterised respectively by a simultaneity of waking or dreaming or sleeping with pure consciousness, refined perception, and unity of knower and known in terms of the Self.

This model of consciousness helps to explain the phenomenon of dual consciousness, at the centre of the paradox of acting in its various forms from Diderot to Barba, as a coexistence of the waking state of consciousness with pure consciousness; in a similar manner, "translumination", "communitas" and "flow" can be explained. Acting from a state of cosmic consciousness takes place in full spontaneity, and with fully concentrated mind. The apparent paradox of spontaneity and discipline disappears. These experiences by actors are clearly related to experiences described by mystics throughout the ages, set in the specific context of theatre.

As far as language is concerned, Vedic linguistics provides a model of language in line with Vedic Psychology, associating the levels of *vaikhari* and *madhyama* with ordinary waking consciousness, the intellect, and the subtler levels of *pashyanti* and *para* with the Self. As the Self, pure consciousness, is universal, language arising from that level, whether verbal or non-verbal, is initially also universal, assuming localised, culture-bound qualities the more it is expressed.

Vedic Psychology describes the function of breathing, and of the physiology in general, in relation to states and levels of consciousness. The interrelation between body and mind, central to Vedic Psychology, provides an explanation for the possibility of affecting the mind, and the autonomous nervous system, by physical movement.

Vedic Psychology shows that the *Natyashastra* has a twofold function: it describes what an enlightened actor does to create a specific reaction in the spectator; it also represents a training guide for an non-enlightened actor to achieve both perfection in his chosen profession, and to gain enlightenment at the same time. The concept of *rasa*, central to the *Natyashastra*, is shown to be an aesthetic experience for both actor and spectator which consist in the coexistence of pure consciousness with aesthetic, performance/theatre-specific contents, stimuli for all levels of the mind.

Looking at the phenomenon of the actor's emotions in the theatre from the perspective of Vedic Science does not only answer many of the questions left open by Western theory, but points well beyond the localised issue towards the general framework of theatre.

1. The model of consciousness proposed by Vedic Psychology is open to emp-irical research. If experiences in the theatre are related to specific states of consciousness as described in Vedic Psychology, then it should be possible to operationalise the theories developed in this study, formulate hypotheses about aesthetic experiences and empirically test the implications.

2. Accepting the model of consciousness proposed by Vedic Psychology on its own and in its applications to theatre allows a reassessment of the function of theatre in society. Currently, the entertainment value of theatre dominates, fol-lowing the sad insight, resulting from failed socialist trends in theatre during the 60s and 70s that theatre can hardly change anything in the "real" world outside theatre. This view is accurate in the ordinary waking state of consciousness. Here, it is indeed difficult, perhaps even impossible, to create change beyond transportation, to use Schechner's term, because theatre affects mainly the intel-lect or the emotions, failing to reach the underlying level of consciousness, pure consciousness or the Self. Vedic Psychology proposes that theatre can be able to reach the Self and thus achieve transformation, a change in both actor and spectator which continues after the performance and which is cumulative, Thus theatre can claim a strong influence in the development of higher stages of consciousness.

3. Whether theatre continues in its current marginal position dominated by commerce and entertainment, or whether the possibilities of theatre highlighted

by its reassessment from the perspective of Vedic Psychology are further developed and tested in their practical applicability, is a matter of choice. The choice, however, has some important implications.

a) Will all plays that have been written so far, be equally suited to serve the purpose of providing a means of development of consciousness and entertainment? If not, which are the criteria of inclusion in or exclusion from a rewritten canon? In this context, aspects of elitism censorship will have to be addressed.

b) Theatre functioning in accordance with the principles of Vedic Psychology will function of a very subtle level of consciousness. The subtler any level of creation, the more powerful it is. It has to be assessed whether theatre functioning on very refined levels of consciousness could be subject to manipulation and misuse.

c) How will the objectives and messages of new playwriting have to be changed to serve the double goal of development of consciousness and entertainment? Will there be a shift towards an as yet only vaguely defined *positive, optimistic* world view?

d) Will there be an increase in productions that combine traditional drama proper with music, and dance, in line with earlier concepts of *Gesamtkunstwerk*?

e) Is a thorough reassessment of actor training necessary to accommodate the demands arising from a Vedic Psychology-oriented theatre?

The present study is only the beginning of a long and potentially very fruitful discussion of the future possibilities of the theatre based on a ancient and yet new understanding of consciousness and the actor.

# Notes and References

## 1. INTRODUCTION

1    Marvin Carlson, *Theories of the Theatre. A Historical and Critical Survey, from the Greeks to the Present* (Ithaca and London: Cornell University Press, 1984), 59-61.
2    *Ibid.*, 65-66.
3    Cf. *Ibid.*, 159.
4    John R. Battista, "The Science of Consciousness", in Kenneth S. Pope and Jerome L. Singer, eds., *The Stream of Consciousness. Scientific Investigation into the Flow of Human Consciousness* (Chichester, New York, Brisbane, Toronto: John Wiley and Sons, 1978), 58.
5    Edoardo Bisiach, "The (haunted) brain and consciousness", in A.J.Marcel and E. Bisiach, eds., *Consciousness in Contemporary Science* (Oxford: Clarendon Press, 1988), 117.
6    *Ibid.*
7    Battista, 57.
8    Cf. *Ibid.*, 58.
9    *Ibid.*
10   *Ibid.*
11   Bisiach, 117.
12   Cf. *Ibid.*
13   Raymond Tallis, *The Explicit Animal. A Defence of Human Consciousness* (London: Macmillan, 1991), 10.
14   Anthony J. Marcel, "Phenomenal experience and functionalism", in A.J.Marcel and E. Bisiach, eds., *Consciousness in Contemporary Science* (Oxford: Clarendon Press, 1988). 121.
15   Cf. Battista, 70.
16   Erika Fischer-Lichte, "Das Theater auf der Suche nach einer Universalsprache", *Forum Modernes Theater* 4:2    (1989), 115.
17   Marvin Carlson, "Peter Brook, *The Mahabharata* and Ariane Mnouchkine's *L'Indiade* as examples of contemporary cross-cultural theatre", in Erika Fischer-Lichte, Josephine Riley, Michael Gissenwehrer, eds., *Theatre, Own and Foreign* (Tübingen: Günter Narr, 1990), 50.
18   Patrice Pavis, *Theatre at the Crossroads of Culture* (London and New York: Routledge, 1992), 4.
19   Cf. *Ibid.*, 5.
20   Cf. *Ibid.*, 185.
21   David Williams, ed., *Peter Brook and the Mahabharata: Critical Perspectives* (London and New York: Routledge, 1991), 24.
22   Cf. Fischer-Lichte, 121.
23   Rustom Bharucha, *Theatre and the World. Essays on Performance and Politics of Culture* (London and New York: Routledge, 1993) 1.
24   Fischer-Lichte, 120.
25   Christopher Innes, *Holy Theatre. Ritual and the Avant Garde* (Cambridge: Cambridge University Press, 1981), 255.

26    Jacqueline Martin, *Voice in Modern Theatre* (London, New York: Routledge, 1991), 119.
27    Cf. Wolfgang Welsch "Postmoderne. Genealogie und Bedeutung eines umstrittenen Begriffs", in Peter Kemper, ed., *Postmoderne, oder: Der Kampf um die Zukunft. Die Kontroverse in Wissenschaft, Kunst und Gesellschaft* (Frankfurt/ Main: Fischer, 1988), 9.
28    *Ibid.*
29    Cf. *Ibid.*, 10.
30    Cf. *Ibid.*
31    *Ibid.*
32    *Ibid.*, 15.
33    Cf. Harold G. Coward, *Derrida and Indian Philosophy* (New York: State University of New York Press, 1990).
34    Anthony Campbell, *The Mechanics of Enlightenment. An Examination of the teaching of Maharishi Mahesh Yogi.* (London: Gollancz, 1975), 11.
35    Cf. Harvey Cox, *Turning East. The Promise and Peril of the New Orientalism* (New York: Simon and Schuster, 1977).

# WESTERN AND INDIAN THEORIES OF THE ACTOR'S EMOTIONAL INVOLVEMENT

## 1. Western Theories in their Historical Contexts

### a. Diderot

1    Denis Diderot, *The Paradox of Acting* (New York: Hill and Wang, 1955), 15.
2    Lionel Gossman and Elizabeth MacArthur, "Diderot's Displaced Paradox", in Jack Undank and Herbert Josephs, eds., *Diderot Digression and Dispersion. A Bicentennial Tribute* (Lexington, Kentucky: French Forum Publishers, 1984), 113-114.
3    Diderot, p. 14.
4    *Ibid.*, p. 19.
5    *Ibid.*, p. 32-33.
6    Allison Grear, "A Background to Diderot's *Paradoxe sur le Comédien*: The Role of imagination in Spoken Expression of Emotion", *Forum for Modern Language Studies* 1:3 (1985), 225.
7    *Ibid.*
8    Cf. *Ibid.*, p. 226.
9    *Ibid.*
10    *Ibid.*, p. 226-227.
11    *Ibid.*, p. 229.
12    Cf. *Ibid.*, p. 233.
13    Joseph R. Roach, "Diderot and the Actor's Machine", *Theatre Survey*, 22:1 (1981), 52.
14    Cf. *Ibid.*
15    Battista, "The Science of Consciousness", 68.
16    *Ibid.*
17    Battista, 70.

18    *Ibid.*
19    D.W.Hamlyn, *The Penguin History of Western Philosophy* (London: Penguin, 1990), 211.
20    Roach, "Diderot and the Actor's Machine", 58.
21    *Ibid.*, 54.
22    *Ibid.*
23    *Ibid.*, 55.
24    Cf. *Ibid.*
25    *Ibid.*, 57.
26    Diderot, 61.
27    *Ibid.*, 62.
28    *Ibid.*, 26.
29    Cf. *Ibid.*, 53.

## b. Stanislavsky

1     Cf. Lee Strasberg, *A Dream of Passion. The Development of the Method.* Edited by Evangeline Morphos (London: Bloomsbury 1988), 84.
2     Cf. Jan Knopf, *Brecht-Handbuch. Theater. Eine Ästhetik der Widersprüche* (Stuttgart: Metzlersche Verlagsbuchhandlung, 1980), 464-468.
3     Constantin Stanislavsky, *An Actor Prepares*. Translated by Elizabeth Reynold Hapgood (London, 1986), 15.
4     *Ibid.*, 14.
5     *Ibid.*, 14.
6     *Ibid.*, 13.
7     Cf. Denis Diderot, *The Paradox of Acting*, 17.
8     Cf. Stanislavsky, *An Actor Prepares*, 13.
9     *Ibid.*, 114.
10    *Ibid.*, 116.
11    *Ibid.*, 15.
12    *Ibid.*, 118.
13    *Ibid.*, 119.
14    Cf. *Ibid.*, 118-119.
15    *Ibid.*, 175.
16    *Ibid.*
17    *Ibid.*, 176.
18    *Ibid.*, 177.
19    *Ibid.*, 168.
20    *Ibid.*, 190.
21    Constantin Stanislavsky, *Building a Character*. Translated by Elizabeth Reynolds Hapgood (New York: Theatre Arts Books, 1949), 266. Methuen is preparing a newly translated edition of the collected works of Stanislavsky, which claims to reveal much new detail. Cf. Sharon Marie Carnicke, "Stanislavsky Uncensored and Unabridged", *TDR* 37:1 (1993), 22-37.
22    Cf. *Ibid.*, 269.
23    *Ibid.*, 181.
24    *Ibid.*, 192.
25    *Ibid.*

26    *Ibid.*, 193.
27    *Ibid.*, 185.
28    Cf. Stanislavsky, *An Actor Prepares*, 249. Stanislavsky uses the terms *mind* synymously with *intellect*, and *will* synonymously with *desire*.
29    *Ibid.*
30    *Ibid.*, 250.
31    *Ibid.*, 247
32    *Ibid.*, 250-251.
33    Cf. *Ibid.*, 274.
34    Stanislavsky, *Building a Character*, 108.
35    *Ibid.*
36    Cf. *Ibid.*
37    Constantin Stanislavsky, *Creating a Role*. Translated by Elizabeth Reynolds Hapgood, Edited by Hermine I. Popper (New York: Theatre Arts Books, 1961), 52.
38    *Ibid.*
39    *Ibid.*
40    *Ibid.*
41    Stanislavsky, *An Actor Prepares*, 267.
42    Diderot, 14.
43    Cf.Marianne Kesting, "Stanislavsky--Meyerhold-- Brecht". *Forum Modernes Theater*, 4:2 (1989), 123..
44    Richard M. Ryckman, *Theories of Personality* (Monterey: Brooks/Cole Publishers, ³1985), 46.
45    Cf. Kesting, 123.
46    *Ibid.*
47    Ryckman, 33.
48    Cf. Bice Benvenuto and Roger Kennedy, *The Work of Jacques Lacan* (London: Free Association Books, 1986), 48.
49    Joseph R. Roach, *The Player's Passion. Studies in the Science of Acting* (Newark: University of Delaware Press, 1985), 205.
50    Lee Strasberg, "Working with Live Material", in Erika Munk, ed., *Stanislavsky and America. The "Method" and its Influence on the American Actor* (New York: Hill and Wang, 1966), 198, quoted in Roach, *The Player's Passion*, 206.
51    Roach, *The Player's Passion*, 205.
52    Cf. Strasberg, 111.
53    Roach, 204-205.

c.    **Meyerhold**

1    James Roose-Evans, *Experimental Theatre. From Stanislavsky to Peter Brook* (London: Routledge, 41989), 29.
2    Samuel Leiter, *From Stanislavsky to Barrault. Representative Directors of the European Stage*. Contributions to Drama and Theatre Studies No. 34. (London: Greenwood Press, 1991), 56.
3    Roose-Evans, 28.
4    Leiter, 56.
5    *Ibid.*, 57.
6    *Ibid.*, 56.

7   Cf. Johannes Hirschberger, "Materialismus", *Geschichte der Philosophie. Neuzeit und Gegenwart* (Freiburg, Basel, Wien, Herder, 111981), 468.
8   *Ibid.*, 482.
9   Leiter, 56.
10  *Ibid.*
11  Cheshire Calhoun and Robert C. Solomon, *What is an Emotion. Classical Readings in Philosophical Psychology* (New York, Oxford: Oxford University Press, 1984), 126.
12  *Ibid.*
13  *Ibid.*
14  Cf. Nico H. Frijda, *The Emotions* (Cambridge: Cambridge University Press, 1986), 125.
15  Cf. Robert Levenson, Paul Ekman, Wallace V. Friesen, "Voluntary Facial Action Generates Emotion-Specific Autonomous Nervous System Activity", *Psychophysiology*, 27:4 (1990), 363-384.

## d. Strasberg

1   Cf. Lee Strasberg, *A Dream of Passion*, 85.
2   *Ibid.*
3   *Ibid.*
4   *Ibid.*, 60.
5   Stanislavsky, *An Actor Prepares*, 14.

## e. Brecht

1   John Willett, ed. and transl., *Brecht on Theatre. The Development of an Aesthetic* (New York: Hill and Wang, 1978), 14.
2   According to Knopf, Brecht first used the German term *Entfremdung* in 1930, from 1936 to 1940 he used both *Verfremdung* and *Entfremdung*, and eventually settled for *Verfremdung*. The German term *Verfremdungseffekt*, which is commonly translated as *alienation effect*. *Alienation* properly translates as *Entfremdung*, synonymous, in English, with estrangement. The German "fremd" means unfamiliar, strange. "Verfremdung" thus implies defamiliarisation, and in that sense distancing, but not estrangement.
3   *Ibid.*, 137.
4   *Ibid.*
5   *Ibid.* 139.
6   *Ibid.*
7   Innes, *Holy Theatre*, 11.
8   Leiter, *From Stanislavsky to Barrault*, 170.
9   Innes, 11-12.
10  Susan L. Stern, "Drama in Second Language Learning from a Psycholinguistic Perspective", *Language Learning*, 3:1 (1980), 81.
11  Willett, 145.
12  *Ibid.*, 193
13  *Ibid.*
14  Ibid. 94.

15     Cf. Aage A. Hansen-Löve, *Der Russische Formalismus. Methodologische Rekonstruktion seiner Entwicklung aus dem Prinzip der Verfremdung.* Österreichische Akademie der Wissenschaften, Philosophisch-historische Klasse. Sitzungsberichte, 336. Band. Veröffentlichungen der Kommission für Literaturwissenschaft Nr. 5 (Wien: Verlag der Österreichischen Akademie der Wissenschaften, 1978) 19.

16     Cf. *Ibid.*, 361-362

17     Cf. Jan Knopf, *Brecht-Handbuch*, 379.

18     Julian Hilton, *Performance*. New Directions in Theatre. (London: MacMillan, 1987), 61.

19     Cf. Knopf, 379.

20     Edward Braun, *The Director and the Stage. From Naturalism to Grotowski* (London: Methuen, 1982), 168.

21     Daphna Ben Chaim, *Distance in the Theatre. The Aesthetics of Audience Response.* Theatre and Dramatic Studies, No. 17. Series Editor: Bernard Beckerman (Ann Arbor, London: UMI Research Press, 1984), 32.

22     *Ibid.*

### f. Artaud

1     Artaud, Antonin. *The Theatre and its Double*. Collected Works Vol. 4, translated by Victor Corti (London: Calder and Boyars Ltd, 1974), 4.

2     *Ibid*. Innes considers Artaud's position in 20th century theatre history as that of a "theatrical lithmus, sensitive to the cultural physiology of the twentieth century" [Innes, *Holy Theatre*, 109.]

3     Artaud, 4.

4     Cf. Innes, *Holy Theatre*, 110.

5     Artaud, 77.

6     *Ibid.*, 78.

7     *Ibid.*

8     *Ibid.*, 25.

9     *Ibid.*

10     *Ibid.*, 26.

11     *Ibid.*, 100.

12     *Ibid.*, 101.

13     *Ibid.*, 102.

14     *Ibid.*, 75.

15     Innes, 60.

16     Artaud, 62.

17     *Ibid.*, 63.

18     Jacqueline Martin, *Voice in Modern Theatre* (London, New York: Routledge, 1991), 58.

19     Philip Auslander, "*Holy Theatre* and Catharsis", *TRI* 9:1 (1984), 23.

20     Innes, 58.

21     Auslander, 23.

22     Innes, 15.

175

## g. Grotowski

1     Jerzy Grotowski, *Towards a Poor Theatre*. Edited by Eugenio Barba with a preface by Peter Brook. (London, Methuen, 1969), 15.
2     Cf. David Bradby and David Williams, *Directors' Theatre*. Macmillan Modern Dramatists (London: Macmillan, 1988), 124.
3     Grotowski, 18.
4     Bradby and Williams, 124.
5     Cf. Grotowski, 16.
6     *Ibid.*, 7.
7     *Ibid.*
8     Bradby and Williams, 123.
9     *Ibid.*
10    Jennifer Kumiega, *The Theatre of Grotowski* (London, New York: Methuen, 1987), 128-129.
11    *Ibid.*, 139.
12    Grotowski, 16.
13    Cf. *Ibid.*
14    *Ibid.*, 39.
15    Chaim, *Distance in the Theatre*, 40.
16    Grotowski, 43.
17    Jan Kott, "Grotowski or the limit". *NTQ*, 6:23 (1990), 203-204.
18    Brian Bates, *The Way of the Actor. A New Path to Personal Knowledge and Power* (London: Century, 1986), 39.
19    Grotowski, 22-23.
20    *Ibid.*, 23.
21    *Ibid.*
22    James Roose-Evans, *Experimental Theatre*, 147.
23    Richard M. Ryckman, *Theories of Personality*, 65.
24    *Ibid.*
25    *Ibid.*
26    Cf. *Ibid.*, 67.
27    Richard Gilman, "Jerzy Grotowski". *New American Review*, 9 (April 1970), 206, 216.
28    Daniel Davy, "Grotowski's Laboratory. A Speculative Look Back at the Poor Theatre", *Essays in Theatre*, 7:2 (1989), 136.
29    Grotowski, 40.
30    Cf. Chaim, 41.
31    Kumiega, 148.
32    *Ibid.*, 147.
33    Christopher Innes, *Holy Theatre*, 163.
34    Kumiega, 139.
35    Grotowski, 16, 125, 162.
36    Cf. David S. Werman, "The oceanic experience and states of consciousness", *The Journal of Psychoanalytic Anthropology* 9:3 (1986), 339-357.
37    Sigmund Freud, *Civilisation and its Discontents*, The standard edition of the complete psychological works of S.F., translated from the German under the general editorship of James Strachey in collaboration with Anna Freud assisted by Alex Strachey and

Alan Tyson. Volume 21, 1927-1931, (London: Hogarth Press and the Institute of Psycho-Analysis, 1961), 64.

38  Cf. *Ibid.*, 65.
39  *Ibid.*, 68.
40  *Ibid.*
41  *Ibid.*
42  Werman, 348.
43  Cf. Ryckman, 64.
44  Cf. *Ibid.*, 65.
45  Grotowski, 89.
46  Kumiega, 121.
47  Kott, 204.
48  Innes, 175.

## h. Schechner

1   Richard Schechner, *Performance Theory* (New York, London: Routledge, 1988), 72.
2   *Ibid.*
3   Cf. *Ibid.*
4   *Ibid.*
5   *Ibid.*
6   *Ibid.*, 71.
7   Cf. Richard Schechner, *Between Theatre and Anthropology* (Philadelphia: University of Pennsylvania Press, 1985), 35-36.
8   *Ibid.*
9   *Ibid.*
10  Schechner, *Performance Theory*, 175.
11  *Ibid.*
12  *Ibid.*
13  *Ibid.*, 177.
14  Schechner, *Between Theatre and Anthropology*, 36.
15  *Ibid.*, 118.
16  Cf. *Ibid.*
17  Cf. Schechner, *Performance Theory*, 57.
18  Schechner, *Between Theatre and Anthropology*, 125.
19  Victor Turner, *From Ritual to Theatre. The Human Seriousness of Play* (New York: Performing Arts Journal Publications, 1982), 11.
20  Victor Turner, *The Anthropology of Performance* (New York: PAJ Publications, 1986), 74.
21  *Ibid.*
22  Richard Schechner, *Performative Circumstances. From the Avantgarde to Ramlila* (Calcutta: Seagull Books, 1983), 150.
23  Cf. Schechner, *Performance Theory*, 171.
24  Schechner, *Performative Circumstances*, 154.
25  *Ibid.*, 138-139.
26  Cf. *Ibid.*, 227.
27  *Ibid.*
28  Cf. *Ibid*

29    *Ibid.*
30    Turner, *From Ritual to Theatre*, 24.
31    *Ibid.*
32    *Ibid.*
33    *Ibid.*, 52.
34    *Ibid.*
35    *Ibid.*, 47-48.
36    *Ibid.*, 48.
37    Cf. *Ibid.*, 56-58.
38    Cf. Turner, *The Anthropology of Performance*, 163.
39    *Ibid.*, 165.
40    *Ibid.*
41    *Ibid.*, 16.
42    Cf. Richard Schechner, & Willa Appel, eds., *By Means of Performance. Intercultural studies of theatre and ritual* (Cambridge: Cambridge University Press, 1990), 36.
43    Cf. Roland Fisher, "A Cartography of the Ecstatic and Meditative States", *Science* (174:4012), 26.11.1971, 897-904.
44    Schechner, *By Means of Performance*, 37.
45    *Ibid.*
46    Diderot, 14.
47    Cf. E. Jephcott, *Proust and Rilke, The Literature of Expanded Consciousness* (London: Chatto and Windus, 1972).
48    Cf. Abraham H. Maslow, *Towards a Psychology of Being* (New York: Van Nostrand, 1962).
49    R.W. Levenson, P. Ekman and W.V.Friesen, "Voluntary facial action generates emotion-specific autonomic nervous system activity", *Psychophysiology* 27:4 (1990), 363-84.
50    *Ibid.*

**i. Barba**

1    Innes, *Holy Theatre*, 11.
2    Cf. Ian Watson, *Towards a Third Theatre. Eugenio Barba and the Odin Teatret* (London and New York: Routledge, 1993) 101,
3    *Ibid.*, 3-4.
4    *Ibid.*, 149.
5    *Ibid.*
6    *Ibid.*
7    Eugenio Barba and Nicola Savarese. *The Secret Art of the Performer. A Dictionary of Theatre Anthropology.* (London, New York: Routledge, 1991), 8.
8    *Ibid.*
9    *Ibid.*, 8.
10    Eugenio Barba, "Interview with Gautam Dasgupta", *Performing Arts Journal*, January 1985, 12.
11    Cf. Watson, 32.
12    *Ibid.*
13    Cf. *Ibid.*
14    Eugenio Barba and Nicola Savarese. *A Dictionary of Theatre Anthropology*, 188.

178

15    Watson, 33.
16    *Ibid.*
17    *Ibid.*, 34.
18    *Ibid.*, 35.
19    Cf. Eugenio Barba, "The Fiction of Duality", *NTQ*, 5:20 (1989), 312.
20    *Ibid.*
21    Watson, 39.
22    *Ibid.*
23    *Ibid.*
24    Eugenio Barba, *The Floating Islands. Reflections with Odin Teatret.* Edited by
      Ferdinando Taviani (Holstebro, 1979),  134.
25    Watson, 40.
26    *Ibid.*
27    Barba, *The Floating Islands,* 35.
28    *Ibid.* 73.
29    *Ibid.*
30    Eugenio Barba, "The Way of Refusal: the Theatre's Body-in-Life", *NTQ*, 4:16 (1988),
      291.
31    *Ibid.*
32    *Ibid.*
33    *Ibid.*
34    Watson, 18.

## j. Brook

1     David Williams, *Peter Brook. A Theatrical Casebook* (London: Methuen, 21991), 1.
2     *Ibid.*, 74.
3     Martin, *Voice in Modern Theatre*, 76. On similarities and differences between
      Stanislavsky,  Brecht, Grotowski, and Brook, see also Shomit Mitter, *Systems of
      Rehearsal. Stanislavsky, Brecht, Grotowski and Brook* (London and New York:
      Routledge, 1992).
4     Peter Brook, *The Shifting Point. Forty Years of Theatrical Exploration 1946-1987*
      (London: Methuen, 1987), 31.
5     Cf. Jan Kott, "Grotowski or the limit", *NTQ*, 6:23 (1990), 203.
6     Bradby and Williams, *Directors' Theatre*, 31.
7     Brook. *The Shifting Point*, 30
8     Cf. Williams, *Peter Brook. A Theatrical Casebook*, 332.
9     Peter Brook, *The Empty Space* (Harmondsworth: Penguin, 1972) [11968], 151.
10    *Ibid.*
11    Brook, *The Shifting Point*, 41.
12    *Ibid.*
13    Cf. Brook, *The Empty Space*, 151.
14    *Ibid.*, 79-80.
15    Cf. *Ibid.*, 80.
16    *Ibid.*, 47.
17    Eugenio Barba, "Eugenio Barba to Phillip Zarrilli: About the visible and the invisible in
      the theater, and about ISTA in particular", *TDR*, 32:3 (1988), 12.
18    Brook, *The Empty Space*, 63.

19    *Ibid.*
20    Cf. *Ibid.*, 151.
21    Brook, *The Shifting Point*, 233.
22    *Ibid.*
23    Bradby and Williams, 147.
24    Brook, *The Shifting Point*, 128.
25    Cf. Leonard C. Pronko, "L.A. Festival: Peter Brook's *The Mahabharata*". *Asian Theatre Journal*, 5:2 (1988), 110.
26    Innes, *Holy Theatre*, 139.
27    *Ibid.*, 142.
28    Maria Shevtsova, "Interaction- Interpretation. *The Mahabharata* from a social-cultural perspective", in David Williams, ed., *Peter Brook and the Mahabharata: Critical Perspectives* (London and New York: Routledge, 1991), 210.
29    Cf. Pronko, 220-221.
30    Brook, *The Shifting Point*, 164.

**Summary**
1    Diderot, *The Paradox of Acting*, 14.
2    Stanislavsky, *Creating a Role*, 52.

## 2. Western Points of Contact
### a. Altered states of consciousness

1    John J. Miletich, *States of Awareness. An Annotated Bibliography* (New York, Westport, London: Greenwood,1988), ix.
2    Cf. Ludwig, Arnold M. "Altered States of Consciousness", in Charles T. Tart, ed., *Altered States of Consciousness. A Book of Readings* (New York, London, Sydney, Toronto: John Wiley and Sons, 1969), 13-16.
3    Cf. *Ibid.* 10-12.
4    Cf. *Ibid.* 18-20.
5    Cf. Charles Tart, "Some assumptions of orthodox, Western psychology", in Charles Tart, ed., *Transpersonal Psychologies* (London: Routledge and Kegan Paul, 1975), 59-111.
6    Cf. Miletich, contents.
7    John H. Clark, *A Map of Mental States* (London, Boston, Melbourne and Henley, Routledge and Kegan Paul, 1983), 1.
8    *Ibid.*, 2.
9.    *Ibid.*
10    *Ibid.*, 13.
11    *Ibid.*, 13-14.
12    *Ibid.*, 16.
13    *Ibid.*, 20.
14    Cf. *Ibid.*
15    *Ibid.*, 22-24.
16    *Ibid.*, 25.
17    Cf. Humberto R. Maturana and Francisco J. Varela, *Autopoiesis and Cognition. The Realization of the Living* (Dordrecht: Reidel, 1980), and Gebhard Rusch, *Erkenntnis,*

*Wissenschaft, Geschichte: Von einem konstruktivistischen Standpunkt* (Frankfurt: Suhrkamp, 1987).

18   Roland Fischer, "Towards a Neuroscience of Self and States of Self-Awareness and Interpreting Interpretations", in Benjamin B. Wolman and Montague Ullman, eds., *Handbook of States of Consciousness* (New York: Van Nostrand Reinhold Company, 1986), 5.

19   *Ibid.*, 15.

20   *Ibid.*

## b. The phenomenon of pure consciousness

1   Cf. W.T. Stace, *Mysticism and Philosophy* (London: Macmillan, 1960). .

2   Robert K. C. Forman, "Introduction: Mysticism, Constructivism, and Forgetting", in Robert K.C.Forman ed., *The Problem of Pure Consciousness. Mysticism and Philosophy* (New York, Oxford: Oxford University Press, 1990), 7.

3   *Ibid.*, 8.

4   *Ibid.*, 3.

5   *Ibid.*, 28.

6   Charles N. Alexander, Ken Chandler, Robert W. Boyer, "Experience and Understanding of Pure Consciousness in Vedic Science of Maharishi Mahesh Yogi", unpublished paper, 5-6, quoted in Forman, 27-28.

7   Forman, 27.

8   Alexander et.al., in Forman, 27-28.

## c. The mind-body relationship

1   Cf. David Hodgson, *The Mind Matters. Consciousness and Choice in a Quantum World* (Oxford: Clarendon Press 1991), 64-88.

2   Stephen T. De Berry, *The Externalization of Consciousness and the Psychopathology of Everyday Life*. Contributions to Psychology, 17 (New York, Westport, London: Greenwood Press, 1991), 20.

3   Cf. Hodgson, 64-88.

4   Max Velmans, "Consciousness, brain, and the physical world", *Philosophical Psychology*, 3:1 (1990), 77.

5   *Ibid.*

6   *Ibid.* 93.

7   Michael Lockwood, *Mind, Brain and the Quantum. The Compound "i"* (Oxford: Basil Blackwell, 1989), 240.

8   Fred Alan Wolf, *Mind and the New Physics* (London: Heinemann, 1985), 185.

9   *Ibid.* 186.

10   *Ibid.* 196.

11   *Ibid.*

12   Robert C. Jahn and Brenda J. Dunne. *Margins of Reality. The Role of Consciousness in the Physical World* (San Diego, New York, London: Harcourt Brace Jovanovich, 1987), 251.

13   Hodgson, *The Mind Matters.*, 446.

14   David Bohm, "A new theory of the relationship between mind and matter", *Philosophical Psychology*, 3:2 (1990), 271.

15   *Ibid.*, 281.

16   *Ibid.*, 283.
17   *Ibid.*
18   *Ibid.*
19   Raymond Tallis, *The Explicit Animal. A Defence of Human Consciousness* (London: MacMillan, 1991), 247.
20   Jean-Marie Pradier, "Towards a Biological Theory of Performance", NTQ VI:21 (1990), 88.
21   *Ibid.*, 88-89.
22   *Ibid.*, 89.
23   *Ibid.*
24   *Ibid.*, 91.
25   Cf. *Ibid.*, 92.
26   *Ibid.*
27   *Ibid.*, 93.
28   *Ibid.*, 94.
29   *Ibid.*
30   Anthony Frost and Ralph Yarrow, *Improvisation in Drama*. New Directions in Theatre (London: Macmillan, 1990), 1.
31   *Ibid.*, 152.

### d. A synthesis of *biomechanics* and Ekman's research: ALBA- EMOTING

1   Susanna Bloch, "ALBA EMOTING: A Psychophysiological Technique to Help Actors Create and Control Real Emotions", *Theatre Topics* 3:2 (1993), 121.
2   *Ibid.*, 123
3   *Ibid.*, 124
4   *Ibid.*, 125
5   *Ibid.*
6   *Ibid.*, 127
7   *Ibid.*, 130
8   Roxane Rix, "ALBA EMOTING: A Preliminary Experiment with Emotional Effector Patterns", *Theatre Topics* 3:2 (1993), 144.
9   *Ibid.*

### *Indian Theatre Aesthetics And its Influence on Western Theories*
### a. General non-Western influences

1   For general Japanese and Chinese influences on Brecht, see Antony Tatlov, *The Mask of Evil. Brecht's Response to the Poetry, Theatre and Thought of China and Japan* (Bern, Frankfurt, Las Vegas: Peter Lang, 1977) and Sjaak Onderdelinden, "Brecht and Asia" in C.C.Barfoot and Cobi Bordewijk, eds., *Theatre Intercontinental. forms, functions, correspondences* (Amsterdam, Atlanta, GA: Rodopi, 1993), 25-42.
2   Willett, *Brecht on Theatre*, 91.
3   Cf. *Ibid.*
4   Cf. *Ibid.* 91-92.
5   *Ibid.* 94.
6   *Ibid.* 92.
7   Diderot, *The Paradox of Acting*, 14
8   Artaud, *The Theatre and its Double*, 38-39

9     *Ibid.*, 31.
10   Cf. *Ibid.*, 84.
11   *Ibid.*
12   *Ibid.*, 85.
13   *Ibid.*, 100.
14   *Ibid.*

**b. Influences of Indian philosophy**

1    Cf. William S. Haney II, "Unity in Vedic aesthetics: the self-interacting dynamics of the nower, the known, and the process of knowing", *Analecta Husserliana*, 233 (1991), 316.

2    Cf. Martin Mittwede, "Die sechs Systeme der Vedischen Philosophie, Einführung", *Mitteilungsblätter der Deutschen MERU-Gesellschaft*, 10 (1985), 29.

3    Stanislavsky, *An Actor Prepares*, 205.

4    *Ibid.*, 214

5    *Ibid.*

6    Swami Vireswarananda, *Brahmasutras* (Calcutta: Advaita Ashrama, 41970), II.4.8, 252-3

7    Swami Venkatesananda, *The Concise Yoga Vasishta* (Albany: State University of New York Press, 1984), 282.

8    *Ibid.*

9    Stanislavsky, *Creating a Role*, 52.

10   Cf. Haney, 297.

11   Harold Coward, *Jung and Eastern Thought* (Albany: State University of New York Press, 1985), 86.

12   *Ibid.*, 61.

13   *Ibid.*

14   *Ibid.*, 140.

15   Cf. Jonathan Shear, "The universal structures and dynamics of creativity: Maharishi, Plato, Jung and various creative geniuses on the creative process", *Journal of Creative Behavior*, 16:3 (1982), 155-175.

16   Peter L. Brent, *The Indian Guru and his Disciple* (Tunbridge Wells: Institute for Cultural Research, 1971), 2-3.

17   Cf. *Ibid.*, 3-5

18   Cf. *Ibid.*, 17.

19   Cf. Cox, *Turning East*.

20   Jacques Vigne, "Guru and Psychotherapist: Comparisons from the Hindu Tradition". *The Journal of Transpersonal Psychology*, 23:2 (1991), 124. Vigne points to three sources for Western misgivings about Gurus: First, someone guided by a positivist, scientific world view will be suspicious about people being attracted by a Guru, someone not allegedly guided by reason. Second, Vigne argues, many Christians may fear "a competition for power and clientele". Finally, Vigne senses an "apprehension among anthropologists themselves. They have concentrated so much on the differences between societies, and the inner coherence of each culture, that they find it hard to see that some psychological mechanisms are obviously cross-cultural, and that one can use one system to get fresh insight into another".

21   Cf. *Ibid.*, 128-129.

183

22    Cf. *Ibid.*, 129. The nature of the commitment itself is also different: in psychoanalysis, its basis is financial, and the transference which the patient is expected to show does not compare with the profound devotion the disciple is expected to selflessly express towards his Guru, to the point where the disciple sees the Guru's action in every event, and further still, everywhere. This "interpretative delirium" is temporal and limited in time, because in its course the disciple gradually becomes aware "of the impersonal reality of that which he called "Guru," which others may call God, destiny or change; but, unlike an average person, he has actually made friends with that impersonal force through the intermediary of the Guru's apparent personality." (131)
23    *Ibid.*, 130.
24    *Ibid.*
25    Cf. Jacob L. Moreno, *Gruppenpsychotherapie und Psychodrama. Einleitung in die Theorie und Praxis* (George Thieme: New York), 31988.
26    Vigne, 135.

## c. Indian theatre aesthetics: the *Natyashastra*

1     G.K. Bhat, "Natya and Nritya: A Perspective on Inter-Relations", in: *Sanskrit Drama. Problems and Perspectives* (Delhi: Ajanta Publications, 1985), 279.
2     *Ibid.*
3     Ghosh, Manomohan (transl). *The Natyashastra. A Treatise on Hindu Dramaturgy and Histrionics.* Ascribed to Bharata Muni (Calcutta: The Royal Asiatic Society of Bengal, 1950), I. 111-112 (15).
4     Bhat, G. K. "Natya and Nritya. . . ", 280.
5     Srinivasa Ayya Srinivasan, *On the Composition of the Natyashastra* (Reinbek: Dr. Inge Wezler Verlag für Orientalische Fachpublikationen, 1980), 1.
6     Cf. Pramod Kale, *The Theatrical Universe. A Study of the Natyashastra* (Bombay, Popular Prakashan, 1974), 5.
7     Cf. *Ibid.*
8     Cf. Ghosh, *Natyashastra*, I. 17-18 (4).
9     Kale, *The Theatric Universe*, 1.
10    Hari Ram Mishra, *The Theory of Rasa in Sanskrit Drama. With a Comparative Study of General Dramatic Literature* (Bhopal, Sayar, Chhatapur: Vindhyachal Prakashan, 1964).
11    Kapila Chandra Pandey, *Comparative Aesthetics.* Vol. 1: *Indian Aesthetics* (Banaras: The Chowkhamba Sanskrit Series Office, 1950), 10.
12    Mishra, *The Theory of Rasa*, 198.
13    V. Rhagavan, *The Concept of the Beautiful in Sanskrit Literature* (Madras: The Kuppuswami Sastri Research Institute, 1988).
14    *Natyashastra*, VI. 15 (102).
15    *Ibid.*, Prose passage after verse VI. 31 (109).
16    *Ibid.*, Prose passage after verse VI.45 (108-109).
17    *Ibid.*, 109.
18    *Ibid.*, VI. 18-21 (102).
19    *Ibid.*, Prose passage after VI. 45 (109).
20    *Ibid.*, VI.17 (102).
21    *Ibid.*, VI.22 (102-103).
22    *Ibid.*, Prose passage after VI.31 (105).

23    E.W. Marasinghe, *The Sanskrit Theatre and Stagecraft*. Sri Garib Dass Oriental Series No. 78 (Delhi: Sri Satguru Publications, 1989), 198.

24    *Natyashastra*, chapter 14.

25    Cf. *Ibid.*, VII.94 (143).

26    R.R. Ambardekar, *Rasa Structure of the Meghaduta* (Bombay: Andreesh Prakashan, 1979), 26.

27    *Natyashastra.*, Prose passage after VII.93 (143).

28    *Ibid.*

29    Suresh Dhayagude, *Western and Indian Poetics. A Comparative Study.* Bhandarkar Oriental Research Series No. 18 (Poona: Bhandarkar Oriental Research Institute, 1981), 14.

30    *Ibid.*, 172.

31    *Ibid.*, 15.

32    G.K. Bhat, *Rasa Theory and Allied Problems* (Baroda: The MS University of Baroda, 1984), 48.

33    *Ibid.*

34    Rekha Jhanji, *The Sensuous in Art. Reflections on Indian Aesthetics* (Delhi: Indian Institute of Advanced Studies, Shimla in association with Motilal Barnasidass, 1989), 35.

35    *Ibid.*

36    Shveni Pandya, *A Study of the Technique of Abhinaya in Relation to Sanskrit Drama* (Bombay, New Delhi: Somaiya Publications Pvt. Ltd., 1988), 256.

37    *Ibid.*

38    Minakshi Dalal, *Conflict in Sanskrit Drama* (Bombay, Delhi: Somaija Publications Pvt. Ltd., 1973), 36.

39    *Ibid.*

40    G.K. Bhat, *Sanskrit Dramatic Theory.* Bhandarkar Oriental Institute Post-Graduate and Research Series No. 13 (Poona: Bhandarkar Oriental Research Institute 1981), 51.

41    E.W. Marasinghe, *The Sanskrit Theatre and Stagecraft.* 188.

42    Schechner, *Between Theatre and Anthropology*, 136

43    *Ibid.*, 138.

44    *Ibid.*

45    *Ibid.*

46    *Ibid.*, 140.

47    Cf. Padma Subrahmanyam, renowned Bharata Natyam exponent in Madras, India, who produced a 13-part TV series about the *Natyashastra* at the request of Indian Television.

48    Watson, *Towards a Third Theatre*, 14.

49    *Ibid.*

50    *Ibid.*, 15.

51    *Natyashastra*, XIV:63-64 (245-246)

52    Kumiega, *The Theatre of Grotowski*, 116.

53    Peter Brook, lecture at *Temenos Academy*, London, 1.11.1993.

## 4. Indian points of contact
### a. Vedic linguistics

1      Harold G. Coward, *The Sphota Theory of Language. A Philosophical Analysis* (Delhi, Varanasi, Patna: Motilal Banarsidass, 1980), 3.
2      *Ibid.*
3      *Ibid.*, 128.
4      *Ibid.*, 129.
5      Cf. *Ibid.*, 131.
6      *Ibid.*
7      *Ibid.*, 73.
8      *Ibid.*
9      Cf. *Ibid.*, 12.
10     Cf. *Ibid.*
11     *Ibid.*
12     William Haney, II, "Unity in Vedic aesthetics", 316.
13     Coward, 76.
14     Antonin Artaud, *The Theatre and its Double*, translated by Victor Corti (London: Calder, 1977), 45.
15     *Ibid.*
16     Cf. Rekha Jhanji, *Aesthetic Communication. The Indian Perspective* (Delhi: Munshiram Mancharlal Publishers, 1985), 5.
17     *Ibid.*
18     *Ibid.*
19     Artaud, 92.
20     Cf. André Padoux, *Vac. The Concept of the Word in Selected Hindu Tantras.* Trans. Jaques Gontier. (Albany: State University of New York Press, 1990).
21     Cf. Jhanji, *Aesthetic Communication*, 5.

### b. The theatre aesthetics of the *Natyashastra*

1      Richard E. Kramer, "The *Natyashastra* and Stanislavsky: Points of Contact", *Theatre Studies* (1991), 56.
2      *Ibid.*
3      *Ibid.*, 57.
4      Cf. G.K.Bhat, *Rasa Theory and Allied Problems*, 48.

## 5. Interculturalism and Postmodernism
### a. Western positions on interculturalism

1      Cf. Bharucha, *Theatre and the World*, 16.
2      Peter Brook, Platform Performance at the Royal National Theatre, London, 5.11.1993.
3      Barba, Eugenio. *The Floating Islands*, 74-75.
4      Edward W. Said, *Orientalism* (London: Penguin Books, 1991), 2.
5      *Ibid.*, 5.
6      *Ibid.*, 36.
7      Richard Schechner, "The Decline and Fall of the (American) Avant-Garde", in Richard Schechner, *The End of Humanism. Writings on Performance* (New York: PAJ Publications, 1982), 19.
8      Eugenio Barba, "Eurasian Theatre", *TDR*, 32:2 (1988), 127-128.

9     Barba, Eugenio. "Eurasian Theatre: The Dramatic Touch of Difference". in Erika Fischer-Lichte, Josephine Riley, Michael Gissenwehrer, eds., *Theatre, Own and Foreign* (Tübingen: Günter Narr, 1990), 33

10    Barba, "Eurasian Theatre", *TDR*, 130.

11    Cf. Avanthi Meduri, "Bharata Natyam--What Are You?" *Asian Theatre Journal*, 5.1 (1988), 1-2.

12    *Ibid.*, 2.

13    Cf. Avanthi Meduri, "Orientalism, Indian Nationalism and the Revival of Classical Dance in India", unpublished paper, presented in Session II on Wednesday, 10.2.1993, in Toronto at the Conference on *New Directions in Indian Dance*.

14    Kapila Vatsyayan, commentary at the end of session I, on Wednesday, 10.2.1993, in Toronto at the Conference on *New Directions in Indian Dance*.

15    Joan Erdman, commentary at the end of Session I, on Wednesday, 10.2.1993, in Toronto at the Conference on *New Directions in Indian Dance*.

16    Meduri, "*Bharata Natyam* ... ", 11.

17    *Ibid.*

18    Gowri Ramnarayan, "Dancer and Reformer", *Sruti* (July) 1984, 22. Quoted in Meduri, "*Bharata Natyam...*", 11.

19    Meduri, "*Bharata Natyam...*", 11.

20    *Ibid.*

21    Dance drama *The Face* by Prakash Jadagudde and Nina Kumari, London, premiered at the Bharatiya Vidya Bhavan, London, on Saturday, 27.2.1993).

22    Rustom Bharucha, *Theatre and the World. Performance and the politics of culture* (London and New York: Routledge, 1993), 249.

23    Cf. Marvin Carlson, "Peter Brook, *The Mahabharata* and Ariane Mnouchkine's *L'Indiade* as examples of contemporary cross-cultural theatre", 50.

24    Cf. Patrice Pavis, *Theatre at the Crossroads of Culture*, 218.

### b. Bharucha's critique of interculturalism

1     Bharucha, *Theatre and the World*, x.

2     *Ibid.*, 4.

3     *Ibid.*, 14.

4     *Ibid.*

5     Cf. *Ibid.*, 15.

6     *Ibid.*, 22.

7     *Ibid.*, 23.

8     *Ibid.*, 25.

9     Kumiega, *The Theatre of Grotowski*, 116.

10    Bharucha, 25.

11    *Ibid.*

12    *Ibid.*, 26.

13    *Ibid.*

14    *Ibid.*, 28.

15    *Ibid.*

16    *Ibid.*, 28.

17    *Ibid.*

18    *Ibid.*

19    *Ibid.*
20    *Ibid.*
21    *Ibid.*, 31.
22    *Ibid.*, 36.
23    Phillip Zarrilli, "For whom is the "invisible" not visible: Reflections on representation in the work of Eugenio Barba", *TDR*, 32:1 (1988), 101-102.
24    Bharucha, 57.
25    *Ibid.*, 244.
26    *Ibid.*, 68.
27    *Ibid.*, 69-70.
28    *Ibid.*, 70.
29    *Ibid.*, 92.
30    *Ibid.*
31    *Ibid.*
32    *Ibid.*
33    *Ibid.*, 148.

### *c. Postmodernism*

1    Johannes Birringer, *Theatre, Theory, Postmodernism* (Bloomington and Indianapolis: Indiana University Press, 1991), xi.
2    *Ibid.*
3    Bharucha, *Theatre and the World*, 16-18.
4    Cf. Ulrich Broich and Manfred Pfister, eds., *Intertextualität. Formen, Funktionen, anglistische Fallbeispiele* (Tübingen: Narr, 1985), 15.
5    Cf. *Ibid.*
6    Cf. *Ibid.*, 25.
7    Cf. *Ibid.*
8    Cf. David George, "On Ambiguity: Towards a post-modern performance theory", *TRI* 14:1 (1989), 71.
9    *Ibid.*
10   *Ibid.*, 75.
11   *Ibid.*
12   *Ibid.*
13   *Ibid.*, 83.
14   Anika Lemaire, *Jacques Lacan.* Translated by David Macey (London, Henley and Boston: Routledge & Kegan Paul, 1977), 67.
15   *Ibid.*
16   *Ibid.*
17   *Ibid.*, 48.
18   George, 74.
19   David George, "Quantum Theatre--Potential Theatre: A New Paradigm?" *NTQ* 5:18 (1989), 171-179.
20   Natalie Crohn-Schmitt, Natalie. *Actors and Onlookers. Theatre and Twentieth-Century Scientific Views of Nature* (Evanston: Northwestern University Press, 1990), 1.
21   *Ibid.*, 2.
22   *Ibid.*, 9.

23    *Ibid.*, 14.
24    *Ibid.*, 28.
25    *Ibid.*, 130.
26    Birringer, 79.
27    *Ibid.*, 31.
28    *Ibid.*, 100.
29    *Ibid.*
30    *Ibid.*, 8.
31    Madan Sarup, *An Introductory Guide to Post-Structuralism and Postmodernism* (New York, London, Toronto, Sydney, Tokyo: Harvester Wheatsheaf, 1988), 131.
32    *Ibid.*, 132.


**6. Towards a Model of Consciousness**
1    Ralph Yarrow, "Neutral" consciousness in the experience of theatre", *Mosaic* 19:3 (1987), 12. See also Ralph Yarrow, "The potential of consciousness: towards a new approach towards states of consciousness in literature", *Journal of European Studies*, 15 (1985) 1-20.
2    Ralph Yarrow, "Neutral consciousness...", 12.
3    *Ibid.*
4    *Ibid.*
5    *Ibid.*, 13.


**THE ACTOR'S EMOTIONAL INVOLVEMENT FROM THE PERSPECTIVE OF VEDIC SCIENCE**
*1. Vedic Psychology's Model of Consciousness*
a. Vedic Science and the "Turn to the East"
1    Cox, *Turning East*, 75. See also Edward Said, *Orientalism*.
2    Cox, 18.
3    Jürg Kollbrunner, *Das Buch der Humanistischen Psychologie: Eine ausführliche einführende Darstellung und Kritik des Fühlens, Denkens und Handelns in der Humanistischen Psychologie* (Eschborn, 1987), 66.
4    Cf. Fritjof Capra, *The Turning Point* (London: Wildwood House, 1982).
5    Cf. Marilyn Ferguson, *The Aquarian Conspiracy: Personal and Social Transformation in the 1980s* (London: Routledge and Kegan Paul, 1981).
6    Cf. Christof Schorsch, *Die New Age Bewegung. Utopie und Mythos der Neuen Zeit. Eine kritische Auseinandersetzung.* (Gütersloh: Gütersloher Verlagshaus G. Mohn, 1988), 20-73.
7    Apart from Bharucha's criticism of Brook's *Mahabharata*-production, see Gautam Dasgupta, Peter Brook's *'Orientalism'*, *Performing Arts Journal* No. 30 Vol. 10 no. 3 (1987).
8    Cf. Bharucha, *Theatre and the World*, 240
9    R. K. Wallace, "Physiological Effects of TM", *Science* 167 (1970), 1751-1754.
10   Cf. David W. Orme-Johnson, et. al., eds., *Scientific Research on the Transcendental Meditation Program. Collected Papers, Vol.* 1 (Rheinweiler: MERU Press, 1977; Roger A. Chalmers, G. et. al., eds., *Scientific Research of Maharishi's Transcendental Meditation and TM-Sidhi Program.* Collected papers, vol. 2 (Vlodrop: MVU Press, 1989); Roger A. Chalmers, et. al., eds., *Scientific Research of*

*Maharishi's Transcendental Meditation and TM-Sidhi Program.* Collected papers, vol. 3 (Vlodrop: MVU Press, 1989); Roger A. Chalmers et. al., eds., *Scientific Research of Maharishi's Transcendental Meditation and TM-Sidhi Program.* Collected papers, vol. 4 (Vlodrop: MVU Press, 1989); Robert Keith Wallace, et. al., eds., *Scientific Research of Maharishi's Transcendental Meditation and TM-Sidhi Program.* Collected papers, vol. 5 (Fairfield, Iowa: MIU Press, 1992).

### b. Vedic Science in the Context of Vedic Literature

1   Cf. Harold G. Coward, *The Sphota Theory of Language,3.*
2   *Ibid.,* 7.
3   *Ibid.*
4   Maharishi Mahesh Yogi, *Life Supported by Natural Law,* (Washington: Age of Enlightenment Press, 1986).
5   Cf. Robert Keith Wallace, *The Physiology of Consciousness* (Fairfield, Iowa: Maharishi International University Press, 1993), 213-233.
6   Maharishi Mahesh Yogi. *On the Bhagavad-Gita. A New Translation and Commentary, Chapters 1 - 6* (Harmondsworth: Penguin, 1969), 482-3.
7   Deepak Chopra, *Perfect Health. The Complete Mind/Body Guide* (Toronto, New York, London, Sydney, Auckland: Bantam Books, 1990), 25.
8   Cf. John Hagelin, "Restructuring Physics from its Foundation in Light of Maharishi's Vedic Science", *Modern Science and Vedic Science,* 3:1 (1989), 32.
9   Chopra, 61-66
10  Cf. Vasant Lad, *Das Ayurveda Heilbuch. Eine praktische Anleitung zur Selbst-Diagnose, Therapie und Heilung mit dem ayurwedischen System* (Haldenwang: Edition Shangrila, 1986), 50-52.

### c. Pure Consciousness and the Structure of the Mind

1   David W. Orme-Johnson, "The Cosmic Psyche as the Unified Source of Creation", *Modern Science and Vedic Science,* 2:2 (1988), 168-169.
2   Cf. John Hagelin, "Is Consciousness the Unified Field? A Field Theorist's Perspective", *Modern Science and Vedic Science,* 1 (1987), 29-88.
3   Orme-Johnson, "The Cosmic Psyche as the Unified Source of Creation", 175.
4   David Bohm, "A new theory of the relationship between mind and matter". 283.
5   Cf. Michael C. Dillbeck, "The Self-Interacting Dynamics of Consciousness as the Source of the Creative Process in Nature and in Human Life", *Modern Science and Vedic Science,* 2:3 (1988).
6   Bohm, 283.
7   Cf. *Ibid.,* 280.
8   Travis, Orme-Johnson."Field Model of Consciousness: EEG Coherence Changes as Indicators of Field Effects", *International Journal of Neuroscience,* 49:3,4 (1989), 203.
9   R.W. Hood, "The construction and validation of a measure of reported mystical experience" *Journal for the Scientific Study of Religion* 24 (1975), 31-32, quoted in Paul Gelderloos, and Zaid H.A.D. Beto, "The TM and TM-Sidhi Program and Reported Experiences of Transcendental Consciousness", *Psychologia* 32:2 (1989), 91-103.
10  Gelderloos, 93.

11    *Ibid.*
12    *Ibid.*
13    *Ibid.*
14    *Ibid.*
15    *Ibid.*
16    *Ibid.*
17    *Ibid.*
18    P.V.Karambelkar, *Patanjali's Yoga Sutras. With Devanagari Text, Transliteration, Word Meanings and Translation* (Bombay: Kaivalyadhama, 1986).
19    *Ibid.*
20    Gelderloos, 93.
21    *Ibid.*
22    *Ibid.*
23    *Ibid.*
24    *Ibid.*
25    *Ibid.*
26    *Ibid.*
27    *Ibid.*
28    Travis, Orme-Johnson."Field Model of Consciousness: EEG Coherence Changes as Indicators of Field Effects", 203.
29    Cf. Charles N. Alexander , Robert W. Cranson, Robert W.Boyer, David W. Orme-Johnson, "Transcendental Consciousness: A Fourth State of Consciousness beyond Sleep, Dream, and Waking", in Jayne Gackenbach, ed., *Sleep and Dream. A Sourcebook* (New York, London: Garland Publishing Inc., 1986), 291.
30    Charles N. Alexander et.al., "Growth of Higher Stages of Consciousness: Maharishi's Vedic Psychology of Human Development", in Charles N. Alexander and Ellen J. Langer, eds., *Higher Stages of Human Development. Perspectives on Human Growth* (New York, Oxford:Oxford University Press, 1990), 290.
31    Cf. Nandalal Sinha (transl.), *The Samkhya Philosophy* (New Delhi: Oriental Books Reprint Company, 1979). I. 63 (102-103) and II.16 (251) for *ahamkara* and II.18 (251) for *manas*.
32    Alexander et.al, "Growth of Higher Stages of Consciousness", 290.
33    Bohm, p. 282.
34    Maharishi Mahesh Yogi, *Bhagavad-Gita*, 481.
35    Michael C. Dillbeck, "The Self-Interacting Dynamics of Consciousness... "264.
36    Charles N. Alexander et.al., "Growth of Higher Stages of Consciousness...", 290.
37    *Ibid.*
38    *Ibid.*
39    Michael C. Dillbeck, "The Self- Interacting Dynamics ...", 264.

## c. Higher Stages of Human Development

1    Charles N. Alexander, Steven M. Druker, Ellen J. Langer, "Introduction: Major Issues in the Exploration of Adult Growth", in Charles N. Alexander and Ellen J. Langer, eds., *Higher Stages of Human Development. Perspectives on Human Growth.* (New York, Oxford: Oxford University Press, 1990), 3.
2    Niralemba-Upanishad of Sukla Yajurveda, 41, in H.N.Aiyar, ed. and transl., *Thirty Minor Upanishads* (Delhi: Arcade Book Company, 1914), 23.

3    Alexander, "Introduction", 3.
4    *Ibid.*, 5.
5    *Ibid.*
6    *Ibid.*, 3.
7    Cf. *Ibid.*, 9-10.
8    Charles N. Alexander, and Robert W. Boyer, "Seven States of Consciousness: Unfolding the Full Potential of the Cosmic Psyche in Individual Life through Maharishi's Vedic Psychology", *Modern Science and Vedic Science* 2:4 (1989), 342.
9    Juan Mascaro (transl.), *The Bhagavad-Gita* (Harmondswortth: Penguin Books, 1962), 3:29, 101.
10   Charles N. Alexander et.al., "Transcendental Consciousness...", 295.
11   Thoreau, H.D., *Walden* (New York, NAL, 1960) (Original Work published 1854), 94-95.
12   Jiminez, trans. Carlos de Francisco Zea, quoted from Robert Bly, "A wrong turning in American poetry", repr. in Dobald Hall, ed., *Claims for Poetry* (Ann Arbor: Univ. of Michigan Press, 1984), 17-37 [original work published 1963].
13   B.J. King and K. Chapin, *Billie Jean* (New York: Harper & Row, 1974, 199. Quoted in Charles N. Alexander et. al., "Growth of Higher Stages of Consciousness: Maharishi's Vedic Psychology of Human Development", 318.
14   Alexander and Boyer, "Seven States of Consciousness", 348.
15   *Ibid.*, 355.
16   Kathleen Raine, *The Land Unknown* (New York: George Braziller, 1975), 119.
17   Johann Gottlieb Fichte, in R.M.Chrisholm, ed., *The Vocation of Man* (Indianapolis: Bobbs-Merrill, 1956), 150-151; quoted by Alexander, "Growth of Higher Stages...", 322-323.
18   Alexander and Boyer, 359.
19   *Ibid.*
20   *Ibid.*, 360.
21   Jayadayal Goyandka, *Shrimad Bhagavadgita As It Is. With English Translation* (Gorakhpur: Gita Press, 1984), 6:29, 106.
22   Maharishi Mahesh Yogi *Bhagavad-Gita*, 441.
23   *Yoga-Vasishta*, ed. Ventkatesananda, p. 393-4.
24   Niralemba-Upanishad of Sukla Yajurveda, 41 (ed. Aiyar,    1914), 23.
25   Tejobindu-Upanishad of Krishna Yajurveda, III, in Aiyar, 86.
26   Rhoda Orme-Johnson, "A Unified Field Theory of Literature", *Modern Science and Vedic Science* 1:3 (1987), 339.

## 2. The Actor's Emotions and Vedic Psychology
### a. The Paradox

1    Roach, "Diderot and the Actor's Machine", 61.
2    Cf. *Ibid.*, 62.
3    Diderot, *The Paradox of Acting*, 14.
4    Ronald Harwood, *The Dresser* (Ambergate: Amber Lane Press, 1980), 70.
5    G. Richards, "The world a stage: A conversation with Ray Reinhardt", *San Francisco Theater Magazine* Winter 1977, 43.
6    Schechner and Appel, eds., *By Means of Performance*, 36.
7    Diderot, 19.

8     Turner, *From Ritual to Theatre*, 48.

9     Cf. *Ibid.*, 56-58. .

**b. The *Natyashastra* from the Perspective of Vedic Science**

1     Gabriel Hartmann, *Maharishi-Gandharva-Ved. Die Klassische Musik der Vedischen Hochkultur: Eine Einführung in die musiktheoretischen Grundlagen* (Vlodrop: MVU Press, 1992), 49-51

2     Maharishi Mahesh Yogi, Interview on Gandharva Veda, WDR and Deutsche Welle, 8.2.91

3     Cf. Hartmann, 41.

4     Sarngadev, *Sangita Ratnakara*, ed. and transl. P. Sharma & R. R. Shringy. Vol. I (Delhi: Motilal Banarsidass, 1984).

5     Cf. Hartmann, 57.

6     *Ibid.*, 69.

7     *Natyashastra*, ed. Ghosh, S, 8:19-21, pp. 150-151

      Hartmann, 62

9     *Ibid.*

10    Cf. *Natyashastra*, VI.15 (p.102).

11    J.L. Masson and M.V.Patwardhan, *Santarasa and Abhinavagupta's Philosophy on Aesthetics*. Bhandarkar Oriental Series No. 9 (Poona: Bhandarkar Oriental Research Institute, 1969), 92-93.

12    Samkhya Sutra 1.74, (p. 118).

13    *Ibid.*, 1.19 (p. 37-38).

14    *Ibid.*, 1.164 (p.229).

15    *Ibid.*, 1.148 (p. 205).

16    *Natyashastra*, VI.17 (p.102).

17    *Ibid.*, Prose passage after VI.31 (p.109).

18    Yogashiromani Shri Shri Ravi Shankar, Rig-Veda Pundit and disciple of Maharishi Mahesh Yogi, Interview with Daniel Meyer-Dinkgräfe, 5.8.1992.

19    *Ibid.*

20    *Ibid.*

21    *Ibid.*

22    Cf. Peter Brook, *The Shifting Point*, 164.

23    Maharishi Mahesh Yogi, *Bhagavad-Gita*, 1.1, p. 26.

24    *Ibid.*, 3:8, p. 191

25    B. Kuppuswami, *Dharma and Society. A Study in Social Values* (Columbia: South Asia Books, 1977), 24ff.

26    Sudhir Kakar, *The Inner World. A Psycho-Analytic Study of Childhood and Society in India* (Delhi: Oxford University Press, 21981), 37.

27    Kuppuswami, 129

28    Kakar, 37

29    *Ibid.*

30    Kuppuswami, 183.

31    Wendy Doniger with Brian K.Smith, transl., *The Laws of Manu* (Harmondsworth: Penguin Books, 1991).

32    Kuppuswami, 183.

33  Cf. Padma Subrahmanyam, renowned Bharata Natyam exponent in Madras, India, who produced a 13-part TV series about the *Natyashastra* at the request of Indian Television.

34  Maharishi Mahesh Yogi, *Bhagavad-Gita*, 15.

35  *Ibid*, 135.

36  *Ibid.*, 390.

37  Cf. *Ibid.*

38  Cf. G.K.Bhat, *Sanskrit Dramatic Theory.*

39  Maharishi Mahesh Yogi, *Bhagavad-Gita*, 128.

40  *Ibid.*, 27.

41  Zarrilli, Phillip B., "What does it mean to "become the character": power, presence, and transcendence in Asian in-body disciplines of practice". in Schechner and Appel, 131-148. here: 142.

42  *Ibid.*

## 3. Interculturalism and Postmodernism

1   Bharucha, 16.

2   Cf. *Ibid.*

3   Cf. Fischer.Lichte "Das Theater auf der Suche nach einer Universalsprache", 117-121.

4   Hartmann, *Maharishi Gandharva-Veda*, 62

5   Maharishi Mahesh Yogi, *Bhagavad-Gita*, 470-472. 15, p.

6   *Ibid.*, 486.

7   Bharucha, 166.

8   *Ibid.*, 167

9   Cf. Rustom Bharucha, Interview with Daniel Meyer-Dinkgräfe, May 1993.

10  Cf. Crohn-Schmitt, *Actors and Onlookers*, 28.

11  Cf. Padoux, *Vac.*

12  Cf. Hagelin, "Is Consciousness the Unified Field?" , 80.

13  Cf. Lemaire, *Jacques Lacan*, 67.

14  Cf. *Ibid.*, 48.

**BIBLIOGRAPHY**

**Aiyar**, H.N., ed. and transl., *Thirty Monor Upanishads*. Delhi: Arcade Book Company, 1914.

Alexander, Charles N, Robert W. Cranson, Robert W. Boyer, David W. Orme-Johnson. "Transcendental Consciousness: A Fourth State of Consciousness beyond Sleep, Dream, and Waking", in Gackenbach, Jayne, ed., *Sleep and Dream. A Sourcebook*. New York, London: Garland Publishing Inc., 1986, 282-315.

Alexander, Charles N. and Robert W. Boyer. "Seven States of Consciousness: Unfolding the Full Potential of the Cosmic Psyche in Individual Life through Maharishi's Vedic Psychology", *Modern Science and Vedic Science* 2:4 (1989): 324-371.

Alexander, Charles N., Steven M. Druker, Ellen J. Langer. "Introduction: Major Issues in the Exploration of Adult Growth", in Charles N. Alexander and Ellen J. Langer, eds., *Higher Stages of Human Development. Perspectives on Human Growth*. New York, Oxford: Oxford University Press, 1990, 3-32.

Alexander, Charles N. et.al. "Growth of Higher Stages of Consciousness: Maharishi's Vedic Psychology of Human Development", in: Charles N. Alexander and Ellen J. Langer, eds., *Higher Stages of Human Development. Perspectives on Human Growth*. New York, Oxford: Oxford University Press, 1990, 286-341.

Ambardekar, R. R. *Rasa Structure of the Meghaduta*. Bombay: Prakashan, 1979.

Armstrong, D.M. "Mind-Body Problem: Philosophical Theories", in Gregory, Richard L., ed., *The Oxford Companion to the Mind*. Oxford, New York: Oxford University Press, 1987, 490-1.

Artaud, Antonin. *The Theatre and its Double*. (Collected Works Vol. 4, translated by Victor Corti). London: Calder and Boyars Ltd., 1974.

Auslander, Philip. *"Holy Theatre* and Catharsis". *TRI* 9:1 (1984): 16-29.

**Barba**, Eugenio. *The Floating Islands. Reflections with Odin Teatret*, ed. Ferdinando Taviani. Holstebro: 1979.

Barba, Eugenio. "Interview with Gautam Dasgupta", *Performing Arts Journal* January 1985.

Barba, Eugenio. "The Way of Refusal: the Theatre's Body-in-Life". *NTQ* 4:16 (1988): 291-299.

Barba, Eugenio "Eurasian Theatre". *TDR* 32:2 (1988): 126-130.

Barba, Eugenio. "Eugenio Barba to Phillip Zarrilli: About the visible and the invisble in the theater, and about ISTA in particular", *TDR* 32:3 (1988): 7-14.

Barba, Eugenio. "The Fiction of Duality", *NTQ* 5:20 (1989): 311-314.

Barba, Eugenio. "Eurasian Theatre: The Dramatic Touch of Difference". in Fischer-Lichte, Erika, Josephine Riley, Michael Gissenwehrer, eds., *Theatre, Own and Foreign*. (Serie Forum Modernes Theater, 2) Tübingen: Günter Narr, 1990, 31-36.

Barba, Eugenio, and Nicola Savarese. *The Secret Art of the Performer. A Dictionary of Theatre Anthropology*. London and New York: Routledge, 1991.

Bates, Brian. *The Way of the Actor. A New Path to Personal Knowledge and Power*. London: Century, 1986.

Battista, John R. "The Science of Consciousness", in Pope, Kenneth S. and Jerome L. Singer, eds., *The Stream of Consciousness. Scientific Investigation into the Flow of Human Consciousness*. Chichester, New York, Brisbane, Toronto: John Wiley and Sons, 1978, 55-87.

Bharucha, Rustom. *Theatre and the World. Essays on Performance and Politics of Culture.* London and New York: Routledge, 1993.

Bhat, G. K. *Sanskrit Dramatic Theory.* (Bhandarkar Oriental Institute Post-Graduate and Research Series No. 13) Poona: Bhandarkar Oriental Research Institute, 1981.

Bhat, G. K. *Rasa Theory and Allied Problems.* Baroda: The MS University of Baroda, 1984.

Bhat, G. K. *Sanskrit Drama. Problems and Perspectives.* Delhi: Ajanta Publications, 1985.

Bice, Benvenuto, and Roger... *The Work of Jaques Lacan.*London: Free Association Books, 1986.

Bisiach, Edoardo. "The (haunted) brain and consciousness", in Marcel, A.J., and E.Bisiach, eds., *Consciousness in Contemporary Science.* Oxford: Clarendon Press, 1988, 101-120.

Birringer, Johannes. *Theatre, Theory, Postmodernism.* Bloomington and Indianapolis: Indiana University Press, 1991.

Bloch, Susanna. "ALBA EMOTING: A Psychophysiological Technique to Help Actors Create and Control Real Emotions", *Theatre Topics* 3:2 (1993): 121-138.

Bohm, David. "A new theory of the relationship between mind and matter". *Philosophical Psychology* 3:2 (1990): 271-286.

Bradby, David and David Williams. *Directors' Theatre* (Macmillan Modern Dramatists). London: Macmillan, 1988.

Braun, Braun. *The Director and the Stage. From Naturalism to Grotowski.* London: Methuen, 1982.

Brent, Peter L. *The Indian Guru and his Disciple.* Tunbridge Wells: Institute for Cultural Research, 1971.

Broich, Ulrich and Manfred Pfister, eds. *Intertextualität. Formen, Funktionen, anglistische Fallbeispiele.* Tübingen: Narr, 1985.

Brook, Peter. *The Empty Space.* Harmondsworth: Penguin, 1972 [11968].

Brook, Peter. *The Shifting Point. Forty Years of Theatrical Exploration 1946-1987.* London: Methuen, 1987.

Brook, Peter. Lecture at *Temenos Academy*, London, 1.11.1993.

**Calhoun**, Cheshire and Robert C. Solomon. *What is an Emotion. Classical Readings in Philosophical Psychology.* New York, Oxford: Oxford University Press, 1984.

Campbell, Antony. *The Mechanics of Enlightenment. An Examination of the Teaching of Maharishi Mahesh Yogi.* London: Gollancz, 1975.

Capra, Fritjof. *The Turning Point.* London: Wildwood House, 1982.

Carlson, Marvin *Theories of the Theatre. A Historical and Critical Survey, from the Greeks to the Present.* (Ithaca and London: Cornell University Press, 1984.

Carlson, Marvin. "Peter Brook, *The Mahabharata* and Ariane Mnouchkine's *L'Indiade* as examples of contemporary cross-cultural theatre". in: Erika Fischer-Lichte, Josephine Riley, Michael Gissenwehrer, eds., *Theatre, Own and Foreign* (Serie Forum Modernes Theater, 2). Tübingen: Günter Narr, 1990, 49-56.

Carnicke, Sharon Marie, "Stanislavsky Uncensored and Unabridged", *TDR* 37:1 (1993): 22-37.

Chaim, Daphna Ben. *Distance in the Theatre. The Aesthe tics of Audience Response* (Theatre and Dramatic Studies, No. 17). Ann Arbor, London: UMI Research Press 1984.

Chalmers, Rogar A., et. al., *Scientific Research of Maharishi's Transcendental Meditation and TM-Sidhi Program.* Collected papers, vols. 2, 3 (Vlodrop: MVU Press, 1989).

Chopra, Deepak. *Perfect Health. The Complete Mind/Body Guide*. Toronto, New York, London, Sydney, Auckland: Bantam Books, 1990.

Chrisholm, R.M., ed., *The Vocation of Man*. Indianapolis: Bobbs-Merrill, 1956.

Clark, John H. *A Map of Mental States*. London, Boston, Melbourne and Henley: Routledge and Kegan Paul, 1983.

Coward, Harold G. *The Sphota Theory of Language. A Philosophical Analysis*. Delhi, Varanasi, Patna: Motilal Banarsidass, 1980.

Coward, Harold G. *Jung and Eastern Thought*. Albany: State University of New York Press, 1985.

Coward, Harold G. *Derrida and Indian Philosophy*. New York: State University of New York Press, 1990.

**Dalal**, Minakshi. *Conflict in Sanskrit Drama*. Bombay, Delhi: Somaija Publications Pvt. Ltd., 1973.

Dasgupta, Gautam. "Peter Brook's *'Orientalism'*, *Performing Arts Journal* No. 30 Vol. 10 no. 3 (1987): 9-16.

Davy, Daniel. "Grotowski's Laboratory. A Speculatove Look Back at the Poor Theatre". *Essays in Theatre* 7:2 (1989): 127-138.

De Berry, Stephen T. *The Externalization of Consciousness and the Psychopathology of Everyday Life*. (Contributions to Psychology, 17). New York, Westport, London: Greenwood Press, 1991.

Dhayagude, Suresh. *Western and Indian Poetics. A Comparative Study* (Bhandarkar Oriental Research Series No. 18). Poona: Bhandarkar Oriental research Institute, 1981.

Diderot, Denis. *The Paradox of Acting*. New York: Hill and Wang, 1955.

Dillbeck, Michael C. "The Self-Interacting Dynamics of Cosnciousness as the Source of the Creative Process in Nature and in Human Life". *Modern Science and Vedic Science* 2:3 (1988): 245-278.

Dillbeck, Michael. "Experience of the Ved. Realization of the Cosmic Psyche by Direct Perception: Ooening Individual Awareness to the Self-Interacting Dynamics of Consciousness". *Modern Science and Vedic Science* 3:2 (1989): 116-152.

Doniger, Wendy, with Brian K.Smith, transl., *The Laws of Manu*. Harmondsworth: Penguin Books, 1991.

**Erdman**, Joan. Commentary at the end of Session I, on Wednesday, 10.2.1993, in Toronto at the Conference on *New Directions in Indian Dance*.

**Ferguson**, Marilyn. *The Aquarian Conspiracy: Personal and Social Transformation in the 1980s*. London: Routledge and Kegan Paul, 1981.

Fischer, Roland "A Cartography of the Ecstatic and Meditative States", *Science* (174:4012), 26.11.1971: 897-904.

Fischer, Roland. "Towards a Neuroscience of Self-Experience and States of Self-Awareness and Interpreting Interpretations". in Wolman, Benjamin B. and Montague Ullman, *Handbook of States of Consciousness*. New York: Van Nostrand Reinhold Company, 1986. 3-30.

Fischer-Lichte, Erika. "Das Theater auf der Suche nach einer Universalsprache". *ForumModernes Theater* 4:2 (1989): 115-121.

Florey, Ernst, and George B. Stefano, eds. *Comparative Aspects of Neuropeptide Function* Manchester: Manchester University Press, 1991.

Freud, Sigmund. *Civilization and its Discontents*, The standard edition of the complete psychological works of S.F., translated from the German under the general editorship of James Strachey in collaboration with Anna Freud assisted by Alex Strachey and Alan Tyson. Volume 21, 1927-1931, London: Hogarth Press and the Institute of Psycho-Analysis, 1961,

Frijda, *The Emotions*. Cambridge: Cambridge University Press, 1986.

Forman, Robert K.C., ed., *The Problem of Pure Consciousness. Mysticism and Philosophy*. New York, Oxford: Oxford University Press, 1990.

Frost, Antony and Ralph Yarrow. *Improvisation in Drama. New Directions in Theatre*. London: Macmillan, 1990.

**Gelderloos**, Paul, and Zaid H.A.D. Beto: "The TM and TM-Sidhi Program and Reported Experiences of Transcendental Consciousness", *Psychologia* 32:2 (1989): 91-103.

George, David. "On Ambiguity: Towards a post-modern performance theory", *TRI* 14:1 (1989): 71-85.

George, David. "Quantum Theatre--Potential Theatre: A New Paradigm?" *NTQ* 5:18 (1989): 171-179.

Ghosh, Manomohan, ed. and transl., *The Natyasastra. A Treatise on Hindu Dramaturgy and Histrionics*. Calcutta: The Royal Asiatic Society of Bengal, 1950.

Gilman, Richard. "Jerzy Grotowski". *New American Review* 9 (April 1970): 206, 216.

Gossman, Lionel, and Elizabeth MacArthur, "Diderot's Displaced Paradoxe", in Jack Undank and Herbert Josephs, eds., *Diderot Disgression and Dispersion.A Bicentennial Tribute*. Lexington, Kentucky: French Forum Publishers, 1984), 106-119.

Goyandka, Jayadayal. *Shrimad Bhagavadgita As It Is. With English Translation*. Gorakhpur: Gita Prress, 1984.

Grear, Allison. "A Background to Diderot's *Paradoxe sur le Comédien*: The Role of Imagination in Spoken Expression of Emotion, *Forum for Modern Language Studies* 21:3 (1985): 225-238.

Grotowski, Jerzy. *Towards a Poor Theatre*, ed. Eugenio Barba with a preface by Peter Brook. London: Methuen, 1969.

**Hagelin**, John. "Is Consciousness the Unified Field? A Field Theorist's Perspective", *Modern Science and Vedic Science* 1 (1987): 29-88.

Hagelin, John. "Restructuring Physics from its Foundation in Light of Maharishi's Vedic Science", *Modern Science and Vedic Science* 3:1 (1989): 3-74.

Hamlyn, D.W. *The Penguin History of Western Philosophy*. London: Penguin, 1990.

Haney, William II. "Unity in Vedic aesthetics: the self-interacting dynamics of the knower, the known, and the process of knowing". *Analecta Husserliana* 233 (1991): 295-319.

Hansen-Löve, Aage H. *Der Russische Formalismus. Methodologische Rekonstruktion seiner Entwicklung aus dem Prinzip der Verfremdung* (Österreichische Akademie der Wissenschaften, Philosophisch-historische Klasse. Sitzungsberichte, 336. Band. Veröffentlichungen der Kommission für Literaturwissenschaft Nr. 5.). Wien: Verlag der Österreichischen Akademie der Wissenschaften, 1978.

Hartmann, Gabriel. *Maharishi-Gandharva-Ved. Die Klassische Musik der Vedischen Hochkultur: Eine Einführung in die musiktheoretischen Grundlagen*. Vlodrop: MVU Press, 1992.

Harwood, Ronald. *The Dresser*. Ambergate: Amer Lane Press, 1980.

Hilton, Julian. *Performance*. New Directions in Theatre.MacMillan: London, 1987.

Hirschberger, Johannes. *Geschichte der Philosophie. Neuzeit und Gegenwart*. Freiburg, Basel, Wien: Herder, 111981.

Hodgson, David. *The Mind Matters. Consciousness and Choice in a Quantum World*. Oxford: Clarendon Press 1991.

Hood, R.W. "The construction and validation of a measure of reported mystical experience" *Journal for the Scientific Study of Religion* 24 (1975), 29-41.

**Innes**, Christopher. *Holy Theatre. Ritual and the Avant-Garde*. Cambridge: Cambridge University Press, 1981.

**Jahn**, Robert G. and Brenda J. Dunne. *Margins of Reality. The Role of Consciousness in the Physical World*. San Diego, New York, London: Harcourt Brace Jovanovich, 1987.

Jhanji,Rekha. *Aesthetic Communication. The Indian Perspective*. Delhi: Munshiram Mancharlal Publishers, 1985.

Jhanji, Rekha. *The Sensuous in Art. Reflections on Indian Aesthetics* (Indian Institute of Advanced Studies). Delhi: Shimla in association with Motilal Barnasidass, 1989.

Jephcott, E.F.N. *Proust and Rilke. The Literature of Expanded Consciousness*. London: Chatto and Windus, 1972.

**Kakar**, Sudhir. *The Inner World. A Psycho-Analytic Study of Childhood and Society in India*. Delhi: Oxford University Press, 21981.

Kale, Pramod. *The Theatrical Universe. A Study of the Natyasastra*. Bombay: Popular Prakashan, 1974.

Karambelkar, P.V. *Patanjali's Yoga Sutras. With Devanagari Text, Transliteration, Word Meanings and Translation*. Bombay: Kaivalyadhama, 1986.

Kesting, Marianne. "Stanislavsky--Meyerhold--Brecht". *Forum Modernes Theater* 4:2 (1989): 122-138.

King, B. J. and K. Chapin. *Billie Jean*. New York: Harper & Row, 1974.

Knopf, Jan. *Brecht-Handbuch. Theater. Eine Ästhetik der Widersprüche*. Stuttgart: J.B.Metzlersche Verlagsbuchhandlung, 1980.

Kollbrunner, Jürg. *Das Buch der Humanistischen Psychologie: Eine ausführliche einführende Darstellung und Kritik des Fühlens, Denkens und Handelns in der Humanistischen Psychologie*. Eschborn, 1987. Verlag!

Kott, Jan. "Grotowski or the limit". *NTQ* 6:23 (1990): 203-206

Kramer, Richard E. "The *Natyasastra* and Stanislavsky: Points of Contact", *Theatre Studies* (1991). pages!

Kumiega,Jennifer. *The Theatre of Grotowski*. London, New York: Methuen, 1987.

Kuppuswami, B. *Dharma and Society. A Study in Social Values*. Columbia: South Asia Books, 1977.

**Lad**, Vasant. *Das Ayurveda Heilbuch. Eine praktische Anleitung zur Selbst-Diagnose, Therapie und Heilung mit dem ayurwedischen System.* Haldenwang: Edition Shangrila, 1986.

Leiter, Samuel. *From Stanislavsky to Barrault. Repre sentative Directors of the European Stage* (Contributions to Drama and Theatre Studies No. 34). London: Greenwood Press, 1991.

Lemaire, Anika. *Jacques Lacan*, trans. David Macey. London, Henley and Boston: Routledge & Kegan Paul, 1977.

Levenson,Robert , Paul Ekman, Wallace V. Friesen, "Voluntary Facial Action Generates Emotion-Specific Autonomous Nervous System Activity", *Psychophysiology* 27:4 (1990): 363-384.

Lockwood, Michael. *Mind, Brain and the Quantum. The Compound "I".* Oxford: Basil Blackwell, 1989.

Ludwig, Arnold M. "Altered States of Consciousness", in Tart, Charles T., ed. *Altered States of Consciousness. A Book of Readings.* New York, London, Sydney, Toronto: John Wiley and Sons, 1969, 9-22.

**Maharishi** Mahesh Yogi, *On the Bhagavad-Gita. A New Translation and Commentary, Chapters 1 - 6.* Harmondsworth: Penguin, 1969.

Maharishi Mahesh Yogi, *Life Supported by Natural Law.* Washington: Age of Enlightenment Press, 1986.

Maharishi Mahesh Yogi, Interview on Gandharva Veda, WDR and Deutsche Welle, 8.2.91

Marasinghe, E. W. *The Sanskrit Theatre and Stagecraft* (Sri Garib Dass Oriental Series No. 78). Delhi: Sri Satguru Publications, 1989.

Marcel, A.J., and E.Bisiach, eds., *Consciousness in Contemporary Science.* Oxford: Clarendon Press, 1988.

Martin, Jaqueline. *Voice in Modern Theatre.* London and New York: Routledge, 1991.

Mascaro, Juan., transl. *The Bhagavad-Gita.* Harmondsworth: Penguin Books, 1962.

Maslow, Abraham H. *Towards a Psychology of Being.* New York: Van Nostrand, 1962.

Masson, J.L. and M.V.Patwardhan, *Santarasa and Abhinavagupta's Philosophy on Aesthetics* (Bhandarkar Oriental Series No. 9) Poona: Bhandarkar Oriental Research Institute, 1969.

Maturana, Humberto R. and Francisco J. Varela, *Autopoiesis and Cognition. The Realization of the Living.* Dordrecht: Reidel, 1980.

Meduri, Avanthi. "Bharata Natyam--What Are You?" *Asian Theatre Journal* 5:1 (1988): 1-26.

Meduri, Avanthi. "Orientalism, Indian Nationalism and the Revival of Classical Dance in India", unpublished paper, presented in Session II on Wednesday, 10.2.1993, in Toron to at the Conference on *New Directions in Indian Dance.*

Miletich, John J. *States of Awareness. An Annotated Bibliography.* New York, Westport, London: Greenwood, 1988.

Mishra, Hari Ram. *The Theory of Rasa in Sanskrit Drama. With a Comparative Study of General Dramatic Literature.* Bhopal, Sayar, Chhatapur: Vindhyachal Prakashan, 1964.

Mitter, Shomit. *Systems of Rehearsal. Stanislavsky, Brecht, Grotowski and Brook.* London and New York: Routledge, 1992.

Mittwede, Martin "Die sechs Systeme der Vedischen Philosophie---eine Einführung". *Mitteilungsblätter der Deutschen MERU-Gesellschaft* 10 (1985): 28-48.
Moreno, Jacob L. *Gruppenpsychotherapie und Psychodrama.Leinleitung in die Theorie und Parxis* New York: George Thieme, 31988.

Onderdelinden, Sjaak "Brecht and Asia" in C.C.Barfoot and Cobi Bordewijk, eds., *Theatre Intercontinental. forms, functions, correspondences* (Amsterdam, Atlanta, GA: Rodo pi, 1993), 25-42.
Orme-Johnson, David W., et. al., eds., *Scientific Research on the Transcendental Meditation Program. Collected Papers, Vol.* 1. Rheinweiler: MERU Press, 1977.
Orme-Johnson, David W. "The Cosmic Psyche as the Unified Source of Creation". *Modern Science and Vedic Science* 2:2 (1988): 168-169.
Orme-Johnson, Rhoda. "A Unified Field Theory of Literature", *Modern Science and Vedic Science* 1:3 (1987): 323-373.

Pandey, Kapila Chandra. *Comparative Aesthetics.* Vol. 1: *Indian Aesthetics.* Banaras: The Chpwkhamba Sanskrit Series Office, 1950.
Pandya, Shveni. *A Study of the Technique of Abhinaya in Relation to Sanskrit Drama.* Bombay, New Delhi: Somaiya Publications Pvt. Ltd., 1988.
Pavis, Patrice. *Theatre at the Crossroads of Culture.* London and New York: Routledge, 1992.
Pronko, Leonard C. "L.A. Festival: Peter Brook's *The Mahabharata*". *Asian Theatre Journal* 5:2 (1988): 220-224.
Pradier, Jean-Marie "Towards a Biological Theory of Performance", *NTQ* 6:21 (1990): 86-98.

Raine, Kathleen. *The Land Unknown.* New York: George Braziller, 1975.
Ramnarayan, Gowri "Dancer and Reformer", *Sruti* (July) 1984: 17-26.
Rhagavan, V. *The Concept of the Beautiful in Sanskrit _ Literature.* Madras: The Kuppuswami Sastri Research Institute, 1988.
Richards, G. "The world a stage: A conversation with Ray Reinhardt". *San Francisco Theater Magazine* Winter 1977, 46.
Rix, Roxane. "ALBA EMOTING: A Preliminary Experiment with Emotional Effector Patterns", *Theatre Topics* 3:2 (1993): 139-146.
Roach, Joseph R., Jr. "Diderot and the Actor's Machine" *Theatre Survey* 22:1 (1981): 51-68.
Roach, Joseph R. *The Player's Passion. Studies in the Science of Acting.* Newark: University of Delaware Press, 1985.
Roose-Evans,James. *Experimental Theatre. From Stanislavsky to Peter Brook.* London: Routledge, 41989.
Rusch, Gebhard. *Erkenntnis, Wissenschaft, Geschichte. Von einem konstruktivistischen Standpunkt.* Frankfurt: Suhrkamp, 1987.
Ryckman, Richard M. *Theories of Personality.* Monterey: Brooks/Cole Publishers, 31985.

Said, Edward W. *Oirentalism.* London: Penguin Books, 1991 (11978, London: Routledge and Kegan Paul)
Sarup, Madan. *An Introductory Guide to Post-Struc turalism and Postmodernism.* New York, London, Toronto, Sydney, Tokyo: Harvester Wheatsheaf, 1988.

Schechner, Richard. *The End of Humanism. Writings on Performance.* New York: PAJ
  Publications, 1982,
Schechner, Richard. *Performative Circumstances. From the Avantgarde to Ramlila.* Calcutta:
  Seagull Books, 1983.
Schechner, *Performance Theory.* New York and London: Routledge, 1988.
Schechner, Richard and Willa Appel, eds., *By Means of PErformance. Intercultural Studies of
  Theatre and Ritual.* Cambrdige: Cambridge University Press, 1990.
Schorsch, Christof. *Die New Age Bewegung. Utopie und Mythos der Neuen Zeit. Eine
  kritische Auseinandersetzung.* Gütersloh: Gütersloher Verlagshaus G. Mohn, 1988.
Shankar, Yogashiromani Shri Shri Ravi, Rig-Veda Pundit and former disciple of Maharishi
  Mahesh Yogi. Interview with Daniel Meyer-Dinkgräfe, 5.8.1992.
Shear, Jonathan. "The universal structures and dynamics of creativity: Maharishi, Plato, Jung
  and various creative geniuses on the creative process", *Journal of Creative Behavior*
  16:3 (1982): 155-175.
Shevtsova, Maria. "Interaction- Interpretation. *The Mahabharata* from a social-cultural
  perspective" in Williams, David, ed., *Peter Brook and the Mahabharata: Critical Per
  spectives.* London and New York: Routledge, 1991.
Sinha Nandalal (transl.), *The Samkhya Philosophy.* New Delhi: Oriental Books Reprint
  Company, 1971.
Srinivasan, Srinivasa Ayya. *On the Composition of the Natyasastra* (Studien zur Indologie
  und Iranistik Monographie 1). Reinbek: Dr. Inge Wezler Verlag für Orientalische
  Fachpublikationen, 1980.
Stace, W.T., *Mysticism and Philosophy.* London: MacMillan, 1960.
Stanislavsky, Constantin. *Building a Character.* Translated by Elizabeth Reynolds Hapgood.
  New York: Theatre Arts Books, 1949.
Stanislavsky, Constantin. *Creating a Role.* Translated by Elizabeth Reynolds Hapgood, Edited
  by Hermine I. Popper. New York: (Theatre Arts Books. 1961.
Stanislavsky, Constantin. *An Actor Prepares.* Translated by Elizabeth Reynold Hapgood.
  London: Methuen, 1986.
Stern, Susan L. "Drama in Second Language Learning from a Psycholinguistic Perspective",
  *Leanguage Learning* 3:1 (1980): 77-100.
Strasberg, Lee. "Working with Live Material", in Munk, Erika, ed., *Stanislavsky and America.
  The "Method" and its Influence on the American Actor.* New York: Hill and Wang,
  1966.
Strasberg, Lee *A Dream of PAssion. The Development of the Method,* ed. Evangeline
  Morphos. London: Bloomsbury, 1988.
Subrahmanyan, Padma. Interview with Daniel Meyer-Dinkgräfe, March 1992.

**Tallis**, Raymond. *The Explicit Animal A Defence of Human Consciousness.* London:
  Macmillan, 1991.
Tart, Charles. *Transpersonal Psychologies.* London: Routledge and Kegan Paul, 1975.
Tatlov, Antony. *The Mask of Evil. Brecht's Response to the Poetry, Theatre and Thought of
  China and Japan.* Bern, Frankfurt, Las Vegas: Peter Lang, 1977.
Thoreau, H.D., *Walden.* New York, NAL, 1960 (Original Work published 1854),
Travis, Orme-Johnson. "Field Model of Consciousness: EEG Coherence Changes as
  Indicators of Field Effects". *International Journal of Neuroscience* 49:3,4 (1989):
  203-211.

Turner, Victor. *From Ritual to Theatre. The Human Seriousness of Play.* New York:
Performing Arts Journal Publications, 1982.
Turner, Victor. *The Anthropology of Performance.* New York: PAJ Publications, 1986.


Vatsyayan,Kapila. Ccommentary at the end of session I, on Wednesday, 10.2.1993, in
Toronto at the Conference on *New Directions in Indian Dance.*
Velmans, Max. "Consciousness, brain, and the physical world". *Philosophical Psychology* 3:1
(1990): 77-99
Vigne, Jaques. "Guru and Psychotherapist: Comparisons from the Hindu Tradition". *The
Journal of Transpersonal Psychology* 23:2 (1991): 121-137.

Wallace, Robert Keith. "Physiological Effects of TM", *Science* 167 (1970): 1751-1754.
Wallace, Robert Keith, et. al., eds. *Scientific Research of Maharishi's Transcendental
Meditation and TM-Sidhi Program.* Collected papers, vol. 5. Fairfield, Iowa: MIU
Press, 1992.
Wallace, Robert Keith. *The Physiology of Consciousness.* Fairfield, Iowa: Maharishi
International University Press, 1993.
Watson, Ian. *Towards a Third Theatre. Eugenio Barba and the Odin Teatret.* London and
New York: Routledge, 1993.
Welsch, Wolfgang. "Postmoderne. Genealogie und Bedeutung eines umstrittenen Begriffs". in:
Peter Kemper, ed., *Postmoderne, oder: Der Kampf um die Zukunft. Die Kontroverse
in Wissenschaft, Kunst und Gesellschaft.* Frankfurt/ Main: Fischer, 1988, 9-36 .
Werman, David S. "The oceanic experience and states of consciousness", *The Journal of
Psychoanalytic Anthropology* 9:3 (1986): 339-357.
Willett, John, ed. and transl., *Brecht on Theatre. The Development of an Aesthetic.* New
York: Holl and Wang, 1978.
Williams, David. *Peter Brook. A Theatrical Casebook.* London: Methuen, 21991.
Williams, David, ed., *Peter Brook and the Mahabharata: Critical Perspectives.* London: and
New York: Routledge, 1991.
Wolf, Fred Alan. *Mind and the New Physics.* London: Heinemann, 1985.

Yarrow, Ralph. "Neutral" consciousness in the experience of theatre", *Mosaic* 19:3 (1987):1-
20.
Yarrow, Ralph. "The potential of consciousness: towards a new approach towards states of
consciousness in literature", *Journal of European Studies*, 15 (1985): 1-20.

Zarrilli,Phillip "For whom is the "invisible" not visible: Reflections on representation in the
work of Eugenio Barba" *TDR* 32:1 (1988): 95-106.
Zarrilli, Phillip B., "What does it mean to "become the character": power, presence, and
transcendence in Asian in-body disciplines of practice". in Schechner and Appel, 131-
148.